THE FIFTH GOSPEL

Other works by Fida Hassnain

Buddhist Kashmir (1973)
British Policy Towards Kashmir (1974)
Ladakh Moonland (1975)
Hindu Kashmir (1977)
History of Ladakh (1977)
Gilgit—The Northern Gate of India (1978)
Kashmir Misgovernment (1980)
Heritage of Kashmir (1980)
Shri Amarnath Cave (1987)
History of Freedom Struggle (1988)
The Fifth Gospel (1988)
Islamic Revolution in Iran (1989)
Beautiful Valley of Kashmir (1992)
Cultural History of Kishtawar (1992)
Encyclopaedia of Kashmir (1992)
Search for Historical Jesus (1994)
Bhaisajva-Guru-Sutra (Sanskrit, 1995)
Kashgar—Central Asia (1995)
La Otra Historia de Jesus (Spanish, 1995)
Jezusa (Polish, 1996)
Gesu 'I' Esseno (Italian, 1997)
Shah Hamadan of Kashmir (1998)
Kashmir Valley (2002)
Historic Kashmir (2002)
Arts and Crafts of Kashmir (2005)
Sufi Alchemy of Peace (2005)

THE
FIFTH
GOSPEL

*New Evidence from the Tibetan, Sanskrit,
Arabic, Persian and Urdu Sources
about the Historical Life of Jesus Christ
after the Crucifixion*

FIDA HASSNAIN & DAHAN LEVI

REVISED AND EDITED BY
AHTISHAM FIDA

BLUE DOLPHIN PUBLISHING

Published by Blue Dolphin Publishing, Inc.
P.O. Box 8, Nevada City, CA 95959
Orders: 1-800-643-0765
Web: www.bluedolphinpublishing.com

ISBN: 978-1-57733-181-0

First printing, September, 2006
Second printing, February, 2008

Library of Congress Cataloging-in-Publication Data

Hassnain, F. M., 1924-
    The fifth gospel : new evidence from the Tibetan, Sanskrit,
    Arabic, Persian, and Urdu sources about the historical life of
    Jesus Christ after the crucifixion / Fida Hassnain & Dahan Levi ;
    revised and edited by Ahtisham Fida.
        p. cm.
    Includes bibliographical references.
    ISBN-13: 978-1-57733-181-0 (pbk. : alk. paper)
    1. Jesus Christ—Biography—Apocryphal and legendary lit-
    erature. I. Levi, Dahan, 1920- . II. Fida, Ahtisham. III. Title.
    BT520.H3 2006
    232.9—dc22

                                                        2006030277

Cover art: "Jesus Meditating," by Bruce Harman,
www.harmanvisions.com

The photographs reproduced in this book
are available in color on-line at
http://www.bluedolphinpublishing.com/5thGospelphotos.html

Printed in the United States of America

10   9   8   7   6   5   4   3   2

Dedicated to

Pandit Sutta, the author of *Bhavishya-maha-parana* – 115 A.D.
Nicolas Notovich, the author of *The Life of St. Issa* – 1890 A.D.
Mirza Ghulam Ahmad, the author of *Messih Hindustan Mein* –
    1908 A.D.

for opening new vistas of research
into the hidden life of Jesus Christ

Table of Contents

Acknowledgments

WE ARE GRATEFUL TO THE FOLLOWING for photographic material included in this book.

Persian History of Mulla Nadri: Khwaja Nazir Ahmad, Tibetan Manuscript: Rev. S.S. Gergan, Degree of 1766: Khwaja Nazir Ahmad, Rider with the Cross: The British Museum, London, Crosses in Ladakh: Rev. S.S. Gergan, Grave Slab at Char-saddah: Archaeological Survey of Pakistan, Thomas at Julian: Archaeological Survey of Pakistan, Peter: Director of Museum, Goa, Sepulcher of Mary at Muree: Mumtaz Ahmad Farouqui, wooden door with six panels: Director of Museum, Goa, Takhat-i-Sulaiman: Franz Sachse, Sepulchre of Aroan at Harwan: Holger Kersten, Stone of Moses: Holger Kersten.

For other photographs, we are indebted to Andreas Faber Kasier, Maria Teja, and Franz Sachse. For line drawings we are indebted to Peloubet's Selected Notes on the International Lessons, Boston 1918. For photographs about the Flight of the Holy Family to Egypt, we are grateful to H.H. Pope Shenouda III, 117th Pope of Alexandria and Patriarch of the See of St. Mark the Evangelist and His grace Bishop Mettaos, Bishop of St. Mary Syrian Monastery, Cairo, Egypt. Our thanks are due to Fathy Saiid Georgy and Lehnert and Landrock, Cairo, Egypt.

For other photographs of archaeological and historical interest, we are grateful to the Director General, J&K Tourist Corporation and Director of Archives and Archaeology, J&K Government.

Introduction

What thou seest, write in a book.
The Book of Revelation

WE DO NOT CLAIM TO BE THE INVENTORS of any theory nor the discoverers of any truth. As such, this book does not owe its origin to any sect, group or movement. It is merely the result of our personal efforts to find out and then compile source material about the lost years of Jesus Christ. It was by chance that in 1965 one of us found a reference to a visit of Nicolas Notovitch to Hemis monastery of Ladakh and his discovery of the Buddhist scrolls about Jesus. Since then, we have been examining evidence about the survival of Jesus Christ at the time of crucifixion and subsequent departure towards the East.

But we must stress that our book is not the last word in the domain of researches on the subject. It only presents startling evidence about the tomb of Jesus in Kashmir. Our research would remain incomplete till this tomb is opened for scientific investigation. The conditions are such that nobody will permit us to open this sacred grave. Both Muslims and Christians are against the very idea, which they term as "desecration of the sacred remains."

Eric von Daniken writes: "The crucifixion, theologians assure us, is to be understood only symbolically." Why is this not made clear in religious teaching? My daughter Lela learned—like all previous generations—that Jesus was the only begotten son of God made flesh, that he suffered every pain (for the oppressing original sin) as a man, that he died as a man, struggled as a man, with all the attendant torments and miseries. But how can God, who knowingly let his own son be tortured—because Adam and Eve committed a sin that he could easily have prevented through his foreknowledge—be reconciled by Christ's death with the very men who killed him?[1]

It is evident that during modern times it has become difficult to believe that Jesus Christ was massacred for our sins. Such theories propounded by the Church, in Rome, 150 years after the death of Jesus Christ, have created misgivings in the minds of sincere Christians. S. Basker writes, "I believe in God and follow Christianity, but I do not like to go the Church and hear the sermons of the father of the Church. I hate these preachers!"[2]

Such sentiments, as expressed above, do not arise until something serious occurs. It may be probable that either the original doctrine, as propounded by Jesus Christ, is not placed before us, or mixed-up truths are presented which cannot be digested easily. Helmut Goeckel has expressed the same sentiments, when he writes: "It must be made possible to reconstruct the legitimate doctrine in the original form. The surest way to succeed is to find again the historical personality of Jesus."[3]

Now, where are the original doctrines? More than one billion people in the world have no other holy book except the Bible. It is considered to be the original text on the life and mission of Jesus Christ. The faithful believe that the Bible has always existed in the form in which they see it today. They further believe that there are no other holy books except the Bible. They do not know that not only was the Bible changed, altered and shortened from time to time, but many other scriptures and Gospels were banished from circulation, and destroyed by burning, as ordained by the Church.

From the start, Christian Councils have met and taken decisions on doctrines from time to time, with the result that the Christian faith, as it exists today, is the faith imposed on us by the ecclesiastical priests. The net result has been that Jesus Christ, as presented today, appears to be some other personality from the one which existed two thousand years ago. As such, what is needed, is to search the real Jesus Christ. By searching the real Jesus Christ, we do not intend to do away with all that Christianity stands for today. We plead to make a dispassionate study of the life and mission of Jesus Christ, who has declared, "I am the Way, the Truth and the Life."[4]

We have no hesitation in declaring that Jesus Christ was the way, the truth and the life. Many people in the world, despite their religious beliefs, loved him and continue to love him. Many are re-searching him and in this respect, we quote from the letter of one of our sincere friends, Lina Ada Piantanelli:

> Since my childhood, I have been searching Jesus Christ. It is my sincere wish to get more knowledge about him, because I always fore-casted that Jesus did not die on the cross. It is my best desire to dedicate my life to Jesus and publish all the truths discovered about him.[5]

We are astonished to find that many hurdles are placed in our way to find the truth. We admit that some may defile the sacred name of Jesus Christ, in their so-called research work. We also ad-mit that some revealing facts may bring a setback to Christianity. But, we must also declare in confidence that the true doctrines of Jesus Christ will surely flourish and flower, and shall exist forever. Anyway, no research is final and no research is the last word! But, we must allow people to open their hearts and write whatever they like. It is very sad that this is not being done. Here is a friend writing from Brazil:

> Two years ago I wrote a book about the resurrection of the Lord. I sent the book to the St. Paul's Order and they did not approve it, be-cause I brought to light many explanations that they could not accept. For instance I discovered the models that the Indians used to paint the Virgin of Guadalupe. I also found that this Indian had painted our Lady of the Angels. I also discovered that our Lady of Guadalupe has a close relation with the spaceship, located in a tomb stone in Palenque, Chiapas, Mexico. This resemblance is sharp about forms and other details put in by the shifty Indian. He was a faithful prehistoric believer and when he had accepted the new religion, he did mix the two faiths but also the spaceship altogether in one painting: Our Lady of Guadalupe.
>
> You can well imagine the strong reaction of the Church, when they sent my book to Mexico, and kept it out of sight. My efforts to get back the book have not succeeded. Now, if this is the attitude of the Church, one can realize that under such circumstances, no researches are possible.

It is true that the gap in the life of Jesus Christ, between the ages of twelve and thirty, is a most fascinating subject for research, and it is going to have a far-reaching effect on the established beliefs of

Christians. In this regard, we quote the feelings of our friend, Joshua Rochstein:

> While it is true that the effect on Christianity's credibility is, at best, secondary to the importance of the research into the historical facts, one cannot avoid speculating on the former. The Church has always preached that Jesus died on the cross, in order to bring salvation to men's souls. Well, what happens to this promise of salvation and belief in it, vis-a-vis Jesus' death on the cross, if research should establish or demonstrate to be very probable that Jesus did not die on the cross at all, but went away to a faraway land like Kashmir, for a second career? In the realm of religion, this would indeed be a major happening. Would it contribute to secularist skepticism or would it influence disillusioned and disappointed Christians, to seek salvation elsewhere?

The writer has expressed his genuine fears, when we take into account the tremendous importance of religious movements in our history and the rejection of centuries-old beliefs. Very recently, questions have been raised about the historicity of Jesus Christ. The Gospels do not provide us with a detailed biographical account of his life and work. These scholars are searching Jesus Christ in the West, with the result that they declare: "Without the historical Jesus, the Christ of the Church is shallow, a radiant shell, a mythical hero without historical weight."[6]

The confusion has arisen because scholars are not trying to find Jesus Christ in the East. At the same time, we have not to search the historical person of recent past. Secondly, clinging to the historical Jesus is to remain blind, because professing any religion means belief in its mythology. There could be no religion without mythology and its rejection would mean total denial of that religion. As such, it is necessary to have faith in all scriptures and there is no need to falsify the statements given in them, nor offer apologistic interpretations.[7] The disciples of Jesus Christ wrote what they saw or believed. We cannot pass any judgment on what is written in the Gospels.

Some scholars have stated that the existence of any such personality as Jesus Christ cannot be correlated with historical facts. Also, the supernatural events in the life of the Lord cannot be explained in terms of science. We can only say: there is a mysterious something which even the scientists cannot explain. The present-day knowledge of man is not the end of total knowledge.

Those who have experienced or have some contact with the mystics do acclaim rightly that Jesus Christ was a divine being incarnated in human flesh. One such friend has written:

> Jesus was an Avatara, a manifestation through the form of a human being of a god, of a divinity, one of the spiritual beings controlling our part of the stellar universe.[8]

Questions that have been raised about the authenticity of the Gospels were condemned by the Church. It is also certain that the compilers of the authorized Gospels recorded with sincerity what they heard about Christ, what they knew of him and what they experienced. Had they had to "cook" things, they could not have ignored the gaps in the life of Jesus. This is a conclusive proof of the authenticity of the Gospels, whether they are authorized or unauthorized. As such, it is necessary to compile afresh the Old as well as the New Testament. By doing this, it will be possible for all of us to absorb the real teachings of Jesus Christ, according to our inherent capacity. There is no need for theologians and the so-called Biblical scholars to guide us—we can be our own guides in search of truth. It may be mentioned at the outset that truth is not the monopoly of any sect, religion or church. Humanity has to find God, and this exercise requires that it be done without the uncalled help of the clergy.

Let every truth-seeking innocent man be his own guide. In this way, we are hopeful God will surely come to show him light. Jesus once said:

> He that believeth on me,
> Believeth not on me,
> But on him that sent me.
> And he that seeth me,
> Seeth him that sent me.
> I am come a light into the world,
> That whosoever believeth on me,
> Should not abide in darkness.[9]

It is of peculiar interest to us that both Buddhism and Christianity have many similarities of thought and ideas. Both these religions are good news to suffering humanity. The subject has been fully dealt with by Hazrat Mirza Ghulam Ahmad in his book, *Mesih Hindustan Mein,* and his thesis is quoted here:

> If Jesus has been called the Master, so the Buddha has been called, *Sasta* or the Master. Both are tempted but could not succumb to such temptations. Like Buddha, Jesus Christ also fasted for forty days. Both taught the same in parables and their teachings have striking similarities.

It is also significant that in some statues termed as "Bodhisattva," their palms show marks which could depict the proof of crucifixion. Can we presume that those Bodhisattvas—or the later Buddhas or "perfect beings"—belong to the Order of Jesus Christ? Do these statues hint to the piercing of hands or feet of Jesus Christ?

It requires to be noted that Jesus has been mentioned in the Oriental manuscripts differently. He is called *Issa, Isa, Issana-deva, Isha Natha, Ishai, Isa Masih, Yusu, Yuzu, Yuzu-Kristo, Yuz-Asaph,* and *Yusu Masih.* In some works, he is mentioned as *Eshvara-putram,* or the Son of God, and *Kanaya-garbum* or Born of a Girl. In some ancient manuscripts he is called *Metteyya,* which is equivalent to Messiah.[11] In some Persian works, he is known as *Nasrani* or *Kristani,* which is equivalent to "of Nazareth" or Christian. It is also interesting that the Christians are known in the East as Nasaran and Kira. Jesus is also titled in the East as *Ibn-i-Maryam* or the Son of Mary.

Father Peter Hebblethwait of the Jesuit Order in Farm Street, England writes:

> I am not at all perturbed or shocked by speculations of Dr. Hassnain since it is open to anyone to ask questions.

Rev. Lionel Swain of the Roman Catholic College of St. Edmund's Ware, Hertfordshire states:

> The least that one must say about Dr. Hassnain's views is that history about Jesus of Nazareth, especially about His survival of the Crucifixion, is pure fiction. It has no basis in history.

Rev. Dewi Morgan. Rector of Flett Street's Church, St. Bride, states:

> There is nothing outrageous about the suggestion by Dr. Hassnain that Christ went to India, in what I prefer to call the hidden years. Prof. Hassnain need not fear that the Christian Church will be upset by his observations. On the contrary, the Church is only too anxious to continue researching. We are concerned only with the truth.

Canon Pearce-Higgins takes a different view when he states:

> Jesus had all the gifts of the spirit (healing clairvoyance and precognition) and He was not a medium in the modern sense of the word. He does appear to have revealed powers and qualities claimed for Indian Yogis. Like the Yogi, He spent hours in prayers and meditation with His disciples and His pattern of teaching was not dissimilar to that of the Hindu holy man. For that reason it is possible that there is substance to the claim that His last years in India, where He may, as Dr. Hassnain claims, have studied the techniques and beliefs of Eastern religions—although His spiritual teaching appears to have been His own.

The distinguished Methodist leader, Lord Donald Soper says:

> I am certainly not offended by Professor Hassnain's views and I have read them with interest. But I am sure that there is far too much evidence against them.
> Thus, whether Jesus Christ did or did not die on the cross is a vital question in which not only the Christians but others are alike keenly interested for the sake of truth. After all, it would not be particularly heretic if the Church in particular, and humanity in general, had one day to accept the truth. That would not in any case alter the basic greatness of Jesus Christ and his teachings.

Much evidence on the life of Jesus Christ has been destroyed with the main aim to separate the real Jesus from the Jesus of the accepted four Gospels. Their technique is to seek out and destroy all evidence. After we photographed two pages from the diaries of the Moravian Mission doctors, the diaries were removed and are no longer there in Ladakh. The same calamity fell on the Tibetan scrolls which were discovered by Nicolas Notovitch. The wooden cross which was photographed by us lying in the sarcophagus over the grave of Yuzu-Asaph has also been stolen. So is the case with ancient damaged manuscripts which were on the sarcophagus. Most of our photographs are missing after we took them to Europe to show them to the publishers.

We acknowledge and express our profound appreciation for those who helped us in many ways to continue our researches. Miss Iris Bolt, who is a specialist in etymology has shown continued interest in this project. Dr. Franz Sachse not only obtained rare and out-of-print books for us but also came to Kashmir for discussion of topics dealt with in this work. We are grateful to him for support and guidance. He has also provided photographs, for which we are indebted to him. Helmut Goeckel, G. Vansister, Prof. Miguel Diaz, Rabbi Elyahn Avihail, Khan Roshan Khan, Sheikh Abdul Qadir, Mirza Wasim Ahmad, Kurt Berna, Syed Abdul Hye, and M.A. Faruqie also helped us by providing research material, for which we express our sincere thanks to them. There are some friends who have given us much moral support and encouragement and they are:

Rev. Otlega I. Nakano
Rev. George I. Morshitta
Ms. Claire Miller
Dr. Ahtisham Fida
Ms. Mary Leue
Dr. Gunter Ammon
Dr. Jose Hermogenes
Dr. John Hill
Mm. Christianne T. de Reyes
Rev. Sundara Aish Muni
Maj. Gen. Habibullah

Other friends who have been a source of inspiration to us are too many to mention here.

It is not our intention to shake your faith in Jesus Christ or his mission. Our main aim in writing this book is to inform the West that we in the East have some source material about the historical Jesus who lived on after the crucifixion. This book was not written in one day but is a result of many years' continued search for evidence. We are searching truth and we wish other seekers to join with us in this noble venture.

We must point out that the life and works of Jesus are of vital interest to the people of the world. It is in this spirit that we have compiled this book, piece by piece, and our work has no connection whatsoever with any religious conviction or bent of mind. We do not belong to any cult or society. As such, we pray that our sins, which are many, may be forgiven in the name of Jesus Christ.

Fida Hassnain
Dahan Levi

CHAPTER ONE

Sources

What thou seest, write in a book, and send it
Unto the seven churches which are in Asia.
The Book of Revelation

THAT WE DO NOT HAVE FULL INFORMATION about the life and works of
Jesus Christ has created a yearning among scholars and devotees to
know more about him. The quest for the historical Jesus began at
the end of the 18th century in the West and it continues unabated.
His biography is still incomplete because there is no source material
to fill in the gaps. The first person to obtain information about Jesus
Christ was Paul and he lived in the same period. As such, the Epistles
of Paul are the earliest source material on the subject. From him, we
learn that God sent forth Jesus Christ in the capacity of his son, *"made*
of a woman, made under the law." He had brothers and one among
them was James. Paul further informs us that Jesus Christ chose
twelve Apostles for preaching the Kingdom of God. According to
Paul, the Jews conspired against Jesus and got him crucified, but he
rose on the third day and met his apostles, about eleven times.

In the first Epistle of Peter, it is written that *"Christ also had once*
suffered for sins; so that he might bring us to God." In the Acts of the
Apostles, the following scanty information is given about Jesus:

> *Ye men of Israel. Hear these words;*
> *Jesus of Nazareth, a man approved of God,*
> *Among you by miracles and wonders and signs,*
> *Which God did by him in the midst of you,*
> *As ye yourselves also know:*
> *Being delivered by the determinate counsel,*
> *And foreknowledge of God,*

Ye have taken,
And by wicked hands have crucified and slain.

Among the earliest Christian writings, the Gospels are the primary source of information about Jesus. We are told about his genealogy, birth and migration to Egypt. All these events cover four years of his life and after that there is a gap of eight years, when at the age of twelve, Jesus visits the Temple in Jerusalem. After this, his life becomes obscure for about seventeen years and there is no information available to fill in this gap. No record of any kind as to where he was or what he was doing during this period is available in the Christian writings of the West. We are only informed that he began a mission at the age of thirty and gathered many followers. At the insistence of the Jewish priests, the Roman governor ordered him to be put on the Cross. He was crucified by four Roman soldiers but was taken down at the behest of Joseph of Arimathea. He rose from the dead and lived with his followers for forty days. What happened after resurrection, nobody knows, except that he disappeared! Strange enough, the Gnostics have their own version of the crucifixion. In a manuscript found at Nag Hammadi in Egypt, we are informed that:

> *I did not succumb to them as they had planned. I did not die in reality but in appearance and it was another who drank the gall and the vinegar. It was another Simon who bore the cross on his shoulder. It was another upon whom they placed the crown of thorns. I was laughing at their ignorance.*

From the above it is evident that there are many contradictory reports about the life of Jesus Christ, which require a thorough probe. It is also possible that our quest for the lost years in the life of Jesus may go against the popular Christian beliefs. The Western sources available to clear this mystery are scanty. However, the source material, both from the West and the East, available so far, which can be consulted is described below.

The Authorized Gospels

The Gospels of Mark, Matthew, Luke and John are the authorized Gospels, included in the New Testament. Originally written in Greek, the scriptures were printed in the 14th century. The above Gospels were compiled before the start of the second century, as may be seen below.[1]

Mark: 60–70 A.D.
Matthew: 85 A.D.
Luke: 90–95 A.D.
John: 110 A.D.

More or less, the Gospels may be termed as the contemporary sources of information on the life and mission of Jesus Christ. Unfortunately, the Gospels provide little or, rather, no information about the childhood of Jesus until the age of twelve, when he went to Jerusalem for the Passover. John the Baptist appears, in about 28 A.D., and as such, no information is available about Jesus up to the year of Baptism, and before the beginning of his ministry. We need not deal with the Hebrew sources due to the obvious reasons. Historically, the Apocryphal Gospels are important, because they were written by the Jewish Christians in the middle of the first century A.D. Similarly, the Dead Sea Scrolls are also important and deserve attention.

Historicity of the Gospels

Did Jesus Christ commit his teachings to writing? Are his doctrines free from error? Such like questions are being asked by those who aim at the critical study of the Gospels. It is a historical fact that twenty-five years after the departure of Jesus Christ, devotees began to collect fragmentary records of his words and deeds.[2] It is Paul who occasionally quotes words of the Master, and his Epistle falls within the above-mentioned period. As such, his work is authentic and authoritative. Then it was Peter who wrote down some events in the life of Jesus Christ. It was Matthew who composed the life and teachings of Jesus Christ in the Hebrew dialect.[3] But no version is available and we have only the Greek version of the first Gospel. As such, we can safely presume that the Gospel according to Matthew was written earlier than 85 A.D. The Gospel of Mark is authentic and authoritative, for he compiled it after getting first-hand information from Peter, who was an eye-witness. As such, Mark has preserved for us some of the most accurate events in the life of Jesus Christ. His Gospel has been dated before the destruction of Jerusalem, 70 A.D. Luke clearly states that his compilation is based on earlier and authentic writings about the words and deeds of Jesus. He states:

> For as much as many have taken in hand,
> To set forth in order a declaration of those things,
> Which are most surely believed among us,[4]
> Even as they delivered them unto us,
> Which from the beginning were eye-witnesses,
> And ministers of the word;
> It seems good to me also,
> Having had perfect understanding.
> Of all things from the very first,
> To write unto thee in order,
> Most excellent Theophilus,
> That thou mightest know certainty of those things,
> Wherein thou hast been instructed.[5]

From the above, two things are clear: that many authors had undertaken to construct the life of Jesus Christ and that they derived information from the narratives of previous authors. Unfortunately, the writings of most of these earlier authors were declared inauthentic by the Church and were destroyed. The authorship of the Gospel according to John is under dispute. However, this Gospel provides us with authentic information about the first disciples of the Lord, about Nicodemus, about the women of Samaria, about the healing of Paul, about the details of crucifixion, about the second coming of Jesus Christ and meeting his disciples, and about the final sermon he gave before parting from them. The details provided in this Gospel are of utmost importance, for Jesus told them not to tarry but follow him, probably on a long journey.

> Thus spake he,
> Signifying by what death he should glorify God.
> And when he had spoken thus,
> He saith unto him,
> Follow me.[6]

Apocryphal Gospels

The search for the historical Jesus by scholars continues. This quest has resulted in the discovery of many writings. However, all these writings are not available, for these were destroyed under orders of the Church. Tradition has handed down a list of 26 Apocryphal Gospels, 7 Acts and 10 Epistles, which were used during the early days of Christianity. These writings, which were rejected by the Church, retain their originality to a great extent, but all of these are not available to us. Some of these original writings exist in name only, and of some, we have only a few fragments.

It may be pointed out that most of these Gospels do speak of Jesus as a man and not as a mythical person. For instance, the Gospel of James informs about the marriage of Mary with Joseph. In the Gospel of the Ebionites, Jesus is believed to have been born in a normal way as a son of Joseph and Mary.

The Gospel of Philip informs us that the Lord migrated towards the East, with his mother and with his consort, Mary Magdalene. It is a historical fact that the Church, in its various councils held from time to time, rejected some Gospels and accepted some Gospels. In the process of drawing such lists, it went on changing entries with the result that now we have only four Gospels, which are considered official and all the rest have been declared heretical. The net result of this suppression has been that we have been deprived of much useful and authentic source material, which could have filled in the gaps in the earthly life of Jesus.

Five Gospels of Tation

Tation, the famous Syric scholar of Edisa, compiled a volume containing five Gospels, in the second century A.D. After thorough research into the Greek and the Hebrew sources, he compiled his Bible, which remained in vogue for several hundred years among followers of the Syrian Church. With the coming of the Roman Church to power, the Bible compiled by Tation was ordered to be destroyed. As such, all its copies were collected and destroyed by fire. It appears that Tation had mentioned that after resurrection,

Jesus Christ did meet his disciples, and especially his mother Mary, several times, and he was a living being and not a spirit. The Roman Church did not like such ideas, and as such, got the Five Gospels of Tation destroyed.

There are about fifty Apocryphal works, discovered so far, which have been denied official patronage because they do not give any support to the revised doctrines formulated by the Church. The most important Apocryphal Gospels are the following:

1. The Gospel of the Hebrews.
2. The Gospel of the Egyptians.
3. The Gospel of Nicodemus.
4. The Gospel of Thomas.
5. The Gospel of James.
6. The Gospel of Barnabas.
7. The Gospel of Peter.
8. The Gospel of the Ebionites.
9. The Gospel of Philip.
10. The Gospel of Mary Magdalene.

The Gospel of the Hebrews was originally written in Aramaic and then translated into Greek and Latin. It gives prominence to James, the brother of Jesus Christ. The Gospel of Nicodemus gives the account of Jesus Christ's descent to the underworld. The Gospel of James provides information about the childhood of the Lord. Among these Gospels, special mention may be made of the Gospel of Thomas and the Gospel of Philip, which are termed as the Coptic Gospels, because they are in Coptic and were discovered at Al-Hammadi in Egypt.

An Italian manuscript of the Gospel of Barnabas exists in the Hofbibliothek in Vienna. Its paper is Italian and the pages are decorated in later periods with Arabic sentences in the margin. It is believed that the manuscript was obtained by an Italian priest Fra Marino from the private library of the Pope. The Gospel was compiled by Joses, a Levite surnamed by the apostles as Barnabas, meaning the son of consolation.[7] As a missionary to Antioch, he accompanied Paul several times but separated from him due to differences. He was stoned to death by the Jews at Slamis in Cyprus.

In his Gospel, Joses mentions himself as an Apostle of Jesus Christ and says that he was directed by the Lord himself to pen down the life and works of Jesus. The Gospel of Barnabas was banned in 382 by the Decree of Western Churches. However, its manuscripts existed in the private library of Pope Damasus (383 A.D.), in the shrine of Barnabas and the Pope V (1585-90). Its English translation was published at Oxford in 1908 by Lonsdale Ragg and Lura Rubert. Soon after, its Arabic translation was published in Egypt.

Testaments of the Twelve Patriarchs

This was one of the scriptures considered authentic by the early Christians. Paul seems to have used these Testaments and even copied some portion out of it while compiling his letters. Even Matthew, while composing his Gospel was indebted to the Testaments of the Twelve Patriarchs. These Testaments were later on left out of the Bible.[8]

The Dead Sea Scrolls

In 1947, a number of manuscripts were discovered from a cave of Wadi Qumran, in the Dead Sea. In 1949, some fragments of the Old Testament were recovered from the Qumran Cave. Later, in 1952, a considerable number of fragments and coins were discovered from the caves of Wadi Murabbaat These manuscripts, which are popularly known as the Dead Sea Scrolls, are compilations of the saints, known as the Essenes, whose monastery, known as the Khirbet Qumran, was destroyed by the Romans in about 70 A.D. Among the scrolls are those called the Lamech scrolls, which are written in Aramaic and contains chapters from the book of Genesis.

The Essenes believed in the Teacher of Righteousness, who was to come and explain the wisdom of all previous prophets. He would be the Anointed One, who would inaugurate a new world order. As such, the Dead Sea Scrolls are a better pointer to understand the background of the New Testament. There are parallels between the doctrines of the Essenes and the earlier Christian doctrines. In the Dead Sea Scrolls, there exist many sentences, which are recorded in the Gospels and attributed to Jesus Christ. In fact, the Gospels of

John and the Dead Sea Scrolls have similar style and similar thinking. As such, for better understanding of the New Testament, study of the Dead Sea Scrolls is essential.

The Dead Sea Scrolls were written before the advent of Jesus Christ. The First Enoch was written in 170-64 B.C. and the Testament of the Twelve Patriarchs was compiled between 109-107 B.C.

Ancient Historical Works

Among the ancient historical works, mention may be made of:

a) *Quod Omnis Probus Liber*, written by Philo of Alexandria in 20 A.D. It provides us with detailed information about the Essenes, who lived in Palestine and Syria.

b) *Historica Naturalis*, by Pliny the Elder, written in 70 A.D., tells us about the Essenes living near Jerusalem.

c) *Wars of the Jews*, written by Josephus in 94 A.D., provides us with information about the Jews and their sects. It also tells us about the Essenes and their tenets and beliefs.

d) *Antiquities of the Jews*, by Josephus, contains some scanty information about Jesus Christ, which seems as interpolation.

The Acta Thomae

Written by Leucius in the beginning of the second century A.D., it is based on letters written by Thomas from India. It was translated into German by Max. Donnet and published at Leipzig in 1883. Though read as the Gospel of Thomas, it was proscribed by the Roman Catholic Church, for it denies the virgin birth of Jesus. It also provides information about the meeting between Jesus Christ and Thomas at Taxila in the Punjab. It was Thomas, who introduced Christianity in the south of India in about 52, and he built many churches but suffered martyrdom in 72. He was buried at Mylapore, where the San-Thome Cathedral Basilica stands at present. The Acta Thomae was denounced in 495 as heretical by a Decree of Gelasius. The information given in it, about the encounter between Jesus Christ and Abdagases is very interesting. This encounter took place soon after the marriage of Abdagases was solemnized. Thomas, under whose supervision the palace at Taxila had been built, performed the marriage but left after the ceremonies.

When Abdagases came to meet the bride, he saw a saintly person there. Recognizing him as Thomas, he asked him as to how he was still there when he had left earlier. But the saintly person replied:

I am not Thomas but his brother.

This incident took place in about 49, and the saintly person was no other than Jesus Christ.[9]

The Gospel of Thomas was translated from Greek into Russian in the 13th century. The Acta Thomae informs as to how the Apostles divided the world for preaching purposes. At the time of this decision, India fell to the lot of Thomas. Jesus is said to have told Thomas:

Fear not, Thomas; proceed to India and proclaim the word, for my grace shall be with thee.

The Syrian Christians of Malabar, India, claim that Thomas was their founder. It must be noted that the Gospel according to Thomas, dating about third century was discovered in 1947 from Luxer in Egypt.[10]

Sanskrit Sources

The following table of inscriptions will show the life of a particular ancient language:

1. Sumerian   4,000 B.C.
2. Elematic   2,000 B.C.
3. Cossean   1,600 B.C.
4. Chinese   1,500 B.C.
5. Hittite   14,000 B.C.
6. Sanskrit   12,000 B.C.
7. Avesta   600 B.C.
8. Arabic   328 B.C.

It is clear that Sanskrit is one among the ancient languages of the world.[11] As Sanskrit was written and read in India, we have to search for documents relating to Jesus in this language. Fortunately, we were able to locate some rare Sanskrit manuscripts, written in the *Sharda* alphabets, in Kashmir.

The Bhavishya-Maha-Purana

In Sanskrit, the word "Purana" means ancient history. The Puranas are considered sacred by the Hindus. Out of the eighteen volumes, the ninth of this series is named *Bhavishya Maha Purana,* which means "prophecies about the future." Among other things, it mentions that in India, in addition to the area under the Brahmanic rule, the devotees of Moses were spread over the rest of the land. It is evident that this refers to the Jewish settlements in the northern regions of India. The *Bhavishya Maha Purana* is an ancient Sanskrit work ascribed to Suta, said to have been compiled in 3191 Laukika year corresponding to 115 A.D. Though the manuscript is written in the *Sharda,* its language is Sanskrit. It was sent by the Maharaja of Kashmir to the Research Institute, Poona, for translation and was published at Mumbai in 1910. It was also translated into Hindi and its two commentaries have been published so far. The *Bhavishya Maha Purana* is one of the most important and independent original sources of information about the visit of Jesus Christ to Kashmir. It may be remarked that the manuscript was written by a Hindu saint long before the advent of Islam. Further, the Hindus have no religious connections with either the Jews or the Christians or the Muslims. Hence, information provided in the *Bhavishya Maha Purana,* though very brief, is historically important. It relates to the meeting of Jesus Christ with the Raja of the Sakas, or the Scythian tribes, who had conquered northern India and Kashmir during the first century. The translation of the relevant verses is given below:

> *O, King!*
> *I hail from a land, far away;*
> *Where there is no truth,*
> *And evil knows no limits.*
> *I appeared in the Mleecha country:*

And I suffered at their hands.
I am known as the Son of God, (Ishvara—Putram)
I am born of a virgin. (Kanya—Garbam)
I teach love, truth, and purity of heart,
I ask human beings to serve the Lord.
The Lord is in the center of the Sun,
And the elements;
And God;
And the Sun are forever.
Bliss giving God being always in my heart,
My name has been established as Isa-Masih.[12]

The Rajatarangini

It is an important historical work in Sanskrit written by Kalahana in about 1148. The *Rajatarangini* is the oldest available history of Kashmir from earliest times. It has been translated from Sanskrit into English by Aurel Stein in 1900 and by Dr. Tokan Sumi into Japanese in 1970. This historical work elaborately describes the crucifixion of a saint, surnamed *Samdhimatti*, meaning the Spirit of God, the disciple of the *Guru* Isana. While the saviour is named as Isana, the crucified is named as *Samdhimatti*, Prince of the Aryas. However, this tradition regarding putting a saint on the cross, documented in an ancient recording, is reproduced here:

> At that time there spread by the force of future events, a mysterious report from house to house declared; To Samdhimatti will belong the Kingdom.
>
> The king thereupon threw him into prison, and there he pined with his legs tormented by cruel fetters. The king thereupon thought that the only way to frustrate the decree of fate was to kill him.
>
> If foolish men prepare a device to work off a coming event, one may be sure that fate intends to open new avenues. Then under the orders of the king, Samdhimatti, the sage, was put on the cross by savage executioners.
>
> The news reached Isana, the great guru, and he proceeded to the place of execution, where his disciple Samdhimatti had suffered without a sympathizer. He found him reduced to a skeleton on the cross.
>
> > Woe, that I see thee today,
> > O, dear, in this condition.
>
> He then drew forth the bone, which the cross had pierced through. He carried away the skeleton, but on his forehead he read inscribed as below:

He will have a poor life, imprisonment, death on the cross and still thereafter a throne. Fate is the embodiment of all miracles; what else but fate would bring him to life again.

Then he stayed at that very place, in his anxiety to see the fulfillment of the prediction and watched the Skeleton. He smelt a heavenly perfume of incense in the middle of the night. Hidden behind a tree, he then saw the skeleton being fitted up with all its limbs. He resembled a person just arisen from deep sleep, covered with heavenly ointments. Then Samdhimatti, wearing a magnificent dress and a wreath, recovered memory of his past and bowed with reverence before his Guru, Isana.

The above narration thereby reveals that Samdhimatti, also known as the spirit of God, was put on the stake, but resurrected like Jesus.

Natha Namavali

Jesus belonged to the sect of the Essenes, of which John the Baptist was also a member. John baptized Christ in a river, and the ceremony employed was very similar to that which is performed to this day among the *yogis* when they take their ablutions in the sacred rivers of India. In the *Song of the Yogi,* which the Natha Yogis sing, there are also references to Isha and to John the Baptist.

My friend, to what country did Ishai go, and to what country went John? My friend, where is the guru of the gurus and where is your mind resting? My friend, Ishai has gone towards Arabia, John towards Egypt. My friend, Ishai is the Guru of my gurus. The mind of the yogi rests only in the yogi.

The Natha Yogis of the Vindhyachal Mountains name their scripture as the *Natha Namavali.* Among the lives of the great *gurus* of this cult, described in this *Sutra,* is a *guru* named Ishai Natha. He came to India at the age of fourteen, and after sixteen long years of *Tapsiya* he came to understand the science of *Samadhi.* After this he went back to his own country and began his ministry. Soon, however, the Jews, who were his enemies, conspired against him and had him crucified. At the time of crucifixion Ishai Natha entered into *Samadhi.* Seeing him thus, the Jews presumed he was dead and buried him in a tomb. At that very moment, however, one of his

Gurus, the great Chetan Natha happened to be engaged in profound meditation in the Himalayas. He saw in a vision the tortures Ishai Natha was undergoing. He therefore made his body lighter than air and flew over to the land of Israel. The day of his arrival was marked with thunder and lightning, for the gods were angry and the whole world trembled. The Chetan Natha took the body of Ishai Natha from the tomb and woke him from his *Samadhi,* and led him off to the sacred land of the Aryans.

The above information given in the *Natha Namavali* establishes survival of Jesus on the cross and his departure towards the East. It is interesting that we are further informed in this *Sutra* that Ishai Natha established his Ashram in the lower regions of the Himalayas.

Tibetan Sources

The message of Jesus Christ was carried by his disciples and devotees to Parthia, Sogdiana, Gandara and other regions of central Asia during the first century. The Buddhists of these countries were well acquainted with Jesus, because for them, he was the future Buddha. There is a very old mention by Hippolytus of the *Book of Revelation* from the land of the Seres in Parthia. We even learn from Hippolytus that the *Book of Elxai* itself originated from Parthia. According to this author, Elxai had received it from the Seres of Parthia. At that time *Seres* was a designation of a nation which produced silk and lived above India, i.e., the Chinese or Tibetans. As the trade in silk passed through Parthia, the Seres of Parthia are the Chinese or Tibetans, who came to the Parthian territory. Thus, the *Book of Elxai* was supposed by its readers or by its author to be a sort of Chinese or Tibetan Gospel.[13]

It is a historical fact that Hippolytus was the Bishop of Rome in about 220 A.D. His specific mention of the *Book of Revelations* shows that the Western Christians of the third century knew of Eastern books of Judaeo-Christian content. Elxai was the incarnation of God, and his sect believed in successive incarnation of the heavenly beings. We also know that the Buddhists believe in the incarnation of Buddha or Bodhisattvas, and parallelism in both the doctrines cannot be doubted. History records that the Ebionites also cherished such beliefs. As such, there is no wonder that our search among the fragments from the Buddhist monasteries will tell us something in detail about the unknown life of Jesus Christ. Hence, there is every need to find out documents which would be lying buried under the huge collections of manuscripts in the *Gumpas* of Ladakh and Tibet.

One such manuscript is entitled *Grub-tha Thams-chand kyi Khuna dan Dod-thsul Ston-pe Legs Shad Shel-gyi Melon*, which means: the History of Religion and Doctrines—the Glass Mirror. Originally, it is an ancient Chinese manuscript which was translated into the Tibetan by Le-zan Cbhes-Kyi Nima.[14] It gives the following information:

> *Yesu, the teacher and founder of the religion, who was born miraculously, proclaimed himself as the Saviour of the world. He commanded his disciples to observe the ten vows, among which he prohibited manslaughter and attainment of eternal joy and happiness through good deeds. He preached that evil deeds plunge one into hell, full with eternal torment and misery. A sin committed in a state of consciousness cannot be condoned and is unpardonable. This is one of the virtuous results emerging out of the doctrines of our Buddha. His doctrine did not spread extensively but survived in Asia for a long period. The above information is derived from the Chinese texts about the religions and doctrines.*

Tibetan manuscript about Jesus

The above would clearly reveal that the Buddhists had great reverence for Jesus, who has been mentioned as Yesu, the Aramaic adoption of his name. It also shows that the Chinese also knew about the miraculous birth of Jesus.

The Unknown Life of Jesus Christ

Nicolas Notovitch, who was a Russian traveller, visited Afghanistan in 1887. From that country he reached Kashmir in the same year. As he decided to return to Russia via Karakoram, he departed for Ladakh, via Zojila and reached Leh on the 1st of November, 1887. He remained in the Hemis monastery for some days with the Buddhist *Lamas* or monks.

During his stay, he discovered the Tibetan manuscripts about the earlier life of Jesus Christ in the Hemis monastery. He transcribed these manuscripts with the help of an interpreter, Dr. Marx, of the Morovian Mission of Leh, attended him during his illness and made a note about the findings of Notovitch in his diary.[15]

Nicolas Notovitch returned to Russia and showed his manuscript to the authorities at Kiev, who told him not to publish the account. He then went to Rome and a Cardinal at the Vatican offered to bribe him for the manuscript, but he refused to comply. He went to Paris to seek some publisher for his work, but no one was ready to help him. Ultimately, in 1890, he got his notes published in New York, under the title of *The Life of Saint Issa*. This very work, published under the title of *The Unknown Life of Jesus Christ* in 1894, can be divided into three parts. The first part deals with the condition that led to his reincarnation. The second part deals with his travels and studies in India up to the age of twenty-nine. The third part deals with his ministry in Palestine. After its publication, this book created a lot of controversy among the Christian scholars. The presence of Jesus in India prior to his crucifixion had shaken the foundation of Christianity. Some among the Christian scholars cast doubts about the existence of any author named Notovitch, and the others doubted even about the existence of any monastery having the name of Hemis. They claimed that *The Unknown Life of Jesus Christ* was a forgery and a fraud. In response to all these allegations, Nicolas Notovitch announced his existence and also gave the names of various people he had met during his travels. But he was condemned and criticized by the Anglican Church. For this purpose it obtained the services of the famous Orientalist from Oxford, Max Muller, to refute the findings of Notovitch.

During this period, India was a part of the British Empire, and they could do anything to remove these documents from Ladakh. Accordingly, the Christian Church Mission in India engaged the services of Ahmad Shah, a neo-Christian, and Professor Douglas of the Government College, Agra, to refute the Tibetan texts found by Nicolas Notovitch. Ahmad Shah lived in Ladakh from 1894 to 1897 and published a book entitled, *Four Years in Tibet*. He admits that his sole aim to visit Ladakh was to refute the find of Notovitch, a Russian, of a hitherto-unknown manuscript of a Tibetan version of the life of Christ between the ages 12 and 30. Professor Douglas visited Ladakh in 1895 for necessary investigations. Later he wrote that the work of Notovitch was a literary forgery.[16] On the strength of his article, a further wave of condemnation and insults swept over Notovitch. Since then, it has been a continuous practice with the

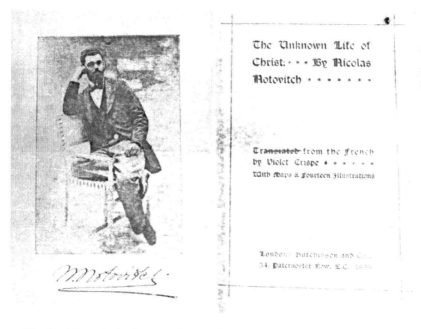

Nicolas Notovitch, the translator of Hemis monastery Buddhist scrolls

Church to trace, buy, confiscate and steal ancient documents referring to Jesus' life in the East.[17]

Central Asian Manuscripts

Central Asia has been the home of several exotic civilizations. It has also remained a seat of vast empires. There was a period when many cultures, the Greek, the Buddhist, the Islamic, flourished in this region. It has been a birthplace of many prophets, philosophers and great men. The vastness and richness of its various cultures can be proved with only one sentence: that all great museums of the world do possess treasures of this region without which all these museums would look poor. It is a historical fact that the Western treasure seekers have stolen caravan-loads of priceless treasures from the Central Asian temples, mosques, tombs, caves and sites. Among the chief robbers, mention may be made of Aurel Stein of England, Albert von LeCoq of Germany, Seven Hedin of Sweden, Paul Pelliot of France, Langdon Warner of the United States and Otani of Japan.

In 1907, Stein ravaged thousands of manuscripts and documents from the Tunhang caves. These manuscripts were written in several Semitic alphabets. It is certain that some manuscripts written in Aramaic pertained to Jesus. Stein intentionally concealed this information from the world for the sake of Christianity by declaring that *"these manuscripts embody teachings of Mani, which are almost the same as those of Jesus Christ."*[18] His statement, though half-true, served as a warning to the Church, who started employing special missions to search out documents relating to Jesus for destruction. In this way, much information about Jesus has been either destroyed or kept concealed.

Persian Works

There are several rare Persian and Arabic works which provide valuable information about Jesus. These works come from Iran, Central Asia, and Kashmir. As regards the Kashmiris, their written records, both ancient and modern, establish their descent from one of the tribes of Israel. The foremost historian of Kashmir was

Mulla Nadri, who began his *Tarikh-i-Kashmir* in the reign of Sultan
Sikander (1378–1416). The next historian was Mulla Ahmad, who
wrote his book *Waqaya-i-Kashmir* in 1426. In both these works, it is
categorically stated that the inhabitants of Kashmir are of Semitic
stock. Another book of history which mentions this fact is *Hashmat-
i-Kashmir*, written by Abdul Qadir in 1748. He states that the inhabitants of Kashmir are the Children of Israel, and that they came
from the *Holy Land*. Some of the most important and rare Persian
works, which provide useful information about Jesus Christ, are
given below:

Rauza Tus-Safa

This is a biography of the prophets, kings and caliphs in seven
volumes, written by Mir Mohammad in the year 836 A.H. (1417 A.D.).
It deals with the odyssey of Jesus Christ from Jerusalem to Nisibis.

Tawarikh-i-Kashmir

This is the famous work by Mulla Nadri, the first Muslim historian of Kashmir. It deals with the events leading to the declaration
of the second ministry in Kashmir, when Jesus Christ arrived in
Kashmir and declared himself as the Son of God, named as Masiah,
and as the Prophet sent to the valley. Mulla Nadri records in his
Tawarikh-i-Kashmir as follows:

> *During this time Hazrat Yuzu-Asaph, having come from the Holy Land to
> this Holy Valley, proclaimed his prophethood. He devoted his days and nights
> in prayers, and having attained higher sphere of spiritual virtues, declared
> himself a prophet for Kashmiris.*
> *I have seen in a book of the Hindus that this prophet was really Hazrat
> Issa, the Spirit of God, who had assumed the name of Yuzu-Asaph in Kashmir.
> He spent his life in this valley and after his demise was laid to rest in the local-
> ity of Anzimar, Srinagar. It is also said that the aura of prophethood emanates
> from the tomb of this prophet.*

Late Sahibzada Basharat Salim of Srinagar, Kashmir, who claimed
to be a descendant of Hazrat Yuzu-Asaph, has the following remarks
about the *Tawarikh-i-Kashmir* by Mulla Nadri:

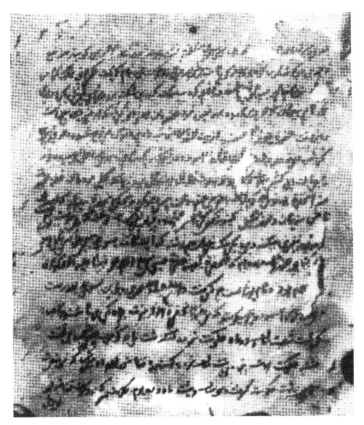

Tawariki-i-Kashmir by Mulla Nadri

Mulla Nadri's Persian book Tawarikh-i-Kashmir is an authentic historical document with enormous and convincing details of our family, i.e. the family of Holy Yuza Asaf. In fact this precious historical document is our family's property and has been in the private possession of my reverenced late father, Sahibzada Ghulam Mohiyuddin.[19]

Kamal-ud-Din

Kamal-ud-Din, also known as *Kashful Hairat* or *Ikmal-ud-Din* in Persian, was written by the great Oriental writer and historian Al-Shaikh-us-Sadiq Abi-Jafar Muhammad known as Al Shaikh Said-us-Sadiq, who died at Khurassan in 962. He has described the travels of Yuzu-Asaph in this famous book. This important source is considered by Western Orientalists to be of great value. It was first printed by Aga Mir Baqar in the Sayyid-us-Sanad Press in Iran in 1782 and was later translated into German by Professor Muller of Heidelberg University. Al Shaikh Said-us-Sadiq had travelled a good deal during his lifetime and collected much material for this and his other 300 works.

In this book is mentioned the first trip of the Jesus to Sholabeth, or Ceylon, and other places. The second journey of the Lord, terminating finally in Kashmir, is also mentioned. His sayings and teachings are also briefly mentioned, which are similar to the sayings of Jesus as given in the Gospels. It is also mentioned that at the approach of death, Yuzu-Asaph sent for his disciple Thomas and expressed his last will to him about carrying on his mission. He directed Thomas to prepare a tomb for him at the very place he would breathe his last. He then stretched his legs towards the West and kept his head towards the East, and passed away.

> *Then Yuzu-Asaph after roaming about in many cities, reached that country which is called Kashmir. He travelled in it far and wide and stayed there and spent his remaining life there, until death overtook him, and he left the earthly body and was elevated towards the Light. But before his death he sent for a disciple of his, Ba'bad by name, who used to serve him and was well-versed in all matters. He expressed his last will to him and said: My time for departing from this world has come. Carry on your duties properly and directed Ba'bad to prepare a tomb over him at the very place he died. He then stretched his legs towards the West and head towards the East and died. May God bless him.*

Ahwal-i-Ahrliyan-i-Paras

Written in Persian, by Agha Mustaffa, it narrates the parables of Yuzu-Asaph as recorded in the Persian traditions. It mentions that he came from the West to Persia, preached there, and many became his devotees. It was published in Tehran in 1909.

Tarikh-i-Azami

Khawaja Muhammad Azam of Deedamari is one of the famous historians of Kashmir. He completed his history of Kashmir in 1827, which is known as *Tarikh-i-Azami*. The work was first printed at Lahore in 1814 A.D. He writes,

Besides that grave (of Syed Nasir-ud-Din in Khaniyar) there is a tomb. It is well known amongst the people of the locality that here lies a Prophet who had come to Kashmir in ancient times. It is now known as the place of the Prophet. I have seen in a book of history that he had come, after great tribulations, from a great distance.

It is said that a prince, after undergoing a good deal of penance and perseverance and through devotion and prayers, had become the Messenger of God to the people of Kashmir. On reaching Kashmir, he invited people to his religion and after death was laid to rest in Anzmarah. In that book the name of the Prophet is given as Yuzu Asaph. Anzmarah is in Khanyar. Many pious people and especially the spiritual guide of the author, Mulla Inayatullah Shaul, says that while visiting the tomb, Divine grace and blessings of Prophethood were witnessed.

Ain-ul-Hayat

Ibn-i-Muhammad Hadi Muhammad Ismail, the author of *Ain-ul-Hayat,* devotes a chapter to Yuzu Aspah under the caption: *Description of the Events concerning Yuzu Asaph,* in which he mentions the various journeys of Yuzu Asaph and gives details of his teachings.

He went to many cities and preached to the people of those cities. At last he reached the city of Kashmir. He invited its inhabitants to righteousness and resided there till death approached him, and his Holy Spirit departed from his earthly body and went to rest with God. But before his death he called his companion Ba'bad and made a will and directed him to construct a tomb for him. He laid himself with his head towards the East and stretched his legs towards the West, and went to the place of Eternity.

Wajeez-ut-Tawarikh

Khwaja Nabba Shah alias Ghulam Nabi Khanyari wrote his history of Kashmir in 1896 under the title of *Wajeez-ut-Tawarikh.* While referring to the tomb of Sayyid Nasir-uddin, he also describes the Tomb of Yuzu-Asaph in these words:

The tomb of Syed Nasir-uddin is in Mohalla Khanyar and is also known as Razabal. There is also the tomb of Yuzu-Asaph, the Prophet. He was a prince and had come to this place. Through prayers and because of his piety he had come as a messenger to the people of Kashmir, and he preached to them. It is said that at that time Raja Gopadatta was the ruler. There was a hole in the

western wall of the Tomb, out of which the aroma of musk used to emanate. A
woman with an infant child came to pay her respects. The child passed urine
and it went into the hole. The woman became insane!

Tawarikh-i-Kashmir

Pir Ghulam Hassan Khuihami (1833-1898) was a noted historian
of Kashmir, who compiled his monumental history of Kashmir in
four volumes. The first volume deals with geography and the second volume deals with political history of Kashmir from earliest
times to 1896. The third and the fourth volumes are devoted to the
life and works of saints, scholars and poets of medieval and modern
times. Volume III is entitled as the *Tarikh-i-Aulia-i-Kashir.* In it, he
refers to the tomb of Yuzu Asaph in these words:

> *It is said that therein lies buried a Prophet who, in ancient times, was*
> *raised for the people of Kashmir.*

Pirzada Ghulam Hassan then quotes Khwaja Muhammad Azam
and says:

> *This man was a prince and through extensive prayers reached the stage*
> *of prophethood (Darja-i-Paighambari). His burial place is in Khanyar and it is*
> *known as Tomb of a Prophet (Qabr-i-Paighambar).*

Hasmat-i-Kashmir

Abdul Qadir wrote a book in Persian on the history of Kashmir
in 1748 entitled: *Hashmat-i-Kashmir.* In it, he refers to the grave of a
prophet, from the *People of the Book,* which is situated at Khanyar in
Srinagar, Kashmir. The term *People of the Book* is applied to the followers of Judaism and Christianity, by the Muslims. He writes:

> *The Tomb is described by the people of the locality to be that of a Paigham-*
> *bar-i-Ahl-i-Kitab (Prophet of the People of the Book).*

The term *Ahl-i-Kitab* means the people, who were blessed with
revealed scriptures like the *Holy Tora,* the Holy Bible and the Holy
Quran.

Waqiat-i-Kashmir

Bad-uddin Qasim (1741-1781) wrote a book in Persian, entitled *Waqiat-i-Kashmir, Janat Nazir.* While referring to the tomb of Yuzu Asaph, he says:

> *The assertion of the people of knowledge is that one of the disciples of Jesus is buried there, from whose tomb emanates Divine grace and blessings.*

It is noteworthy that he connects this tomb with one of the disciples of Jesus Christ, without mentioning his name. However, it is significant that he refers to the Tomb having existed during the period of Jesus Christ.

Travels in Central Asia

Travels in Central Asia by Meer Izzut-oollah, in the years 1812-1813, was translated into English by Captain Henderson, attached to the Foreign Office of the Government of India. It was printed at the Foreign Department Press at Culcutta, India, in 1872. Meer Izzut-oolah undertook his journey to Central Asia on the 20th of April, 1812, and committed to writing all that he himself saw and heard.

His work contains an account of his travel to Bokhara and a description of each day's journey from Attock to Kashmir, from Kashmir to Ladakh, from Ladakh to Yarkand, from Yarkand to Kashghar and from that place to China. He travelled from Kashghar to Samarkand, from Samarkand to Bokhara, from Bokhara to Balkh, and from there to Kabul. He has provided an interesting and thought-provoking account of the similarities between the Buddhists and the Christians. Among other things, he tells us about the sculptured figure, representing Jesus Christ, the Trinity and the Bible, which was revealed to the Tibetans, in a language which has now become unintelligible. Hippolytus had made mention of *The Book of Revelation* and the *Book of Elxai,* to have originated from the land of the Seres in Parthia. The term Seres refers to the silk producing nation of the Chinese and the Tibetans. Both the above books are supposed to be a sort of the Chinese or the Tibetan Gospels.

The Crucifixion by an Eyewitness

The above title was published by the Indo-American Book Co., Chicago, in 1907 as a second edition in the Supplemental Harmonic Series. It is stated in its introduction that the substance given in the book was first published there in 1873 but was withdrawn from circulation, and all its copies, along with its plates, were destroyed. But one copy found its way into the possession of a prominent Mason in the State of Massachusetts and remained with him until 1907. The book is a translation from the Latin manuscript in possession of the Masonic Fraternity in Germany. Accordingly, it was republished in 1907. The above work contains the translation of the letter written by a member of the Essene Order to another member in Alexandria just seven years after the crucifixion. It gives an eyewitness account of the crucifixion, and the method by which Jesus Christ was saved from death on the Cross.

The Aquarian Gospel of Jesus the Christ

The Aquarian Gospel of Jesus the Christ was compiled by Levi H. Dowling before 1907, after many years of study and silent meditation. The Gospel tells us the story of Jesus Christ and also gives a complete record of the period spent by him in Tibet, India, Persia, Egypt and Greece. Levi was a student of world religions and it is possible that he may have borrowed information for his Gospel from the following works:

1. *Crucifixion by an Eyewitness*, 1873.
2. *Life of Saint Issa*, 1890.
3. *The Unknown Life of Christ*, 1894.

Masih Hindustan Mein

In Urdu, *Masih Hindustan Mein* is a work of research by Mirza Ghulam Ahmad, the founder of Ahmadiyas in Islam. This treatise has been translated from Urdu into English, entitled *Jesus in India*. The original work was published in 1908. The main thesis expounded in this research work is the escape from death of Jesus Christ on the cross and his subsequent journey to India in quest of the lost tribes of Israel. The most important portion of the treatise deals with similarities between Buddhism and Christianity. The author is of the opinion that Jesus Christ came to India after the crucifixion, and his teachings were imbibed into the Buddhist scriptures by the followers of that religion. This important research work deals with the escape of Jesus Christ from death, his recovery and healing of the wounds from the crucifixion, his journey towards the East in search of the lost tribes, and his demise in Kashmir. As the founder of a new sect in Islam, Mirza Ghulam Ahmad writes with religious zeal, which is mingled with his beliefs, aspirations and teachings. That is the reason why the arguments produced in this work have tremendously affected Muslim thought and disturbed Christian thinking.

The Gates of India

The Gates of India by Colonel Sir Thomas Holdich, was published by Macmillan and Co., London, in 1910. He investigated the routes which were used by explorers into the hinterland of India. He states that during ancient times, a variety of people or tribes either migrated or were deported from the Middle East, through Persia to North West India. He has further stated that there was an easy highway from Mesopotamia to Afghanistan for centuries. He says:

> *Thus it was that the people of Western Asia—Egyptians, Israelites, Jews, Phoenicians, Assyrians. Babylonians, and even Greeks—were transported over vast distances by land, and a movement given to the human race in that part of the world which has infinitely complicated the science of ethnology. There is not an important tribe of people in all that hinterland of India that has not been drafted from somewhere. From Persia and Media, from Aria and Skythia, from Greece and Arabia, from Syria and Mesopotamia they have come and their coming can generally be traced historically, and their traditions of origin proved to be true. But there is one important people, who call themselves Ben-i-Israel, who claim a descent from Kish, who adopted a strange mixture of Mosaic law and Hindu ordinance in their moral code, who keep a feast which strangely accords with the Passover, who hate the Jews with a traditional hatred, and for whom no one has been able to suggest any other origin than the one they claim and claim with determined force, and these people rule Afghanistan.*

Qabr-i-Masih

Based on the ethnological studies of the Kashmiris, Mufti Mohammad Sadiq wrote a book in Urdu entitled *Qabr-i-Masih,* which
was published in 1936. Being a scholar of repute, he has provided
evidence to prove the thesis that the Kashmiris are a Semite race. He
deals with this at length to show parallel words in the Hebrew and
Kashmiri languages. By providing conclusive evidence, he showed
that the Kashmiris have adopted the same rituals, customs and man-
ners that are a hallmark of the Jews. He gives a chapter on the Tomb
of Yuzu Aspah and historical evidence to show that Yuzu Aspah is
the name given by Kashmiris to Jesus Christ.

As he was a missionary of the Ahmadiyas, his work is mingled
with his personal beliefs and thinking. However, the *Qabr-i-Massih*
is a very useful work which formed the basis of a more elaborative
work by Khwaja Nazir Ahmad, who wrote *Jesus in Heaven on Earth,*
in 1952.

The Passover Plot

In this book, Hugh J. Schonfield has given a novel interpretation
about the events in the life of Jesus Christ. To him, Jesus was an actor
who deliberately undertook to fulfill the prophecies contained in
the Old Testament regarding the coming of the Messiah and deliberately planned to get himself crucified. There is a tendency among
some European scholars to weave out such fantastic tales around
the life of Jesus Christ.

New Testament Christology

The Foundations of New Testament Christology by R. H. Fuller is a
fine study of the historical Jesus in the light of the message and witness of the post-resurrection Church. It seeks to connect the teachings contained in the Gospels with the old and ancient scriptures of
the Hellenistic Judaism and other mystery cults.

The Nazarene Gospel Retold

Robert Graves and Joshua Pedro, working together, have made an objective study of the teachings of Jesus Christ, and their work includes some of the original apocalyptic books which had been dropped under orders of the Bishop of Rome. Both the above mentioned authors wrote another book, entitled *Jesus in Rome,* which deals with the post-crucifixion period in the life of Jesus Christ. The Jesuits have burnt both the books.

Asrar-i-Kashir

Written in Urdu, *Asrar-i-Kashir* by Dr. Aziz Ahmad, published in 1964, is the first anthropological and ethnological study of Kashmir. It is an attempt to make a comparative study of rituals, customs, art, architecture, ornaments, and rites of the Israelites and the Kashmiris. The author has taken up numerous topics, with the result that he has not been able to do justice with each subject. Secondly, where the author does not succeed in getting an authority or reference, he takes the help of a divine inspiration or a dream and tries to prove his point. As such the work by the author is defective and incomplete. However, the book is valuable, for it encourages us to look for those subjects—linguistics, ethnology, culture—which have remained overlooked until now.

A Mission to Bokhara

A Mission to Bokhara was originally published in 1845. Joseph Wolf, himself a Christian Jew and an Anglican clergyman, tells us that he came across Israelites in Persia, Kurdistan, Khurasan, Kokand, Bokhara, and Samarkand. He found the Jews of Bokhara and Khurasan to be quite ignorant of certain facts of history involving the Jews, for example, the story of Jesus. He felt that this proved their descent from the ten tribes who never returned to Palestine after their Babylonian captivity.

Jesus Nichtam Kreuz Gestorben

In the Cathedral of St. John in Turin, Italy there is a religious relic of world importance reputed to be the burial cloth of Jesus Christ. This linen is 14 feet, 3 inches long and 3 feet, 7 inches wide, carrying a negative image of a man with wounds similar to those suffered by Jesus. This burial cloth is unquestionably very very old and its history is known since 544, when Bishop Eulalio declared that the portrait found in Edessa in 540 was an impression not made by human hands. In 1898, when this holy relic was again shown to the public in Italy, a photographer named Secondo Pia photographed it in detail. After developing the glass plates in his dakroom, he discovered the imprinted face of a crucified person with a close likeness to the pictures of Jesus. The photograph showed the body with wound marks, the spear mark in the right side and the bloodstains caused by nails. Since then scientists, doctors and scholars have come up with their findings contrary to or in favor of the religious belief of the Christians.

Jesus Nichtam Kreuz Gestorben, by Kurt Berna, written in German and published by Verlag Hans Naber, Stuttgart, Germany, came out in 1952. It is a scientific study of the Turin Shroud, the marks of burning, bodily impression, and the marks of blood on it. Subsequently, Kurt Berna has come to the following conclusions:

a) The Holy Shroud is the original burial cloth of Jesus Christ.
b) He, having been removed from the Cross, was laid in this linen.
c) He was not dead at that time, and the blood marks on the linen show the existence of the flow of blood.

Jesus in Heaven on Earth

This is a standard work of research by Khwaja Nazir Ahmad, first published by the Woking Mission and Literary Trust, the Mosque, Woking, England in 1952. Since then many editions have appeared. The book is well-documented and contains an exhaustive bibliography. As the author belongs to the Ahmadiya community, he has mixed his own beliefs with facts of history, aiming at destroying Christian doctrine. He says:

> *The enquiry upon which I am about to enter may result in the annihilation of the greatest and most valuable part of that which Christians have been wont to believe concerning their saviour Jesus.*

Despite this major defect, the book contains valuable source material on the unknown life of Jesus Christ. The material pertaining to the lost ten tribes and their racial connections with the Afghans and the Kashmiris is a valuable contribution to the historical research.

The Crumbling of the Cross

Written by Mumtaz Ahmad Faruqui and published by the Ahmadiyya Anjuman Ishaat-i-Islam, Lahore, Pakistan in 1973, this book is basically a summary of the above-mentioned book, but contains a resumé of scientific studies done on the Holy Shroud at Turin. The author has given translated extracts from *Jesus Nicht am Kreuz Gestorben* ("Jesus Did Not Die on the Cross") by Kurt Berna, in the Appendix. As the name of the book suggests, the author, who is a member of the Ahmadiya community, is out to destroy Christian beliefs.

Jesus Died in Kashmir

This work by Andreas Faber Kaiser appeared first in Spanish under the title of *Jesus Vivo Y Murio En Cashemira*, in 1976, from ATE, Barcelona, Spain. Its English version was published by Gordon and Cremonesi, London, in 1977. The author has tried to compile a concise documentary dossier of all that is known about the second life of Jesus Christ and his demise in Kashmir. The main aim of the book is to inform the West about the matters which have an important bearing on Christian beliefs. In the end, he says:

> *Definitive proof is lacking, and for this reason I believe that the tomb in question should be opened for scientific investigation. In addition I propose that, in order to search out the truth in a scientifically objective manner, a world congress of Bible scholars, linguists, orientalists, and specialists in Islam and*

ancient history should be convoked. Only by these means is it possible to arrive at a firm, unbiased conclusion.

The author was provided with all useful research material on the subject by Professor Hassnain, and he acknowledges it, in his book.

Professor Hassnain is an authority on archaeology and anthropology in Kashmir. He has carried out an extensive research on the past history of this land and its people, with much care and sincerity. He is the only living authority after Khwaja Nazir Ahmad, who has conducted extensive researches on the Tomb of Jesus in Kashmir. He provided me with all precious source material and helped me to produce this book.

The Turin Shroud

In his book on the Holy Shroud, Ian Wilson has drawn together all the historical and scientific facts about the burial cloth of Jesus Christ, which is preserved in the Cathedral of St. John in Turin, Italy. This valuable book informs about the presence of human blood and pollen grains on the cloth, which shows that the Shroud may have once wrapped the body of Jesus Christ. It took him twelve years to investigate the truth about the relic. He has traced the history of the Shroud during the last two thousand years.

Die Messias Legitimation Jesu

This work by Helmut Goeckel deals with a number of subjects concerning Christology. The author traces the conception of a Messiah in the Old Testament and the New Testament. After tracing the history of various religions, the author describes in detail the rise and fall of Judaism. This work has a useful chapter on the Essenes of Qumran. After this, the author takes up the life of Jesus Christ, his ministry in Palestine and his mission in the East. The author discusses similarities between Christianity and Buddhism and then closes his book with a chronology.

The Lost Years of Jesus

For the first time, the author Elizabeth Clare Prophet brings together the testimony of four eye-witnesses of the Tibetan scrolls, giving detailed description about the pilgrimage of Jesus Christ from Jerusalem to India. With the thoroughness of a determined disciple turned detective, she tells the intriguing story of the international controversy that arose when the Tibetan scrolls were first discovered in 1887 by Nicolas Notovitch. The author puts together the missing pieces in the early life of Jesus and reveals that from age thirteen to age twenty-nine, he was both a student and a teacher in India. According to her, what Jesus was to say later in Palestine, he had already learned in India among the Buddhists.

The King of the Jews

This book, published in 1987 by Dr. Johan Forsstrom, is in reality a thesis submitted by him for an award of a Degree by the Ruhunu University of Sri Lanka. He has dedicated his book to the *Hebrew Buddhist Jeshua or Jesus, who passed away in Srinagar, Kashmir, in the year 110 A.D.* According to the author, the crucifixion is a "cock and bull" story. He says it was someone else who was crucified and it was Christ who married and migrated to France. According to him, Jesus was another person, who came to India twice and was buried in Kashmir. The 4th and 5th chapters of the book deal with the teachings of Buddhism and the Essenes. The author openly scolds and speaks against Christianity, and this bias has surpassed his thinking. The last chapter provides valuable information on subjects such as *Buddhism and Greek Thought, Buddhism and Islam,* and *Buddhism and Vegetarianism.* Equally important is the information he provides about late Basharat Saleem, who claimed to be the descendant of Jesus Christ. This work contains much information on the books of the Essenes.

Saving the Savior

Abubakr Ben Ishmael Salahuddin, is the author of *Saving the Savior,* published by him in 2001 from Illinois, USA. He examines

the theory about the physical survival of Jesus Christ after crucifixion and his tomb in Srinagar, Kashmir, India. Claiming himself a
staunch Ahmadi Muslim, he feels that he must detach himself from
his personal beliefs and be fair and impartial. The author starts his
discussion by describing Jesus in the light of Islamic sources, such
as the Quran and the *Hadis*. Then he proceeds to explain the connections of Jesus with Buddhism. He quotes from Nicolas Notovitch
and Khwaja Nazir Ahmad's—*The Unknown Life of St. Issa* and *Jesus
in Heaven on Earth*. The ninth chapter deals with important Eastern
sources—documents and manuscripts supplied by Professor Hassnain to him. In *Saving the Savior*, the author has tried to explore
those intimate religious beliefs, which are dear to the followers of
the major religions of the world. In this regard, his book is definitely
against Christian belief and dogma and pro-Ahmadiyya causes and
activities.

Jesus and Moses

Gene D. Matlock has authored a book, *Jesus and Moses Are Buried
in India*, which has been published by Authors Choice Press, New
York in 2000. The book is the result of a long and patient research
conducted by the author by going through all available research
material on Biblical history.

It was in 1980, when the author got *a shock of his life* to find the
location of the Biblical river "Cophen" in India. After this, he decided
to delve further to find the original home of the Hebrews in India.
Basing his theory on the linguistic similarities between Hebrew and
some Indian languages, the author has discovered that the whole
of the Bible-land was colonized by the Indians during prehistoric
times. His theory is that Abraham, called Brahma, the Creator god of
Hinduism was *"the founder of all worlds,"* and major religions, which
includes Judaism, Christianity and Islam also. The lost tribes of Israel
never got lost, but returned to their land of origin. In this regard,
he describes the Yadavas clans, who claim a Hebrew descent. Many
other Indian clans and traditions associated with the Khapirus had
their namesakes in Israel. However, even the roots of the Lost Tribes
are buried deep in Indian prehistory. The Yadavs of India came to
be known as the Yehudis of Palestine.

The author has quoted from a number of books, abundant archaeological and linguistic evidence to discover the traditions and legends about the great Jewish kings, Kish Saul, David and Solomon in Afghanistan, Pakistan and India.

Christ: The Book of Doubts and Book of Truth

Markus von Friedland, a renowned scholar of Switzerland, has authored the following works:

1. Christ – What Happened after Golgatha.
2. Christ – The Book of Doubts.
3. Christ – The Book of Truth.
4. Christ – A Trilogy Narrative.

The above books deal with the life of Christ, before and after crucifixion; with the life of Thomas in South India; and with the three lives of Lars Andronikus Porsenna, an Etruscan prince, who accompanies Jesus Christ during his travels.

The Hidden Years of Jesus

Dr. Hans Juergen Trebst published his research in 2005 on Nicolas Notovitch's *The Unknown Life of St. Issa*, in German and English, entitled *The Hidden Years of Jesus.* His work is a genuine piece of research, even to the minutest detail. The author is balanced and impartial up to the last word.

CHAPTER TWO

Genesis

In the beginning was the Word,
And the Word was with God,
And the Word was God.
St. John

IN THE BEGINNING God made the heaven and the earth. As the earth was invisible, he created the light so as to separate it from the darkness. He also ordered a firmament in midst of the water, so as to make a separation between water and water. Accordingly, the water was gathered into one receptacle and the dry land appeared. Thus the land and the sea came into existence. After having created animal life, God made man after his image.[1]

The above is the story of creation given to us by the early Semites. The whole work of creation was completed in six days and the seventh day was sanctified as the day of rest or the Sabbath. When men began to multiply and daughters were born to them, the sons of God came to this earth. Seeing these daughters of men, they fell in love with them and took them as their wives. These women bore children to them which were perfect human beings or super beings. The story of mating between the sons of God and the daughters of men can be interpreted to mean that God deputed angels to develop the genetic code of human species which lived on this earth. In order to explain the whole position, let us quote from the Old Testament:

> And it came to pass,
> When men began to multiply on the face of earth,
> And daughters were born unto them;
> That the sons of God saw the daughters of men,

That they were fair;
And they took them wives of all which they chose.[2]

The above verses make it clear that the sons of God came to this earth and impregnated virgins. These sons of God were not mythical beings but super beings. Secondly, the taking of wives was not done in a monogamous way, but was a sort of polygamy. The words, 'wives of all' denoted the fact that these daughters of men mated with many pairs of these supermen, with the result that the present human race came into existence. For such a creation, it was necessary to make perfect genes for the human species. The above hypothesis is further amplified in the Old Testament as below:

And the Lord said,
My Spirit shall not always strive with man,
For that he also is flesh:
Yet his days shall be,
A hundred and twenty years.
There were giants
In earth in those days;
And also after that,
When the sons of God,
Came in to the daughters of men,
And they bore children to them,
The same became mighty men,
Which were of old,
Men of renown.[3]

The above reveals that the giants had defiled the women on this earth, and God wanted to again reset the genes of human beings. He sent his sons to impregnate these earthly daughters, who bore a new species of children who could live for nearly one hundred and twenty years. It is also apparent that God modified the age structure of the new human beings, whom he termed men of renown.

Some scholars have tried to explain the above development of genetics as something mystical, declaring that such marriages between the sons of God and the daughters of men are to be taken as mythology, and mating between them is to be termed as spiritual intermixture. Such an explanation is absurd in connection with a

-scientific experiment like the perfection of a gene. It has been explained above that the whole purpose for sending supermen to this
earth was to develop the genetic code of human beings, and for
this purpose, intercourse between the mates was physical and not
spiritual; more so, when God himself admits:

> My Spirit shall not always strive with man,
> For that he also is flesh.[4]

Here, God speaks of man as flesh and of himself as flesh, and
"the word" also encompasses God in the meaning of flesh. It is thus
clear that the sons of God were not spiritual beings or of ephemeral
nature; they were mightier physical beings than giants, and they
had physical intercourse with women of this planet.

The above explanation seems to be in accordance with modern
scientific opinion. The only question relates to the sons of God. Who
were these—or did God actually have sons? The answer to this
question may lie in the existence of human beings and supermen in
other planets who descended on this earth and left the place after
impregnating the daughters of this earth. Where did they go after
producing, what is termed as, *mighty men* or *men of renown*? Either
they perished here at the ripe age of one hundred and twenty or
flew back to other planets!

The Globe

The present distribution of the continents is regarded as a result
of the drifting apart of individual masses of earth. Such drifting occurred millions of years ago. There was a time when Asia, Africa,
America and Australia were tightly wedged together. God created
a firmament in the midst of water, with the result that water was
gathered into one receptacle resulting in the appearance of lands.
Thus the Old Testament clearly hints at the creation of the earth and
drifting of various lands, now known as continents. Even at present,
the organic belts of the high mountain ranges, such as the Himalayas
and the Alps are unilateral and extend over the earth and in the seas.
These ranges pass through the lands and the seas of South America,
Africa, Arabia, India, Australia and Antarctica.

If we go beyond the farthest point that imagination can reach, we will find that the middle of the two Americas were nearer the Mediterranean; Mexico, Spain, Palestine, Ladakh, Korea and Japan were on the same longitude. Thus, there was a period when the world was a single unit of the earth. This may account for the story of Jesus Christ in the ancient traditions of Mexico, Spain, Palestine, Iran, Ladakh, Kashmir, Central Asia and Japan. Far away in the dim past, we may have known Jesus in many lands, and he may have been making only his most recent advent during the days of Herod in the first century B.C.

It would thus appear that we have to search for other sons of God, who made their advent from time to time in the above mentioned countries. Has there been only one Jesus or many? All this is a mystery. If Jesus came to this earth when continents had not drifted, then the tradition about his existence in Mexico, Palestine, Ladakh and Japan can be easily explained. Another conclusion would be that Jesus had lived in former ages, and was reborn several times.

When Jesus Christ was born, the region known now as the Middle East was divided between the Assyrians, Babylonians, Persians, Greeks and Romans. All these people had their own gods and goddesses. All their kings, prophets, lawgivers and teachers were considered gods or the representatives of God. On other occasions, these worldly gods considered themselves as the sons of God. Not only had God made man in his own image, known as Adam, but also had created a woman for him. When Eve gave birth to the first child, she declared that she "got a man from the Lord." Men began to multiply and divided themselves into tribes. These tribes migrated to various parts of the earth and founded many cultures.

For at least half a million years, these human species scattered in various parts of the globe. These groups of people moved from place to place. It is only in the Paleolithic period that they abandoned the life of savagery, and began to settle in the Middle East. The Neolithic period in the region began in 6000 B.C.[5]

Various Cultures

It may be that 20,000,000 years back our ancestors took their first step, but the man who could be termed as the founder of some sort of civilization appeared nearly 500,000 years back. He used stone implements and was a cannibal. He lived in caves and pits. It was in 8000 B.C. that he moved out and started living in villages. This was the beginning of civilization in the Middle East and the Far East. Urbanization started around 7000 B.C. and pottery was introduced some years later. The earliest known Neolithic settlement has been dated at Jericho, and it was from the Middle East that the first agriculturists spread out into Europe, North Africa and India and mixed with the local population.[6] The first irrigation system in the world was started in Mesopotamia in 5000 B.C. It spread to Egypt, Iran, and other countries of the Near East. The name Caucasoid, from the region near the Caucasus, which is used for the Mediterranean race also, stretched from the Atlantic to India. As such, it covers the countries of Spain, Turkey, Arabia, Iran, Armenia, Afghanistan and Kashmir. Since the archaeological finds in Mesopotamia and Turkmania bear evidence to its trans-Asiatic character, it is evident that this culture had close affinity with the Indus civilization. It is also a fact that the Indus culture during its peak period spread far beyond its limits and as such, it can be surmised that the cultures covering Egypt, Iran, Afghanistan, Sind, the Punjab, Kashmir, Ladakh, Tibet, and Central Asia were facets of the same culture, though bearing special features of a particular region. From its epicenter, this civilization moved from region to region and has left its impact on religion, arts and architecture. That is the reason why we now excavate similar or parallel objects of archaeological interest from the whole region at different places or sites. In the late prehistoric period, sedentary cultures emerged in Egypt, Nubia, Palestine, Syria, Armenia, Asia Minor, Mesopotamia and Iran. All these countries were subjected to successive waves of immigration and the rise and fall of many empires.[7]

It is proved beyond doubt that the people from Mesopotamia moved toward the north west of India in about the 3rd century B.C. The skeletons found at Mohenjodaro and Harappa include the Mediterranean stock. This shows that the whole region from Palestine to India had been peopled by the race which should have continued to inherit the same cultural affinity. As such, when we speak of Jesus Christ visiting the East, it need not be considered a unique proposition. The trend of migrations of the tribes during the Mesolithic age has been from the West towards the East, from which side the sun rises, and man had been eager to find out the abode of the Sun god.

Indus Civilization

The Indus civilization grew in about 2000 B.C. with the founding of Mohenjodaro and Harrapa in the north west of India. These people had established trade and cultural relations with the people of Afghanistan, Iran, Syria, and Egypt from earliest time. It was in reality the projection of Mesopotamian civilization. It is thus evident that India had established its relation with the countries of the Middle East and Western Asia long before the advent of Jesus Christ.

Archaeological finds in Kashmir, Ladakh and Central Asia have close connections with the Egyptian, the Assyrian and the Sumerian cultures. Though our researches are meager, still these finds are important to establish the existence of links between the Semites and the Aryans during prehistoric times.

In the cylinder seals of Assyria, we find seven dots or circles along with the Sun, Moon and the Star of Venus. These dots or circles are described as gods or goddesses in mythology. We have found a similar seal at Mohenjodaro, known as the seal of seven sisters. It has been further established that many Indus seals have been unearthed in Mesopotamia. Such seals with circles have been found in Iran also. This would reveal some sort of link between Mesopotamia and Mohenjodaro on the one hand and Iran and Ladakh on other hand. The river Indus flows from Ladakh and Kashmir into the Arabian Sea. The Indus civilization, as we understand it now, is considered to be located in Ladakh, Kashmir, Afghanistan, Punjab and Sind. This civilization flourished during 2400-1700 B.C. and ranks among four widely-known civilizations of the ancient world.

At Hoi-Nar, Phalgham, in Kashmir, the State Department of Archaeology has located a site of importance where brick tiles showing two animals rearing up on their hind legs and entwining their necks so as to make a circle have been found. This motif is of common occurrence in the art of Asia from Egypt to Kashmir. The plaque of king Nar-Mer, preserved in the National Museum in Cairo, depicts two animals entwining their necks in a circle—the same motif which is shown on tiles found at Hoi-Nar in Kashmir. Did Hoi-Nar have some link with Nar-Mer of Egypt? It may be mentioned that Nar-Mer claimed divine advent as an incarnate god.[8]

Similar motifs have been found on jars from Egypt which show two animals in the same posture. The two motifs are so exact and similar that one becomes amazed. This would show that artists from Egypt may have reached Kashmir some time before the first century A.D.

We find such motifs on Tibetan antiquities showing two animals facing each other, rearing on their hind legs. This motif is of common occurrence in the art of Asia, from Mesopotamia to Siberia.[9]

The sphinxes of Egypt are known throughout the world, but it is a strange coincidence that a sphinx showing a lion with a human face lies near the tomb of Kepachen at Chonggye in Tibet.[10]

The bull and the cow were worshipped by Egyptians during prehistoric times. At Mohenjodaro, we have located many seals and terra-cottas with motifs of bulls. The Sumerians assigned the statues of the goddess to the lion, which mythology was copied in the East also.[11]

Ethnologically the people of Iran, Afghanistan and Kashmir are the same people. Political domination of Iran over the northwestern regions of India began with the conquest of Punjab by Darius in 512 B.C., and the region remained under their influence up to the 2nd century B.C. when the Kushanas attained prominence.

During those four centuries, the civilization and culture inherited by Iran from Judah penetrated into the north of India. It was during this period that the Kharoshti script of the Hebrews penetrated into India. The influence of Iran on their art and architecture was great and even the effigies of the four lions on the Ashokan pillar at Sarnath and the famous Dharma Chakra were copied from the pillars of palaces at Persepolis in Iran. It is strange that Kharoshti numerals are found on all the tiles excavated at Harwan, Ahan, Kurhom, Hoi-Nar and Mattan, in Kashmir.

Contacts Between East and West

From time immemorial there have existed contacts between the East and the West. Besides the sea routes, there were land routes for commercial as well as political purposes. It is a historical fact that there have been continuous migrations from West to East during the ancient and medieval period of our history in search of better natural resources of food, water and wood. We have scanty references about actual routes used by nomad tribes during their migrations. However, it is clear that there existed links between the Middle East countries and India, Afghanistan, Central Asia and Tibet. It was Darius Hystaspes who colonized Afghanistan and certain parts of Central Asia with Greek captives and slaves of war. It is also known that sea trade between Egypt, Syria and India and such coastal navigation existed long before the coming of the Europeans into India.

Herodotus also refers to the Greek settlements in Bactria six centuries before the advent of Jesus Christ. Persia deported Syrians to Assyria during ancient times, and after the fall of Sumeria in 721 B.C. the Israeli tribes were forced to disperse into Central Asia, Iran and Afghanistan. The transportation of the Greeks, the Israelites, the Sumerians and the Assyrians into the Far East continued for many centuries. The Kassites known as Kash, Kish or Kush travelled through Persia, Afghanistan and Central Asia to Kashmir. During their travels, they established settlements with the appellation of Kash, Kish or Kush, and such towns, cities and countries are still known as Kashan in Persia, Kashghar in Central Asia and Kashmir and Kishtawar itself. It may be pointed out that, since ancient times, there has existed an easy highway from Arabia to Persia, then to Afghanistan and North India to Kashmir, to Tibet and the Pamirs.

Ancient Gods

Tradition makes it that God blessed Noah and his family and they multiplied and the whole earth was filled by his descendants. Some out of his family settled in the fertile valley of the Tigris and Euphrates, where they built large cities, from which travellers journeyed to Egypt, India and other countries. Abraham, who was the god of one tribe, made a long journey to Canaan along with *his* people. Crossing the Sinai, Abraham and his people went to Egypt. Sarah, the wife of Abraham, being very beautiful, was taken away to the palace of Pharaoh, who met her.[12]

But after some time she was handed back to Abraham, who returned to Canaan with his tribe. When Abraham and Sarah were far advanced in age, God visited Sarah and she conceived.[13] Abraham was one hundred years old when his aged wife bore a son to him, named Isaac. How did God meet Sarah?

> And the Lord appeared unto him,
> In the plains of Mamre:
> And, lo, three men stood by him:
> And they said unto him,
> Where is Sarah thy wife?
> And he said,
> Behold, in the tent,
> And they said,
> Sarah thy wife shall have a son.[14]
> And the Lord visited Sarah as he had said,
> And the Lord did unto Sarah as he had spoken.
> For Sarah conceived,
> And bore Abraham a son in his old age.[15]

From the above, we infer that God, along with two other gods, visited the tent of Abraham in the plains of Mamre. All the three looked like men, and he prepared three measures of fine meal for them. Abraham fetched a tender calf and gave it to one man, who was young. This man dressed it. After the meals were prepared, Abraham set it before them and they did eat.[16]

After having a delicious lunch, they asked him about the whereabouts of his wife and he allowed them to look at her in the tent. Sarah laughed, saying how could she conceive and bear a child?[17] So God visited Sarah at the appointed time, as he had said, and he did unto Sarah as he had spoken.[18] He met her, and she bore a child, who was named Isaac. It is also clear that the Lord who dealt with Sarah, was Yahweh and it was due to him that Sarah conceived and bore a son to Abraham in his old age.[19]

The above is the second incident related in the holy scriptures about the mating of the sons of God with the daughters of men. In various mythologies, we find the heavenly god mated with Ghe, the earthly maiden; Shiva, the sky god, holding the moon in his hand, fell for Parvati, the mountain maiden of the Himalayas.[20]

To some, these sons of God are holy, wise and immaterial beings in a beautiful human form of fiery light. They are also considered direct manifestations of God in a human form. When, as has been clearly revealed above, a special feast was prepared for them and one of them hastened to dress a calf, which was roasted in butter, and all of them ate the lunch, they cannot be considered as immaterial beings. They were also known as angels who visited this earth to convey orders of God to men. Maybe these sons of God were astronauts who visited this earth during prehistoric times!

Moses the Law Giver

Moses was selected by God as his agent to deliver the law to the people. He was a shepherd by profession who tended sheep belonging to his father-in-law, Yethro, a priest of Midian. When he came near the mountain of God, an angel appeared to him in a flaming fire, out of a bush which began to blaze. Then God revealed himself to Moses, and declared:

> I am that I am;
> The Lord God of your fathers,
> The God of Isaac,
> And the God of Jacob,
> This is my name forever,
> And this is my memorial unto all generations.[21]

This mysterious sentence: I am that I am, has been rendered differently by various scholars, as below:

> *Ehyeh Aser Ehyeh.*
> *Ego Eimi Ho On.*
> *I-a-o-u-e.*
> *Ya-weh.*

I-a-v-e.
Ye-uo.
Yav.
Yo.
[yod hay vuv hay: yhvh—Yahweh]

As ordered, Moses and Aaron, his brother, rescued the Children of Israel from the slavery of Pharaoh. He led them away out of Egypt and after wanderings, brought them to Sinai. It was here that Yahweh gave the law to Moses for guidance of the people.

Moses had brought these tribes to the Mountain of God to receive "the foundation of their national unity and the constitution of their religious community. In their state of exaltation, they accepted with readiness the prerogatives and duties of the divine election constituting them a holy nation, the priest-people among mankind, and guardians of the spiritual interests of humanity.[22]

The Ten Commandments

Comparison of the two versions of the Commandments given in Exodus and in Deuteronomy reveals that the number of the Commandments is not ten but more. Here is the version from the earlier scriptures:

1) Thou shalt have no other gods before me.
2) Thou shalt not make unto thee any graven image.
3) Thou shalt not bow down thyself to them, nor serve them.
4) Thou shalt not take the name of thy God in vain.
5) Thou shalt remember the Sabbath day.
6) Thou shalt honor thy father and thy mother.
7) Thou shalt not kill.
8) Thou shalt not commit adultery
9) Thou shalt not steal.
10) Thou shalt not bear false witness against thy neighbor.
11) Thou shalt not covet thy neighbor's house.
12) Thou shalt not covet thy neighbor's wife.
13) Thou shalt not covet any thing that is thy neighbor's.[23]

Here is another version from Deuteronomy:

1) Thou shalt have none other gods before me.
2) Thou shalt not make have any graven image.
3) Thou shalt not bow down thyself unto them.
4) Thou shalt not take the name of the Lord thy God in vain.
5) Thou shalt keep the Sabbath day.
6) Thou shalt honor thy father and thy mother.
7) Thou shalt not kill.
8) Thou shalt not commit adultery.
9) Thou shalt not steal.
10) Thou shalt not bear false witness.
11) Thou shalt not desire thy neighbor's wife.
12) Thou shalt not covet any thing that is thy neighbor's.[24]

These were the Commandments, the statutes and the judgments which were taught by Moses to his people.

It was ordained by Yahweh that the gods of alien nations were not to be worshipped by the followers of Moses. Idolatry was prohibited but the people continued to carve images of wood, stone, and metal for worship. The commandments stressed the sacredness of marriage, and forbade all illicit relations. It was ordained that everyone had to work for six days but the seventh day should be left free for thoughts of God. Thus Yahweh selected the followers of Moses as his special people to spread his words all over world. It was a priestly class like the Brahmanas of India.[25]

The manual of guidance for the nation was called the Torah or book of instructions. It was written without vowels or punctuation, so as to render it capable of many and varied interpretations. It was read to the people and ratified by them. The original words of Yahweh were supplemented from time to time by the priests, who recorded the death of Moses also in the Torah. Naturally, such an event could not form part of the Book during the lifetime of Moses. Incidentally, it may be mentioned that the invention of these Commandments has been attributed to the king Hammurabi of Babylon (1700 B.C.). Moses, who lived in 1220 B.C., appears to have borrowed much from Hammurabi, whose complete text has been found in Susa inscribed on twenty-one horizontal columns.[26]

There is controversy about the fact as to who gave the above Commandments: was he God or Yahweh? It has been stated earlier that it was Yahweh who impregnated the wife of Abraham when he came in the guise of a young man along with two other companions and met Abraham in the plains of Mamre.[27] An anthropologist has remarked that Yahweh was originally the tribal god of Canaan, and Moses had married the daughter of a priest belonging to the Order of Yahweh. He is said to have helped Moses in his combat with the Pharaoh of Egypt. He is also said to have performed many miracles, and it was through his efforts that Pharaoh along with his army perished in the sea. Maybe he was God himself, or God-incarnate or the son of God, or the local god. He is also known as the god of mercy, like Avalokiteshvara Buddha. The Jews have attributed two qualities to God—mercy and power.

It was Moses who bound the Children of Israel into a nation, and in this task, he was helped by Aaron. After having succeeded in leading the Israeli tribes out of Egypt in about 1220 B.C., he gave them the law, by which all these tribes agreed to hold Yahweh as their God. Thus a unity was formed among the scattered people on the religious impulse of a common God, who adopted them eternally as his own children. Moses taught them how to worship and thus laid the basis of spiritual monotheism.

Mary the Consort

Moses was assisted by Aaron because his sister Mary was the chief consort of the former. Miriam is the old form of the name Mary, by which name she is mentioned in the Old Testament. When Moses and his followers crossed the sea, she took a timbrel in her hand, and danced with other women singing thus:

> Sing to the Lord,
> For he hath triumphed gloriously:
> The horse and his rider,
> Hath he thrown into the sea.[28]

Moses made her the chief prophetess of the nation, an honor given to any woman for the first time in history. Up to that time, it had been the privilege of men only to become prophets. Thus

Moses as prophet and Mary as prophetess retained the supremacy over the people, and Aaron acted as the chief priest, to spearhead the supremacy of the two. But the bond between this trio could not continue for long, because Moses became infatuated with the love of an Ethiopian woman. Thus Aaron and Mary began to speak against Moses.[29]

In the meanwhile, the Amalekites led an attack on the followers of Moses and he put Joshua in command of the Israeli nation. Through his intercession and prayers the Amalekites were defeated. Thus, he succeeded in founding the religion as well as a state for the Israeli tribes.

Death of Moses

When Moses was one hundred and twenty, God spoke to him saying:

> Go up the mountain Abarim,
> To that mount Nabo,
> Which is in the land of Moab,
> And take a view of the land of Canaan,
> Which I give to the children of Israel;
> And die on the mount to which thou goest up,
> And be gathered to thy people,
> In the same manner
> As thy brother Aaron died on the mount
> Because you disobeyed
> My word among the Children of Israel,
> Because you did not hallow
> Me among the Children of Israel,
> Thou shalt see the land at a distance,
> But shalt not go in thither.[30]

From the above, we gather that God became angry with Moses because he had disobeyed his word and had not hallowed him among the Israelites. As such, Moses was ordered to migrate to the mount Nebo in the land of Moab and die there. Indeed, it was a terrible trial for Moses, but, as he was always loyal and obedient to the will of God, he left on his last journey. Having reached the fixed place, he died of exhaustion. Let us quote from the Old Testament:

> And Moses went up from the plains of Moab
> Unto the mountain of Nebo to the top of Pisgah.
> So Moses the servant of the Lord died there
> In the Land of Moab according to the word of the Lord.
> And he buried him in a valley in the land of Moab,
> Over against Beth-peor:
> But no man knoweth of his sepulcher unto this day.
> And Moses was a hundred and twenty years old when he died—
> His eye was not dim nor his natural force abated.[31]

The above account, though very brief, is full of meaning. For the first time in the Old Testament, time and space have been shortened to such an extent that it is difficult to apprehend the tragic odyssey which Moses was ordered to perform. He was a hundred and twenty years old, but his eyesight was not dim, nor his natural energy abated. From the description given above, it is evident that he journeyed by land and sea to reach the place of his last destination. Minute examination of the schedule of his travel makes it clear that he proceeded to a city of palm trees; then to Segor or Zoar; then to Jericho wherefrom he proceeded towards the countryside.

From there he had to traverse wilderness and the desert area and all land of Judah unto the utmost sea, meaning thereby the Arabian sea. After crossing the lands of Manasseh and Ephraim, he went to Nephtali. From that place, he even crossed the Dan and Phasga, which is also known as Pisgah. After reaching the top of the Mount Nabo, which is also known as Nebo, he breathed his last and died. He was buried in the land of Moab, over against Beth-peor.

It is evident that in order to find the place for his grave, he conducted a long journey to Moab near Bethpur and died there. It is also stated categorically that no man knows his grave up to this day. Most scholars have tried to locate all the countries which Moses visited, but in vain. Some scholars even had to admit that it was futile to search out the countries and the places, for these were unknown.[32]

Strangely enough, some place names around the grave of Moses can be identified in the valley of Kashmir, from the maps published by the Survey of India. We will revert to this subject towards the end of this chapter.

The Sects

It is necessary to offer some details about the sects or religious communities that lived in Palestine before the advent of the Christian era. Most prominent were the Hebrews, who had restored the Temple at Jerusalem and developed a well-knit society and a religious movement under guidance of the priests, who were known as the priests of Jehovah. Most powerful among the priests were the Levites, who formed a special hereditary caste, supreme in religious hierarchy. The other priestly castes were known as the Zadokites and the Aaronites, said to have been commissioned by Zadok and Aaron. The Jews believed in one God, who was supposed to care for and save the world from destruction. They were divided into a number of tribes and sects. After the imperial census of the year 6 or 7, the Jews understood fully that they were the subjects of the Romans. There were some among them who incited the people in the name of religion and were known as the Zealots. The majority consisted of the Pharisees, who expected termination of the Roman rule through divine intervention. Among them was a section of the Baptists who expected the arrival of the Messiah in the near future. The Sadducees belonged to the priestly aristocratic class who allied themselves with the government. Distinct from them there existed an Order of Essenes who lived in villages of their own. They had a secret lore about angels and other mystic matters. They performed frequent ablutions and wore white garments.[33]

The Essenes professed a severer discipline and were particularly attached to each other. They selected other men's children and fashioned them after their own pattern. Devoted to the works of ancient writers, they could conquer pain by sheer will power.[34]

The Hebrews

Palestine was occupied by the Neolithic tribes in about 4000 B.C. These ancient people lived in caves. The region was later occupied by the tribes from Canaan, North Arabia, Babylonia, Armenia and Egypt. Such waves of new settlers continued up to 1446 B.C. when Moses returned to Egypt. The tribes from Armenia were termed

Khabiru by the Canaanites, which name was changed to Hebrew at a later stage. As such, the earliest Jewish tribes came to be known as the Hebrews and their language also was termed as the Hebrew language. It was Moses who combined all these tribes into one nation and gave them a religion. After having consolidated their position, the Hebrews attacked Egypt, burning and looting many towns. But their supremacy was broken by the Hittites in about 1293 B.C. The Hebrews came to be known as the Jews later on, and they are known as such, even up to present times.

The Jews

The term Jew has been derived from Judah or the follower of Judaism. The word is pronounced in various languages like this:

Judaeus—Latin
Loudaios—Greek
Yhudai—Aramaic
Yhudi—Hebrew
Yahud — Arabic
Yahudi—Urdu
Yehud—Kashmiri

It may incidentally be remarked that Joo or Jeo used to be the prefix of every name in Kashmir in the past.

The Children of Israel

The Israelites or the Children of Israel are known as Bani-Israel in the East. Jacob had twelve sons from his legal wives and concubines and from them are derived the twelve tribes of Israel. Two divisions marked themselves off according to descent from Leah or Rachel. As such, Reuben, Simeon, Levi, Judah, Issachar and Zebulon reckoned themselves as of the former and Joseph and Benjamin as of the latter. The inferior lineage from the concubines consisted of children of two groups: Gad and Asher of one group and Dan and Naphtali of the other group. However, they all knew themselves as children of the same father.[35]

They fought among themselves for the holy land, with the result that Joshua partitioned them into two groups, and got them settled in the divided Palestine. Saul united them and Solomon gave them prosperity. But due to their internal strife, they got divided again, and two tribes were lost to them. Subsequently, the remaining ten tribes became slaves of various kings, with the result that they got scattered in different lands. They also got mixed up with other nationalities and lost their identity. It was only some remnants that remained in Palestine. Thus the fate of the ten tribes has become a mystery.[36] Hence, it became a mission of the Hebrew prophets to search out these tribes and make them settle in the holy land.[37]

In the 6th century B.C., the Jews suffered persecution and had to run away toward Syria and Babylon. In subsequent years, most of them were arrested and made prisoners. Persecution of the Jews continued for centuries: they were either killed, made prisoners or had to run away. During the period of the Indo-Greek kings most of the Jews, who were skilled in many arts, migrated towards Afghanistan, Bactria, and hilly areas of Gilgit. During the succeeding periods, they were lost in various lands, for they had traversed long distances. They are said to have reached Gaznah and the country of the Kush where a river flows.[38]

They also reached the outskirts of Kashmir and settled in Hazara. Definite information is available about the Hebrew tribes of Hazara who mostly occupied themselves in trade and commerce.[39] Hazara is situated towards the southwest of Kashmir. The existence of Jews in Central Asian countries has been testified by various authors.[40]

Hebrews in Egypt

The story of Hebrew settlements in Egypt is very old, when they migrated to that land and worked as agriculturists. It goes to the period when the Hyksos ruled over Egypt. Moses assembled them and induced them to migrate from Egypt. It was Rameses II who utilized them for construction works. In about 1230 B.C. they revolted against the Egyptians. During the days of David, they attained supremacy in the region now known as Israel. David established his camp at Jerusalem, which became a political, as well as a religious center for them.[41] Under Solomon, they built the capital at Jerusalem, with hamlets, markets and the famous Temple. But in later periods, they divided themselves into two major groups, with the result that Egyptians sacked Israel and destroyed the Temple at Jerusalem. During the succeeding period they suffered untold miseries and were transported to foreign lands as slaves. In about 590 B.C. Psametik of Egypt utilized them as mercenaries, but they had to migrate again from that country.

Hebrews in Persia

In about 539 B.C. the Babylonians were defeated by Cyrus the Great. The Jews hailed this defeat, for they had suffered at the hands of the Babylonians, who had burnt the Temple at Jerusalem. Most of them had been carried away as slaves to Babylon and employed as agricultural labor. Cyrus the Great not only liberated them from slavery, but allowed them to settle down in Palestine. They were allowed to establish their state and build the Temple at Jerusalem, under the patronage of the Emperor. Having attained freedom and status, most of them settled in Persia, and established themselves as rich traders. Now, they started to move towards the East and went as far as Central Asia. However, they looked to Jerusalem as their spiritual center, where Menahem had established a subject state of Judea. Sensing that he had become too powerful, the Persians overthrew him in about 485 B.C. Incidentally, it may be mentioned that the Jews thought of Cyrus the Great as their saviour and made him a god in their writings. However, Jews not only influenced the Zoroastrians of Persia, but also were influenced by the foreign doctrines, this resulting in a mixed ethical and religious code. It was a happy blending of Judaic and Zoroastrian thought. It was during this period that Persian art and architecture entered Palestine, and the Jews built large and luxurious villas there. But during the later period, reaction prevailed among the Jews and the priestly class, under the guidance of Ezra, succeeded in establishing orthodoxy among them. He forbade modernism and foreign ideas, and even forced the Jews to abandon Persian wives. This resulted in complete isolation of the Jews of Palestine from Israelis of other lands.

Division Among Bani-Israel

Bani-Israel and its downfall began with the death of Solomon. After having ruled for forty years, Rehoboam, his son, sat on the throne. Various tribes of the Bani-Israel joined to present their demands before the new king, who rejected them with contempt.

Out of these tribes, the ten tribes became angry and declared Jeroboam as their ruler and named their state Israel, while only two tribes who had remained faithful to Rehoboam called their kingdom Judea. From this period, the division started among the Children of Israel. Both the kingdoms fought many battles and destroyed each other. The kingdom of Judea was destroyed in 597 B.C. by Babylon, while the kingdom of Israel was destroyed in 721 B.C. by the Ashureans. It was after this destruction that the remaining ten tribes were made captives and settled in Khurasan, Iran and Sind.[42]

Jews in Greece

It was in about 600 B.C. that the Jewish tribes came into contact with the Greeks. Accordingly, they adopted the Greek architecture and arts. During this period, the Jews quarreled among themselves and were divided into many sects. In 323 B.C. Alexander the Great conquered Egypt and the Egyptian Jews rendered all assistance to him, for which they received many privileges. They considered him as their liberator and joined his army as mercenaries. When Alexander passed through Palestine and Syria, the Jews came forward to welcome him. Alexander marched towards Persia and subdued it very easily. He then followed up his victories with an invasion of what had been the Persian territory in India. He reached the Beas river when his troops refused to go further. He therefore kept some garrisons under the Greek commanders to guard his eastern dominions.[43] In this way, his Jewish mercenaries not only settled in the northwest of India but in other regions also.

It was in about 260 B.C. that the Torah was translated into Greek. It was due to their contact with the Greeks that they spread towards the northern shores of the Mediterranean sea.

Israelis in Afghanistan

The Bactrians and the Scythians are early tribes that settled in the region now known as Afghanistan. The Sumerians, the Persians, the Armenians and the Afghans belong to the same race of the Caucasoids of the Mediterranean stock. However, the Armenoids are predominant among the Afghans. It is a historical fact that Afghanistan was an important country, through which the routes to the Persian region, Asia Minor, Kashmir and Central Asia have passed since ancient times. In fact, the word Afghan comes from the Armenian word, *Aghvan*, meaning "the mountaineers." This establishes a historical connection between the Afghans and the Syrian captives of Armenia.[44]

Some of the Afghan tribes trace their genealogies to the Hebrew prophets and some claim a descent from the Israeli tribe of Kish. This would show that the Afghans are the remnant of the ten lost tribes of Israel. Both Assyria and Persia established their colonies in Afghanistan, with captives from Syria, who were Jews. It is for this reason that some tribes in Afghanistan still call themselves *Bani-Israel*, the Children of Israel. It was during the Arab occupation that they were converted to Islam.[45]

Among the tribes of Afghanistan we find names which indicate their connection with the Greeks from prehistoric times. But it was during the invasion of Alexander that the Greeks not only settled in various parts of Afghanistan but also established their kingdoms in the region. It is interesting to know that about seventy Israeli priests are said to have settled in Herat, Afghanistan. Some Israeli prophets are buried at Balkh, and Ibn-i-Betuta, the famous world traveller, makes special mention about the tomb of Ezekiel there. Another prophet of the Jews, Samuel, is buried on the side of the road leading to Khurasan from Hamadan. Another Israeli prophet is buried at Rang-barang near Bajoor in Afghanistan.[46]

It is interesting to note that the Afghans carry their tribal names even at present and use them as cognomens. Prominent among these tribes are the clans of *Amma-zye, Davood-zye, Abrahim-zye, Shemoo-zye, Yusuf-zye, Ayub-khel, Haroon-khel, Issa-khel, Ishaq-khel, Mysa-khel, Sulaiman-khel Yayah-khel, Yaqoob-khel, Yunus-khel* and *Zakaria-khel*.[47] All these clans possess ancestral pedigrees which carry their ancestral line right back to Jacob. These Records of Rights are also preserved in the Revenue Archives of each region of Afghanistan, Chitral and Peshawar.

The Afghans call themselves *Bani Israel* or the Children of Israel. They say that they migrated to Ghore and Bamean during the reign of Nebuchadnezzar. They were converted to Islam due to the efforts of Khalid ibn al-Walid in about 633 A.D. For their services to him in the wars against the infidels, they were honored with the title of Butan which has changed to Pathan now.[48] Some Afghans claim their descent from Cush and Ham and call themselves *Bani Israel*. They have mixed the Mosaic Law into their moral code.[49]

Jews in India

There is a theory that like the Aryans, the Semites also originated from India, and migrated towards the West. It is further observed that the extraordinary persistence of the Jewish community has its origin in the caste system of the Hindus, where the Brahmanas would never mix with other people nor allow any one to join their caste. However, it cannot be denied that there had been much traffic between the northwest India and the Middle East during ancient times. Even at present, there are Hebrew settlements on the western coast of India, at Bombay, Cochin, Kerala and Tamil Nadu. In Kerala, the Jews are divided into the white Jews and the black Jews. Both groups do not mix, but rather, look down upon each other, each claiming to belong to the original followers of Judaism. They came to Kerala 2,000 years ago and the king granted lands in their favor. One of their chiefs, Joseph Rabban, was granted the title of *Srinadon Moplah*.[50]

Recent researches have revealed the existence of the remnants of *Bani Israel* in Burma, Nagaland and Kashmir. The Pashtoon community living in Gutli Bagh, Ganderbal, in Kashmir have claimed that they are from the Children of Israel. They say that have migrated from Afghanistan, where live the other tribes of *Bani-Israel*. They were once followers of Moses and later converted to Islam.[51]

We are informed that the first two tribes which were deported to Afghanistan were that of Gad and Reuben. This happened when Ashurnazirpal ruled over Assyria. Maybe this migration took place during the last decade of the 8th century B.C. Out of the two tribes mentioned above, the Reubenites proceeded further towards Hazara and Kashmir while the Gaddites permanently settled in Afghanistan. The descendants of the Gaddites are known as Gadd-rani during present times. According to another source, this deportation of Jews to Afghanistan continued in an organized manner up to the reign of Nebuchadrezzer (539 B.C.).[52] It will be of interest to know that Nebuchadrezzer is known in Kashmir as *Bakhatnasser* and there are many stories woven around his name: among the Kashmiris, a person who is a dandy and a rogue is nicknamed as *Bakhatnasser.*

The Israeli tribes who had suffered persecutions got themselves settled in the hilly areas and valleys of Kashmir, Hazara, Gilgit, and Chitral. A majority among them changed their religion from time to time and became Buddhists, Shaivites and Muslims. It has been observed by many writers that their faces, conduct and behavior shows that they are the descendents of the ancient race of Israel.[53]

It has been testified by Christian missionaries that the Kashmiris are the descendants of the Hebrews.[54] Evidence regarding the existence of Jewish literature has also been found. It is related that an old manuscript of the Torah in Hebrew was procured from Kashmir by a Christian missionary.[55]

Another writer, who conducted the land settlement of the Kashmir valley during the 19th century, states that the majority of the Kashmiri people belong to the Semitic race. The facial features of their women are generally like those of their Jewish counterparts. It appears that the Kashmiris are no more than the lost tribes of Israel.[56]

Kashmir

The valley of Kashmir is known by its inhabitants as Kasheer because it was a settlement of a race known as Kash or Cush who were of Semitic origin. These people found the towns of Kash, Kashan and Kashgar. Kash is a town in Bukhara, Kashan exists in Iran, and Kashgar lies in the Chinese Turkistan.

From earliest times, Kashmir is known as a paradise on earth. It has been claimed that many patients who suffered from fever and stomach trouble recovered by drinking water from its springs. Occa-

Scenes of Kashmir

sionally, sterile women got pregnant here. God almighty has given many blessings to this land, and for this reason, Kashmir is called the blessed land. Holy scriptures of the East have acclaimed it as the land of bliss. It is also a historical fact that many prophets and saints of the world have visited Kashmir during their lifetimes.[57]

Kashur means the abode of the Kashur people and Kashur means those who eat meat. The Hindus believe that, as their religious shrines are situated in the valley, Kashmir is also known as the Garden of Solomon, said to have been populated by Solomon in 100 B.C.[58]

In order to save themselves during the invasion of Alexander, some of the Jewish tribes spread into the mountain valleys of the Himalayas. They also reached Kashmir and Tibet via Afghanistan.[59] These people brought their religious relics with them. Claudius found an ancient copy of the Torah in Kashmir which was written on leather and was 48 feet in length.[60]

The Kush Tribe

Kush or Cush was the son of Ham and a grandson of Noah.[61] He was the founder of the Kash or Cush tribe, which settled in the East. This tribe founded Kash, a village near Baghdad. These people named rivers, mountains, cities and countries after the name of their ancestor Kash or Cush. In Mesopotamia, they founded a kingdom, and the Kashan river in that country is a testimony to this fact. Kash-mar, a village near Nishapur in Iran, was also founded by them. This tribe also proceeded towards Central Asia and founded many settlements. Kash-mohra, a village in Merv; Kash, a village in Bokhara; Kash-band and Kash-ania, villages in Samarkand, were their settlements in Central Asia. In Mesopotamia, the tribe founded the towns of Kash-an, Kash-af and Kashi. They also moved towards Afghanistan and founded settlements at Kash-kar, Kash-hil, Kash-ek and Kash-u. While the Hindu-Kush mountains are named after them, they also founded a settlement south of this mountain range known as Kash-mor.

It was Babar, the founder of the Moghul dynasty in India, who pointed out in his memoirs that the etymology of the word Kashmir is derived from the Kash or Cush tribe which inhabited the valley.[62] This tribe settled in the region now known as Kash-tawar, in the Doda District of Kashmir. Crossing the Pir-Panjal range, these people spread in the valley of Kashmir. Kush-tawar, in the Pulwama District, Kash-nag, a spring in the Anantnag District, and Isae-Kush village bear the name of this tribe. These people were led by their leader Kash-yapa into the valley and, according to an old tradition, the name Kashmir is derived from him. However, there is no linguistic evidence to support this idea, because the whole fable of Kash-yapa and his progeny is astronomical.[63] Had Kash-yapa drained the valley of its waters or found his progeny in any part of the valley, its capital would have been termed as Kash-yapa-nagar or Kash-yapa-pur, as is the way with the etymologies of that period. According to the latest geological researches, it has been established that the valley of Kashmir was a lake millions of years back and its water found its outlet by the volcanic agency through a narrow gorge at Baramulla.[64]

However, it cannot be denied that the Kush or Cush tribe established their kingdom in the valley, and history records some kings of this tribe, namely, Utpa-la-Kusha and Hirneya-Kusha.[65] The latter has also been mentioned as the hero of a fairy tale in the *Katha-sarit-sagara*, an ancient Sanskrit work of Kashmir. It also records Kanaka-Kusha, his father, as one of the kings of Kashmir. It is not only that one of the Semitic tribes, namely the Kash or Cush, settled in the valley, then, but there is historical evidence regarding disbursement of the other Israeli tribes around the valley of Kashmir. The tribes mentioned in the Old Testament and those who retained their names in Kashmir are mentioned in other works.[66] The Book of Esther gives an account of a king who reigned from India to Ethiopia and whose kingdom consisted of 127 provinces. It states:

> Now it came to pass in the days of Ahasuerus which reigned from India even unto Ethiopia, over a hundred and seven and twenty provinces, that in those days, when the king Ahasuerus sat on the throne of his kingdom, which was in Shushan the palace in the third year of his reign, he made a feast unto all his princes and his servants; the power of Persia and Media, the nobles and princes of the provinces being before him when he showed the riches of his glorious kingdom and the honor of his excellent majesty many days, even a hundred and fourscore days.[67]

The above account establishes very ancient contacts between India and the Middle East. It was during his reign that the Jews established themselves throughout the empire, with the result that Haman, the new minister at court, complained that these people had scattered abroad and dispersed among the people in all the provinces of the kingdom.[68]

The *Nila-mata-Purana* is an ancient Sanskrit work dealing with the legends concerning the origin of Kashmir, its inhabitants, sacred places and rituals. It makes mention of the following tribes which settled in the valley of Kashmir, when it emerged out of the lake:

1) Nagas, the dragon-worshipers, akin to the Scytho-Median Zohak.
2) Pishacas, the tribes living between the Hindu-kush and Kapisa or modern Kafiristan.
3) Darvas, the sons of Dara, the descendants of Judah.
4) Abhesuerus, the tribe of Ahasuerus, the emperor.
5) Gandharas, the people of Gandhara.
6) Juhundaras, the tribes of Ghazni.
7) Sakas, the Scythians.
8) Khashas, the descendants of the son of Noah, Cush.
9) Tanganas, the Central Asian tribes.
10) Mandaves, the descendants of Mandu.
11) Madras, tribes of ancient Sakala.
12) Antagiris, the mountain tribes.
13) Yavanas, the foreigners or the Ionians.

Out of the list, the Darvas, the Abhesuerus and the Khashas are primarily the Jewish tribes. As regards the Abhesuerus, the tribe after the name of the emperor Ahasuerus deserves special mention. They were the famous people who helped the Assakenoi in offering resistance to the Greeks. Alexander the Great confirmed their ruler under the title of Satrap.[69] It is evident that, like the Cush tribe, the Abhesuerus had attained prominence in Kashmir.

Advent of Buddha

According to the Buddhist chronicles preserved in the Hemis monastery in Ladakh, there have existed many previous Buddhas before the time when *Sakyamuni* Buddha made his advent into this world. He is mentioned as the king over the three thousand worlds of suffering beings. According to these chronicles, there are even Buddhas who are supreme and who have power over transmigration.[70] The rulers of the world divided into the two categories: the Buddha rulers and the non-Buddha rulers. The former came to this world to do good to humanity and save them from sufferings. Sakyamuni Buddha was the Son of God and his mother was the best and purest of the daughters of men. She was a virgin when she gave birth to Buddha.[71] He was tempted several times by the Devil but did not succumb to these temptations. During the period of temptation he was on a fast for forty days. He performed many miracles and gave impressive sermons to the multitude. He talked in parables and explained spiritual matters by means of physical analogies.[72] He showed the way to obtain perfection of virtues, so as to attain *nirvana* or eternal bliss.

Soon after his demise, the leadership of the community came into the hands of Sriputra, who did the same thing as Paul did to the original teachings of Christ. He gave emphasis to orthodox views with the result that a division crept into the Buddhist Sangha. The first Buddhist Council to settle the differences was held at Rajagarha. The second Council was held about a hundred years later at Vashali but without much success. The Buddhists split into two major sects known as Theravadins and Sarvastivadins.

The third Buddhist Council was held at Pataliputra in the 3rd century B.C. It was called by Ashoka the Great for settlement of differences among the orthodox and the progressive schools. Ashoka did invaluable service to Buddhism by deputing missionaries towards the eastern and the western regions bordering India. During his reign, Buddhism got a foothold not only in India but outside in central Tibet, Burma, Thailand, Afghanistan, Persia and Kashmir. We find a Buddhist mission from the river Ganges in India reached the court of Philadelphus (285-246 B.C.) at Alexandria. The king was a patron of culture and had obtained the Hebrew sacred books for translation purposes. The Buddhist mission from India not only found a welcome at his court but patronage also, for he was very much interested in ancient laws and scriptures.[73]

The Jewish population of Alexandria resided in a compact quarter in the north of the city. It is probable the Buddhist mission from India got settled adjacent to the Jewish community. The Theravadins influenced the Essene Order to such an extent that they came to be known as "Therapeuts." Philo speaks of the Therapeuts as those Essenes who of their own free will retired into solitude and who from love of godliness and heavenly things passed their time in studying religion and nature. "They live in several places in Palestine and Egypt, and in this last country their greatest congregation was in the vicinity of the city of Alexandria."[74] It is certain that links between the Indian Buddhists and the communities living in Egypt and Palestine date back to the 3rd century B.C.

The next important event in the history of Buddhism is the conversion of Menandera, a king of a Bactrian dynasty of Greek origin, to Buddhism. The king was defeated by the famous Buddhist philosopher of Kashmir, Nagasena, in a discussion held at a place in the vicinity of Kashmir. Henceforth, the Indo-Greeks appear to have accepted the doctrines of Buddhism.[75] In the first century, the Kushans emerged as the foremost ruling dynasty in the north of India including Afghanistan. It was Kanishka who convened the fourth Buddhist Council in Kashmir. Henceforth the *Mahayana* or the progressive Buddhism penetrated into Central Asia from Kashmir and then spread out in China and Korea and thence to Japan. It is during this very period that we find a saintly person in Kashmir to have come from a far-off land claiming that he is known as *Ishvera-putra* or the Son of God, and *Kanyagarbha* or born of a girl. We will take up this issue in subsequent pages.

Jewish Traits

Many scholars have pointed out that the Kashmiris prepare their graves on the model of the Jewish tombs. Such graves are called *Mosai* graves and are oriented east and west. The Gujjars in Kashmir, who are Muslims, term themselves as the descendants of Israel. Their dress, as well as the fashion of their hair, is peculiar to the Jewish style. The paddle used by the Kashmiri boatmen is on the model of a heart and is in vogue even at present. Such paddles are never used in any country of the world except Palestine and Kashmir. The Kashmiri boatmen call themselves the descendents of the prophet Noah. Old architecture in Kashmir reveals that the stairs leading

to it are always from the west. This is not the case with the ancient Hindu, Muslim or Buddhist architecture.

At Aish Muqam, we have the rod of Moses, which is called Asai-Sharif or the esteemed staff.

Tomb of Moses

The circumstances under which Moses died are shrouded in mystery.[76] Nothing is known about the tomb of Moses, except that he was buried in the valley of Moab near Bethpeor, situated in a far-off land in the east. It is believed that Moses was buried on the hill of Nabu overlooking the valley of Lolab and Bandipur in Kashmir. Some historical material is available to show that Moses came to Kashmir. Some of the towns and hills are still named after him. It is also stated that Moses came to Kashmir in his last days.[77] He was buried on the hill of Nabu in the Bandipur. His tomb is visited by many a Kashmiri devotee.[78] According to some, Moses came to Kashmir to preach them the word of God.[79] The Jews believe that Moses disappeared and went to the Land of Promise, in a far-off land in the East.[80]

It is surprising that the five places mentioned regarding the Land of Promise—Bethpeor, Hesbun, Pisgah, Mount Nabu and the valley of Moab—do exist in Kashmir even at present. According to the Western scholars all these places have remained unidentified. But the Survey of India map would reveal that all these places can be located in the Bandipur area. Bethpeor was known earlier as Behatpur in Kashmir and now is known as Bandipur.[81] Hashbon is now known as Hashba, Pisgah is known as Pish, Moab is known as Mowu and Nabu is known as Nabo or Nil-toop.[82] All the above-mentioned places do exist in the area in which the tomb of Moses is situated.

Moses was a prophet and was ordered by God to refrain from entering Palestine and to die on the hill of Nabo.[83]

> Go thee, unto Mount Nabo and die, but thou shalt not go unto the land which I give to the children of Israel.

He had to obey the commands, and went to Kashmir. People believed in him and his tomb is known as the shrine of the "Prophet of the Book."[84]

Jewish Settlement

The Jews, after having settled in Kashmir, founded many villages and towns, some of which exist even at present. The immigration of Jewish groups into Kashmir continued for many centuries and they continued also to adopt local religions. A stage came when the Kashmiri stopped such infiltration, however, and would allow only one or two Jews to enter the valley every year.[85]

Thus, it is not strange that many place names which have given in the Torah and the Bible also exist in Kashmir. Reference is invited to the following table, which shows still existing settlements:

Ashma	Ashma
Ashar	Ashew
Astera	Astore
Babal	Babel
Balpor	Balpura
Benatpore	Bandipor
Karan	Karan
Mattan	Mattan
Nabo	Nabo
Dore	Dore
Haroon	Harwan
Pisgah	Pis
Uri	Uri
Golgotha	Gilgit

The Jews uphold such things as daily worship, regular prayers, intensive study and dietary laws known as Kashrut. They insist on the separation of men and women in the synagogue. They also do not permit music during religious ceremonies. The same is the case with the Kashmiris, who are very particular about intensive studies, regular prayers, dietary laws and the separation of men and women during prayers. No instrumental music is played at the time of religious congregations.

Impact of Jewish Immigrations

The Jewish immigration resulted in much influence on the language, custom and behavior of the Kashmiris. It is not the scope of this book to give a detailed account of the similarities between the Israelites and the Kashmiris, but a general review of the impact of Jewish influence can be summarized in the foregoing paragraphs.

There are many Hebrew words in the present-day Kashmiri language. The ratio has been fixed at nine percent—and such Hebrew words are still in vogue.[86] Hebrew has influenced the Kashmiri language for nearly two thousand years.[87] The early Jewish tribes who came to Kashmir from Central Asia spoke the Aramaic language, and this language gradually became the Kashmiri language.[88]

The Kashmiri Language

The aboriginal tribes which settled in the valley of Kashmir after its emergence from water evolved their own language, which may be termed as original Kashmiri. But with the advent of other tribes, such as the Khasite Aryans, their language underwent a change. However, research reveals that the original Kashmiri words, idioms and proverbs are a mixture of many languages such as Aramaic, Hebrew, Sanskrit and Persian.[89] The Kassites were a substock of the Aryans whose exploits are shrouded in mystery. We hear of them as Kish in the Old Testament. They established themselves as rulers of Babylonia in about 1780 B.C. and named their capital Kish.[90] They established a settlement in Persia with the name of Kashan. After having crossed the Hindo-Kush, they found Kashgar in Central Asia. Having crossed the Indus, they settled in Kishtawar and

Kashmir. These Kassite tribes have also been termed as Semites who migrated towards the northwest of India and settled in the region. We find traces of the Brahmi and Kharosti in Kashmir in the shape of inscriptions, tiles and numerals. It is a fact that both these alphabets are derived from the Aramaic alphabet, which was prevalent in Mesopotamia in the 5th century B.C. It is for this reason that the present-day Kashmiri language contains 30% Persian, 25% Arabic, and 45% words from Sanskrit and other languages including Hebrew.[91]

Similarly, many ceremonies, like that of birth, marriage, and death are the same in Kashmir as are prevalent in Palestine. The period of purification for women is above one month among both the nationalities. Levirate marriages are a common feature among the Jews as well as the Kashmiris. Mourning for the dead is fixed at forty days among both the people. Even the coffins to carry the dead are of the same design. The Jews always orient their graves from east to west, and such graves have been found in Kashmir with Hebrew inscriptions.

The Jews and the Kashmiris have some similar food habits, such as the eating of smoked fish and the using of oil only for cooking purposes.

Lingam—The Holy Stone

Among the Kashmiri Pandits the worship of the Lingam, the holy stone, is a daily routine. In every shrine, we find a stone on which they pour flowers, incense, water and oil every day. To them it is the phallus of Shiva and a symbol of creation. Every Pandit has great reverence for certain rocks and stones which are raised at sacred places. In the Old Testament this stone is given many names, such as Jegar, Galeed and Mizpah.[92]

Anointing of the sacred stones has been mentioned in the Old Testament at many places, such as the following passage:

> And Jacob rose up early in the morning,
> And took the stone
> That he had put for his pillow,
> And set it up for a pillar,
> And poured oil upon the top of it.[93]

The stone of Moses

In ancient Canaan, the religion of the people was the same type of polytheism as practised among the Shivites of Kashmir. Like Canaan, each spring, lake, hill or city has its divine or devil possessor. These possessors are both male and female in both countries. In Canaan they are known as Baal or Baalah, while in Kashmir they are known as Deva or Devi. For demonic possessors the Kashmiris use the name Beru. The worship of the Sun and the Moon was common both in ancient Canaan and Kashmir.

The temples in both the country had carved images and statues. It is also significant that in every temple there used to be a stone pillar which was known as *Mizpah* in Canaan and Lingam in Kashmir. The Pandits of Kashmir continue to worship this stone pillar even today. It may be noted that in ancient Canaan the sexual manifestations of life were under the patronage of the goddess Astarte. On festive occasions there used to be music and dancing before her altar and men and women gave themselves to orgies. In India the goddess Astarte is still worshipped as *Kumari* or Durga. The Hindus think of Shiva and Durga as the promoters of creation, and for this reason they are represented by the two symbols of the Lingam (phallus) and the Yoni (vagina). Among the Kaulas and the Shaktas, the worship of Shiva and Durga is practised by eating flesh, drinking wine and giving themselves to orgies. Magic and sorcery were rife both in Canaan and India. With the advent of the followers of Judaism, many such practices came to an end. But one point is significant and that is that there exist parallels between Kashmir and Canaan of bygone times.

It is recorded in the Hebrew history that, when Moses was away, the Children of Israel began worshipping a calf. Among the Hindus, the tradition of revering a cow continues even up to this day. After their occupation of Canaan, the Jews could not help adopting some of the old religious practices. They adopted some form of idolatry and created images for worship in the form of a bull or a serpent.[94] Among the Hindus of India in general and among the Kashmiri Pandits, the worship of Shiva's bull and serpents is a common practice. While the followers of Hinduism feel a special fascination for the *Shank*, the followers of Judaism have attached great importance to the *Shofar*. On all festive occasions and religious ceremonies, the Hindus blow the *Shank*, a horn created out of a sea shell. The Jews, on the other hand, blow the Shofar, which is a ram's horn. It is a common practice to blow the *Shofar* in the synagogue each morning at the time of prayers. In the same way the *Shank* is blown each morning in the Hindu temples of Kashmir at the time of recitation of the *Bhajan* or prayers. Both the Jews and the Hindus blow these horns at the climax of their prayers. It is a strange coincidence that both the communities have a special prayer for rain because it is a blessing upon the face of the earth.

Among the Hindus, *Dewali* is the festival of lights, while the Jews have a similar festival known as *Chanu-kah*, during which oil lamps are kindled. Both the festivals commemorate victories.

In the month of *Visakh*, the Kashmiri Pandits observe the festival of Visakh. This day is considered auspicious for drinking and eating special foods. It occurs in the first fortnight of April and is similar to the Jewish festival of *Pesakh*, which is celebrated in early spring. On the occasion of *Pesakh*, the Jews eat a special kind of bread.

Another festival of the Kashmiri Pandits deserves consideration. It is known as *Til-Ashtami*, which is observed on the lunar eighth day of the eleventh month of the year. While lamps are lit and rice is dropped on them, the chief priest pours oil on the sacred stone which is called the lingam. This ceremony is similar to a ceremony of the Jews in which they anoint the tabernacle with oil.

Jesus in Kashmir

In subsequent pages we will be dealing with information about the life of Jesus Christ which will show that he came to Kashmir in search of the lost tribes of Israel. Not only is it believed in Kashmir that Jesus Christ graced this valley after he left Jerusalem, but all over Central Asia, as well as in Ladakh and Tibet, there is a strong belief that Jesus Christ travelled in these countries.[95]

Thus it is not a strange coincidence that there exist a dozen towns and villages in these countries associated with his name or named after him. It may be mentioned at the outset that Jesus is known as Yuzu or Yusu or Issa in Kashmir. Some of the places associated with his name are mentioned below:

Ishabar, meaning the place of Isa.
Ishmuqam, meaning the site of Isa.
Yus midan, meaning the ground of Yusu.
Yusmarg, meaning the garden of Yusu.
Yusnag, meaning the spring of Yusu.

All the above sites are visited by the locals as well as tourists in Kashmir. It may be mentioned that Jesus is called Yusu in Hebrew.

Ancient chronicles of Kashmir tell us that nearly 2000 years ago the famous saint Isana used to live here who would resurrect the dead to life. Isa means Christ, because he is known as such in the East. Now this saint Isana saved the prince of the Aryas from the cross and gave him life. This is the same Bible story of the crucifixion as recorded in the ancient history of Kashmir.

It is a strange coincidence that Christ met the Kashmiri King some time before 78 A.D. Their conversation is reproduced in a manuscript written in 115 A.D.[96]

It may seem strange to Christians to learn that Jesus Christ proclaimed his prophethood in Kashmir and died here. Yet also his

Tomb

tomb with a stone engraved with an impression of his feet exists at Khanyar, in Srinagar, Kashmir.

All these issues will be dealt with in subsequent pages. It is sufficient to say here that research conducted so far on the subject has established two visits of Jesus Christ to India; one at the age of thirteen and the other as a person in his forties. A translation of a poem in Kashmiri about the tomb of Jesus Christ is reproduced below:

> Here lies the Tomb,
> So famous and so illuminant:
> Sanctum of the Prophet.
> Whosoever bows before it,
> receives light and consolation.
> Tradition has it:
> There was a prince,

Accomplished, pious and great:
He received the Kingdom of God;
Was devoted to the Almighty,
Was commanded to be the Prophet,
True guide of the devotees.
Here lies the Tomb of that Prophet,
Who is known as Yuz-Asaph.[97]

CHAPTER THREE

The Son of God

Before anything else existed,
There was Christ with God.
St. John

BEFORE THE SPREAD OF CHRISTIANITY, there existed many mystery cults in the region besides Judaism. It is but natural that such cults could be termed the basis of Christianity. Then there were the imperial cults, which originated from the East and penetrated into the West after Alexander's conquest. These mystery cults originated from India, Iran, Mesopotamia, Egypt and Greece. Even though these mystery cults have affected Christianity in a limited way, still it cannot be denied that they form the basis of Christian thought and mythology. Buddhism also started as a mystery cult, laying much emphasis on *mukti* or the salvation of soul. Hence the usage of the term "saviour" for Jesus Christ has its origin in Buddhist thought.

Mithraism of Iran also began as a mystery cult. The same is the case with the Manichean and Mandean cults of Persia. It may be mentioned that the Manichean cult was greatly influenced by the Buddhist doctrines of *Nirvana* and *Pari-nirvana*. Mani, the founder of this religion, appointed twelve disciples, like Jesus Christ, for propagating his doctrines. Influence of the Hindu mythology is reflected in the writing of the later apostles, when they relate events about the pre-existence of Jesus Christ and his reincarnation into this planet.

Pre-Existence of Jesus Christ

To believe in the pre-existence of Jesus Christ means adherence to Christianity. John hints at the pre-existence of Jesus Christ when he says:

In the beginning was the Word,
And the Word was with God,
And the Word was God.
The same was in the beginning with God.[1]
And the Word was made flesh
And dwelt among us,
Full of grace and truth.[2]

From the above we gather that Jesus existed in the beginning with God. Later he was made flesh and dwelt with us, full of grace and truth. The meaning would be clear if we replace Jesus for the Word thus:

In the beginning was Jesus,
And Jesus was with God,
And Jesus was God.
The same was in the beginning with God.
And Jesus was made flesh
And dwelt among us,
Full of grace and truth.

This would make Jesus Christ equal to God and interconnected with Him. At the same time it would show that Jesus, who was God, came to this earth in the shape of a man and dwelt among us with grace and truth. The life of Jesus in this world was the earthly life of God. This would further mean that God incarnated in the form of a human being. It is further mentioned that Jesus descended from heaven and ascended into heaven. He lived earlier with God in the cosmos and ascended into it.

If I have told you earthly things,
And ye believe not,
How shall ye believe,
If I tell you of heavenly things ?
And no man hath ascended up to heaven,
But he that came down from heaven,
Even the Son of man which is in heaven.[3]

Here, Jesus tells us to believe in his heavenly ascent and descent. There is no reason to disbelieve him, because it is a spiritual allegory. Before his ascension, two men in white apparel said:

Ye men of Galilee,
Why stand ye gazing up into heaven?
Thus came Jesus,
Which is taken up from you into heaven,
Shall so come in like manner,
As ye have seen him go into heaven.[4]

In the above Epistle, the heavenly advent of Jesus Christ has been proclaimed. He was God, came to this earth and went away: such is the mythological event related in Timothy:

God was manifest in the flesh,
Justified in the Spirit,
Seen of angels,
Preached unto the Gentiles,
Believed on in this world,
Received up into glory.[5]

The pre-existence of Jesus Christ has been further asserted by Peter when he affirms that Jesus Christ was foreordained before the foundation of the world, but was made manifest in these last times for us.[6]

Some scholars have suggested that the theory of incarnation is a later addition made by the Apostles. But the very idea of pre-existence and incarnation has been given in the Gospel of John, which is an early and important part of the Holy Bible. The incarnation of gods and goddesses has been the basic dogma of nearly all religions in the world. It is no wonder that the doctrines of the pre-existence and incarnation of Jesus as God also find their rightful place in the Christian mythology.

Explanation

The concepts of God-incarnate, the Son of God and the Messiah have roots in the ancient mythology of Egypt. It is an historical fact that in Egypt the Pharaohs were considered divine beings or gods. The same is the case in Hindu mythology. In Assyria, a king was considered the Son of God. In Israel, even angels were termed "the Sons of God," who had intercourse with human women.[7] In the Old Testament, the term "Son of God" is used as a title for Abraham,

Moses and other prophets. But no prophet in the Old Testament has claimed the position of God or God-incarnate for himself. This is peculiar to Jesus only. The idea of incarnation is the pivot of Hindu mythology and it is probable that Jesus got acquainted with it during his first journey in India. He himself asserts at three places in the Bible that he is the Son of God.

Name

After his advent, Jesus Christ came to be known by various names and titles which may be mentioned here:

God: Timothy believes that Jesus Christ was God, who manifested himself in the flesh, and came to the earth.[8]

Son of God: Jesus himself believed that he was the Son of God. During his discourse with the king of Kashmir, he said that he is known as the Son of God.[9] He addresses God as Abba, which means Father.[10] He mentions God as Father numerous times in the Gospels.

Son of Man: Jesus Christ is called the Son of Man nineteen times in the New Testament.

Immanuel: He is mentioned as Immanuel, a term that refers to the future king who would bring peace and prosperity to the people.[11]

Jesus: This name occurs frequently in the New Testament. Sometimes he is also mentioned as Jesus of Nazareth or Jesus Christ.

Joshua: One of his earlier names was Joshua, but the Gospels refrain from mentioning him as Joshua,[12] for the name Joshua already exists in the Old Testament, and so this would have created confusion.

Jesus: Jesus is called Jesu in Aramaic.

Yusu: In all translations of the New Testament into Urdu, the name of Jesus is given as Yusu.

Yuzu: In Persian, Jesus is called Yuzu or Yuz.

Issa: In Arabic, Jesus is known as Issa or Isha.

Iesus: Among the Greeks, he was known as Iesus.

Christ: In the Gospels, Jesus is called Christ, numerous times. The term is derived from the Hebrew term, Masiah, meaning the anointed one.[13] Jesus himself asserted that he was Christ.[14]

Lord: Jesus was also addressed as Lord during his earthly life. But he resented this honorific title, when he said: "Why do you call me 'Lord, Lord,' and not do what I tell you?"[15]

Messiah: Jesus is also known as the Messiah, for he travelled into the East—and this term signifies a traveller.[16] This term also means a healer in the East, for Jesus was capable of healing ailing persons. This term or title has been used twice in the Gospel of John. During the pre-Christ period the Jews expected two Messiahs; the temporal head and the spiritual head, more or less of equal rank.

Nazarene: According to Matthew, when Jesus came and dwelt in the city called Nazareth, he was called a Nazarene.[17] Accordingly, the early Christians were known as Nazarenes.[18]

It is interesting to note that Christians in the Kashmiri language are called Nasara or Nasarene, which is equivalent to Nazarene. After his arrest by the Roman governor, Paul was accused of sedition among all the Jews and was called the ringleader of the sect of Nazarenes. Thus it is evident that by the end of the first century, the Christians were termed as Nasarene or Nazarene, among the Jews in various parts of the world. It may have been his title which is the same as *nazir* in Arabic, which means the one with the aim of bringing humanity on the right path. In this connotation, Jesus Christ was surely a messenger of God who made his advent in Israel. *Nazar* in Arabic means "a sign" and is derived from the Hebrew word Netzor. Whereas, in regard to Nazareth, which also means "the watchtower," it is possible that the place might have been linked with Qumran, for we know of a tower near the monastery in the area. It is also evident that since his birth, Jesus had been brought up in the surroundings of Qumran, which contained many Essene monasteries.

The use of the name "Jesus" is an invocation for healing and the name "Joshua" comes from the Sumerian language.[19]

According to Matthew, he is to be called a Nazarene, for he came to and lived in a city called Nazareth. This city existed in the central part of Palestine, situated 32°-40° and 35°-30°.

The name "Christ" is a translation of the Greek word *Christos*, meaning a Messiah, or an anointed one.

The Scrolls found at Qumran inform us that there were to be two Messiahs, the priestly and the kingly, who were expected. Their description is as follows:

> And the Priest,
> And the Anointed one,
> Shall come with them,
> For he is the head of the
> Entire congregation of Israel.
> And then shall come
> The Messiah of Israel,
> And before him shall sit
> The heads of the tribes,
> All the heads of the congregation,
> The wise men of Israel,
> Each according to his proper place of rank.[20]

From the above it appears that the Messiah of Israel has great status, for before him the heads of congregations shall have to sit. It is interesting to note that in Kashmir Christians are also termed Kri or *Chri*. This term may have also been applied to them as derived from *Christos* or *Kyrios* of the Greeks and the Egyptians. It may mean Lord or God, which term was applied to the kings during the ancient period of our history.

Yuzu-Asaph

In Kashmir, Jesus is known as Yuzu-Asaph, as well as Juzu-Asaph. The word Yuz or Juz stands for Yusu and Jesu, and Yuzu-Asaph and Juzu-Asaph stands for Joshua, the original name of Jesus. It is necessary to point out that Joshua was an important prophet and the lieutenant of Moses.[21] Asaph (Joshua) composed several of the Psalms in the Old Testament.[22] During the reign of the famous Mughal Emperor of India Akbar the Great, Jesus Christ was known as Yuzu Kristo. In one of the poems by Faizi, the court poet of the Mughals, Jesus Christ is addressed as:

> *Ai ke nami too; Yuzu Kristo*
> Thou, whose name is Jesus Christ.

How Jesus came to be known as Yuzu-Asaph in Kashmir has been explained in one of its early histories. Mullah Nadri writes:

> In the ancient Hindu scriptures, I have found that it was Jesus, the Spirit of God, who assumed the name of Yuzu-Asaph.[23]

Similarly, an inscription inside the temple popularly known as Takhat-i-Sulaiman, in Srinagar, Kashmir, contains the following verses:

> In this period, Yuzu-Asaph proclaimed his ministry; year 54.
> He is Yusu, the prophet of the Children of Israel.

Just as the name Joseph stands for Yosaf in the East, the name Jesus has been transliterated as Yusu. Study of the Dead Sea Scrolls reveals that *Asaph* or *Ya-Asaph* was a mystical name of Jesus Christ.[24]

Bethlehem

Whereas Jesus was the Son of God, his birthplace has become a matter of controversy. Matthew and Luke say that Jesus was born at Bethlehem, while Mark mentions Nazareth as the birthplace.[25] It is evident that the controversy has been created by the compilers of the New Testament. During the period under review, the region was divided into three parts known as Samaria, Galilee and Judea. Matthew gives a positive statement that Jesus was born in Bethlehem during the reign of Herod.[26] Mark mentions Galilee as the country of Jesus, and his statement that a prophet is not without honor save in his own country is significant. Luke has given Nazareth, a city of Galilee, as the place where Mary lived when the angels sent by God visited her.[27] He mentions that Jesus was born at Bethlehem:

> And all went to be taxed,
> Every one into his own city.
> And Joseph also went up from Galilee,
> Out of the city of Nazareth into Judea,
> Unto the city of David
> Which is called Bethlehem,
> To be taxed with Mary his espoused wife,

Being great with child.
And she brought forth her firstborn son
And wrapped him in swaddling clothes,
And laid him in a manager.

John is silent on the subject, but gives certain hints which show that Jesus belonged to Galilee.

For out of Galilee ariseth no prophet.
But some said,
Shall Christ come out of Galilee?
Hath not the scriptures said
That Christ cometh of the seed of David,
And out of the town of Bethlehem,
Where David was?
So there was a division among the people
Because of him.[28]

Jesus is also spoken of as Jesus of Galilee or Jesus of Nazareth.[29] Old Nazareth has left many traces behind. It lay farther up the hill than the modern village, and there, 1200 feet above sea level, its little houses with their clay walls clustered together, one of them belonging to Joseph the carpenter.[30] It is evident that we must locate both Bethlehem and Nazareth in the region.

Bethlehem

Bethlehem known as Nosiriyyah was situated in Galilee, in the valley of Esdrasion. Nazareth was also a town in Galilee about seven miles away from Bethlehem. Hence it is a fact that Jesus belonged to Galilee and he is rightly spoken of as Jesus of Galilee. It is also a fact that he belonged to Nazareth, for his parents lived there and as such, he is rightly spoken of as Jesus of Nazareth.

Jesus was born in Bethlehem, away from his home town. Though his birthplace is termed controversial, there appears to be no need to make capital out of it. There is every justification to believe that the compilers of the Gospels had no axe to grind, and the sincerity of their purpose cannot be questioned.

Joseph and Mary

Matthew and Luke have provided two genealogies of Jesus, and they contain a few discrepancies as well as mistakes. The genealogy of Jesus has been divided by Matthew into three divisions of four-teen names each. Not only has he omitted some other names given in the Old Testament, but has also made a grave mistake in the last division where, from Jeconiah to Jesus, he mentions only thirteen names. It is evident that he is to be censored for his serious omission. Thus Matthew has given a total of forty-one instead of forty-two generations. However, he is frank enough to declare Joseph as the legitimate father of Jesus, where he mentions the names of Christ in the third division saying:

> And Jacob begot Joseph the husband of Mary, of whom was born Jesus, who is called Christ.

It is a point for consideration that in terms of the issue of how Jesus can be believed to be the Son of God, and on what authority, Matthew mentions his name as emerging from the third division of the genealogy. But if this were the case, then the number of the generations would be reduced to twelve only, for one generation has been missed by him already.[31]

It must be noted that Luke also speaks of Jesus as the son of Jo-seph.[32] At the same time, he speaks of Adam also as the son of God.

Joseph in the garb of an angel meets Mary in the temple.

When both Matthew and Luke declare Joseph to be the husband of Mary and the father of Jesus, it is difficult to reconcile this statement with the theory of virgin birth. This problem will be taken up later, after we complete our views on the genealogy of Jesus Christ.

The tradition of compiling genealogies among the Jews of Palestine was very common in those days. Such compilations could be genuine or fictitious, but both served the purpose. Keeping the above custom in view, when we consider the genealogy of Jesus, we come to the conclusion that the Gospel genealogies were not compiled on the basis of biological descent but for the requirements of mythological prophesies. It is for this reason that both the Apostles, soon after their mention of Joseph as the father of Jesus, introduce the subject of virginal conception.

The genealogy prepared by Luke goes in ascending order from Jesus back to Adam and contains seventy-seven names. Moreover, he makes God the ancestor of Jesus. Thus it seems that Matthew and Luke have prepared divergent genealogies. But it is also certain that both the Apostles are trying to establish the Davidic lineage of Jesus Christ.

While the lineage of Joseph has been traced by the Gospels, no exhaustive information is available about Mary. She was the daughter of Joachim by his wife Hannah.[33] Her cousin Elizabeth was married to Zechariah. She belonged to the family of Aaron.[34] Zechariah was a high priest, who lived away from any of the main cities in Galilee. It was at the instance of Zechariah that Joseph married Mary and took her to his own house, from the temple. Jesus was born to her at the time when she was fourteen years of age.[35] A controversy arose for the reason that Mary was engaged during the preparation of a veil for the temple and she was not supposed to have any carnal connections with her husband.

Tradition makes it that Jesus was born in the family of Joseph, who worked as a carpenter at Nazareth. His mother Mary had been betrothed to Joseph, and Jesus is believed to have been born of a virgin. It is a historical fact that the ancestors of Jesus came from Assyria, which is the original home of the religion of Zoroaster. Abraham and the later prophets, including Moses, built the edifice of Judaism on the basis of this primitive religion. The Essenes have also built their philosophy on the primitive forms of Zoroastric rituals. Hence, Joseph and Mary had in their blood these very primitive ingredients.

Born of a Virgin

The question of the virgin birth has come into public discussion, causing uneasiness and doubts. The questioning does not come from non-Christians only but from sincere Christians also, and some have termed the virgin birth as absurd and incredible. This question disturbed Luke also and he gives the following story:

There was a Jewish priest, Zechariah, whose wife Elizabeth also belonged to the priestly class They had no children. One day when Zechariah was burning incense inside the inner sanctuary, an angel came to tell him that his wife would bear him a son. He stayed on at the temple for some days and then returned home. Soon after-

The Son of God 83

wards, his wife became pregnant. In the following month God sent the angel to another virgin, engaged to be married to a man named Joseph.

> The angel started praising her in those words:
> Hail, thou that are highly favored,
> The Lord is with thee:
> Blessed art thou among women.[36]

Mary, not accustomed to such overtures, was troubled at his saying and wondered what such a salutation by the angel could mean. When she thought of leaving, the angel, who wanted her to stay, said unto her:

> Fear not Mary:
> For thou hast found favor with God.
> And behold,
> Thou shalt conceive in thy womb,
> And bring forth a son:
> And shalt call his name Jesus.[37]

In order to reassure her, the angel further said:

> He shall be great!
> And shall be called the Son of the Highest;
> And the Lord God shall give unto him,
> The throne of his father David:
> And he shall reign
> Over the house of Jacob forever;
> And of his kingdom.
> There shall be no end.[38]

Mary was now fully moulded by the angel but, being innocent, expressed her amazement as to how could she have a baby, for she was a virgin. But the angel, who had by now overpowered her, said:

> The Holy Ghost shall come upon thee;
> And the power of the Highest
> Shall overshadow thee.[39]

Luke is talking in allegorical words in describing the whole encounter which the angel had with Mary. The angel "had by now come upon her," and had "overshadowed" her. The angel now reassured her saying:

> That holy thing,
> Which shall be born of thee,
> Shall be called the Son of God.

After coitus with the angel, Mary might have felt distress as to how could she convince her parents—but the angel reassured her that her cousin Elizabeth had conceived a son in her old age in the same manner and this was the sixth month with her. Accordingly, Mary declared that, as she was the servant of the Lord, she was willing to do whatever the angel wanted.[40]

A few days later, Mary hurried to the house where Elizabeth lived. At the sound of Mary's greetings, Elizabeth's baby leaped within her and she gave a wild cry:

> Blessed art thou among women,
> And blessed is the fruit of thy womb.[41]

Mary remained in the house of Zechariah for three months. During this period Elizabeth reassured her, saying:

> There shall be performance of those things
> Which were told her from the Lord.

Marriage

The compilers of the Gospels, for obvious reasons, are mainly interested in the crucified Christ, and as such, provide very little information about Joseph, Mary and their marriage. Hence, we have to search out the required information from other works discarded by the Catholic Church as "unoriginal texts." The family tree of Joseph given by Matthew shows him to belong to the family of David. Similarly, some little information about the genealogy of Mary is given in Luke. Her real name was Miriam or Mari. Her birth is also miraculous and is given as follows:

Joachim and his wife Hannah lived at Nazareth. They had no children and as such, felt gloomy. The Gospel of James, also known as the Protovangelium *Jacobi,* has provided the following information about the birth of Mary.

Reuben, the priest, told Joachim that, as he had not given any offspring to Israel, he was not qualified to present offerings in the Temple. He felt aggrieved and informed his wife, who, when reminded of her barren condition, lamented.

> Woe is me,
> What am I like ?
> I am not like the birds in heaven,
> For the birds of heaven
> Are fruitful before
> Thee, O Lord.

At that time, an angel came from heaven and told her that she would be blessed with a child. She made a promise with the angel that if she was blessed with a child, she would bring it for service in the Temple, as a gift to God.

Thus, owing to the will of God, Hannah gave birth to a daughter, who was named Miriam. When she was three years of age, she was taken to the Temple and entrusted to the priest Zechariah. She remained in the Temple until she was twelve, when the angel sent by God visited her. She discussed the matter with Elizabeth, who greeted her, saying that God had favored her. Now, Zechariah, in conformity with the Jewish custom, summoned the bachelors of the community, and declared:

> Let them bring every man a rod,
> And to whosoever
> The Lord shall show a sign,
> His wife shall she be.[42]
> And Joseph cast down his adze
> And ran to meet the heralds,
> And when they were gathered together,
> They went to the high priest,
> The rods were thrown,
> In the fountain outside the Temple;
> When Joseph's rod emerged,

> A dove came down,
> And sat beside it.

Thus, as ordained by God, Mary was selected by a divine sign to be the wife of Joseph. He being a man of stern principles wanted to break the engagement.[43] But he was charged with incontinence, and questioned as to why he had forgotten the Lord.

> And Joseph was full of weeping,
> And the priest said:
> I will give you to drink
> The water of the conviction of the Lord:
> And it will make manifest your sins
> Before your eyes.[44]

The priest made Joseph drink the holy water, and sent him to the hills. But he returned whole because sin did not appear in him. As such, he was not condemned but asked to carry Mary to his home. So Joseph took Mary to his house rejoicing, and glorifying the Lord of Israel.[45]

Paul, the chief expositor of the Christian dogma, speaks of the descent of Jesus as follows:

> Jesus Christ our Lord
> Which was made of the seed of David,
> According to the flesh.[46]
> God sent forth his Son,
> Made of a woman,
> Made under the law.[47]

As regards the birth of Jesus, Paul makes the following observations:

a) Jesus was made according to the flesh.
b) Jesus was born of a woman.
c) Jesus was born under the law.

The above-mentioned observations of Paul would become clear if we refer to what Jesus Christ has to say about divorce. When Pharisees came to him to enquire about the law, he said:

But from the beginning of the creation,
God made them male and female.
For this cause shall a man leave his father and mother
And cleave to his wife;
And they twain shall be one flesh
So then they are no more twain,
But one flesh.[48]

The assertion that Jesus was born under the law and according to the flesh testifies to the conception of Jesus in the natural way, i.e., by the cohabitation of a male and female, and in the case of Jesus, it could be no other persons than Joseph and Mary.

The Blessed Mary

The Son of God

According to the law, the marital relationship between a man and woman was established at the time of betrothal. It is also a fact that cohabitation between the betrothal and the marriage feast was not prohibited, and they could enter into intimate relations soon after the initial ceremony. The marriage feast could be held later on. The only condition which was upheld by both was that at the time of betrothal, it was obligatory for the groom to pay "compensation" to the bride's father. As soon as the money had been paid, the transaction of marriage would be complete and the husband had full powers over his wife. According to the lay tradition, the groom had the privilege and obligation of cohabitation with his spouse as soon as the betrothal covenant was over.[49]

The mythological theory of virgin birth propounded by the Apostles Matthew and Luke finds no corroboration in the Gospels of Mark and John. We do not, also, find any reference to it in the Epistles. As such, it could be argued that by virgin birth the compilers of the Gospels may have meant miraculous birth, without any physical pain to the mother. It was a divine birth, because God wanted to incarnate through the person of Jesus. Hence, the story that the angel of God came to Mary should not be taken in a literal way. At the most, it was a sort of a dream or an illusion which Mary had at the time of her visit to Elizabeth.

It is also a fact that the conception of divine birth was very popular during the second century, and in order to satisfy the ego of the believers, certain insertions and alterations were made in the Gospels. The net result was nothing else than confusion worse confounded.

The Essenes' Version

The Essenes have a different version about the birth of Jesus. The following passage explains their point of view:

> I will now tell you of the parentage of this man, who loved all men, and for whom we feel the highest esteem, that you may have

full knowledge of him. He was from infancy brought up for our Brotherhood. Indeed, he was predicted by an Essene whom the woman thought to be an angel. This woman was given to many imaginings, delving into the supernatural and into the mysteries of life, and she found deep interest and pleasure in the things she could not explain. Our brother has acknowledged to us his part in these things, and has persuaded the Brotherhood secretly to search for and protect the Child. And Joseph, who was a man of great experience in life, and deep devotion to the immortal truth, through a messenger of our Order was influenced not to leave the woman nor disturb her faith in the sacredness of her experience, and to be a father to the child until our Brotherhood should admit him as novice.[50]

The above passage hints about the advent of Jesus through mystical rituals observed by the Tantrics. In various treatises on Hindu Tantras, the Shakti and the Shakta perform the sacred *Mythuna*, which may be termed as heavenly coitus. The above version creates the impression that Jesus was the son of an Essene whom Mary thought to be an angel. If this version is correct, then we may presume that the chief priest of the Order visited Mary, and Joseph was told to be a father to the child for some years. That establishes a strong connection between the Essenes and Jesus.

When Joseph found that his fiancée was already pregnant, he wanted to leave her. But, he was influenced by the special messenger of the chief priest of the Essenes not to leave her nor disturb her faith.

As Joseph was devoted to the Essenes, he agreed to be the father of the child, until he would be admitted into the Order as a novice. It would then mean that Jesus was protected by the Essene Order throughout his life and also at the time of his crucifixion. This issue will be discussed in subsequent chapters.

Jesus was begotten in a unique way in which the natural process of fertilization had been bypassed. An angel had come from heaven to earth and put the word of God into the vulva of Mary. The net result was that a baby was born to Mary from this divine union. As such, Jesus was designated as the Son of God. This term was only a metaphor but later it assumed a real sense. In the past the Jews had considered themselves as the Sons of Jehovah and all human beings were termed as the Sons of God. It is also significant to note that in Judaism, the designation, the Son of God, was also used for angels, who used to have coitus with human women.

> And it came to pass when the men began to be multiplied on the earth and daughters were born to them, that the sons of God seeing the daughters of men that they were fair, took to themselves wives of all whom they chose.[51]

In the Old Testament, an earthly father is eliminated in case of Isaac. The idea regarding conception by a virgin is contained also in

Mary and Jesus

the scriptures.[52] It was not only that angels visited the virgins on this earth, but God himself visited Sarah in her solitude. "He did unto Sarah as he had spoken and she conceived."[53]

Noah was also born in the same miraculous way. The Genesis apocryphon found among the Dead Sea Scrolls informs us that when the wife of Lamech was made pregnant by an angel, he expressed his suspicion and declared that his wife had been unfaithful to him.[54] But she repudiated him saying that the holy angel had come upon her.

The most formidable difficulty arises when we find that Mark does not mention the virgin birth. It is strange that John is also silent on the subject. Further, Paul does not relate this story. It appears that either the conviction never existed during their times or they did not believe in the birth of a child without the three elements required for creation—the man, the woman, and the creative energy. Only once in Mark is Jesus styled as the Son of David.[55] But Jesus certainly called God his father. At a later stage in his life, when the king of Kashmir asked him about his parentage, he replied that he is known as the Son of God.[56]

The chronological order of the Gospels is given as follows:

Mark	65-70 A.D.
Matthew	85 A.D.
Luke	90-95 A.D.
John	110 A.D.[57]

But the earliest of sources are the Epistles of Paul, for he was one of the contemporaries of Jesus. Why did he remain silent on the subject? Paul was born at Tarsus and was educated under Gamaliel. After his conversion at Damascus, he went to Jerusalem and met Peter and James, the brothers of Jesus. It was possible for him to be informed about the virgin birth of Jesus. According to him, Jesus was born in a Jewish family, was born under the law and had brothers.[58] It is significant that Mark, the first Apostle, and John, the fourth Apostle, also do not make any mention of virgin birth. The issue also never came up for discussion in the Epistles. The question arises as to who invented the story of virgin birth and why?

Someone has tried to solve this puzzle by stating that God descended from the high heaven and become a man in the person of Jesus Christ. If we are to believe in the incarnation of God, as the Hindus believe, then there was no need for God to be conceived in the womb of Mary, for he would straightaway come to the earth without any aid from a woman. Among the Jews, the king was hailed as the Son of God:

> I will be to him a father,
> And he shall be to me a son.[59]

While, among the Egyptians, the king was actually a God; the Assyrians believed him to be the Son of God. It has also been interpreted that Jesus was Son of God in the spiritual sense and not in the literal sense of the word. This title was given to him after his baptism, when he was appointed to play an important part as a prophet of God. As such, the birth of Jesus through a virgin expressed the transcendental origin of Jesus.[60] This at once takes us to Sumer, situated at the terminal of the rivers Tigris and Euphrates, which had developed a rich civilization in about 4000 B.C. The garden of Eden is believed to be situated here, and the region was considered to be the Land of God.[61]

Sumerian Mythology

Some of the Sumerian myths tell us of gods who came down to earth, impregnated the women and then returned to the stars. Enlil, the god of air, impregnated the earthly maiden, Meslamtaea, with divine semen.[62]

The Sumerians, later established their hegemony over Akkad and Elam and influenced the cultural life of all the river basins right up to the northeast of Palestine.

The archaeologists have already found in the region a very high level of the Sumerian civilization in the shape of classical architecture, literary texts, clay tablets and cylinder seals. Some of the seals have been interpreted so as to prove that the genetic code of the humans was perfected by these extraterrestrial visitors.

Perhaps we would have solved the mystery about the virgin birth of Jesus had not the censors of Rome destroyed the existing manuscripts of the mystery cults in 400 B.C. After a few centuries, the Christian compilers threw out the other manuscripts and produced the present New Testament. Accordingly, the Book of Enoch was discarded as unholy. It tells us about the name of the angels who coupled with the virgins of this earth.

Chronology

As Jesus was born under supernatural conditions, his date of birth has created a good deal of confusion. In order to understand his mission, the scholars have tried to find out the chronology of his life. As stated in the beginning, the advent of Jesus was an act of God and must be bracketed with the creation of this planet. If we believe that Jesus was the Word of God, then we must also believe that Jesus existed before the creation of this universe. It is for this very reason that John speaks of the Word which was with God.

> In the beginning was the Word,
> And the Word was with God,
> And the Word was God.
> And the same was in the beginning with God.[63]

Further, says he, about the advent of Jesus Christ:

> And the Word was made flesh,
> And dwelt among us,
> Full of grace and truth.

It is for these very reasons that Luke gives God as the ancestor of Jesus.[64] Despite researches, we have not yet reached a stage when we could gather information about the Jesus of prehistoric times who is spoken of in the ancient mythologies. We have no option but to continue our research on the life and mission of the Son of God who was born in Palestine and is known as Jesus of Nazareth. We have no option but to consider this very Jesus in the framework of historical writings.

Both Luke and Matthew date the birth of Jesus during the reign of Herod, the king of Judea, which lasted between 39 to 4 B.C. Luke provides a further clue:

> When Cyrenius was governor of Syria,
> And Joseph also went to Bethlehem,
> To be taxed with Mary his espoused wife,
> While they were there,
> She brought forth her firstborn son.[65]

Cyrenius is better known as Quirinius, who went as Legate to Syria in 6 A.D., but we know from a Roman inscription discovered at Antioch that he also went to that country on a military mission in about 7 B.C. under orders of Augustus.[66] According to Luke, the above-mentioned census took place about the year Jesus was born. Hence, we have to date the birth of Jesus Christ around 7 B.C.

The Christians celebrate Christmas from the 24th of December to the 25th of December, for they believe that Jesus Christ was born on the 25th of December of the Zero Year. This date was fixed arbitrarily by the Scythian monk Dionysius Exiguus in the year 533 A.D. As he was not a sound mathematician, he did not insert the Zero Year between 1 B.C. and 1 A.D. It is a historical fact that the Romans used to celebrate the 25th of December every year as the birthday of Mithra, whom they worshipped as the Saviour of mankind. They also termed the day as "*Dies Natalis Invicti,*" the birthday of the unconquered. It was a major Roman festival which was taken over by the early Christians to be the birthday of Jesus Christ.[67]

Christmas

It has to be admitted that Jesus Christ was not born on the 25th of December because this date or any other date has not been mentioned in the Gospels. As such, our task in fixing the date of his advent in this world has become very difficult. It may also be mentioned that, according to the Romans, the Sun was born on the 25th of December. The Talmud had predicted that the coming Messiah would be born with the sign of Fishes, which zodiacal constellation is also known as Pisces, and occurs in the middle of June. It cannot be denied that the advent of Jesus had been predicted in ancient scriptures, and Jews were eagerly waiting for this advent. According to Luke, Jesus was born in the season "when shepherds abide in the field and watch over their flock by night." Recordings made by meteorologists show that during December, Palestine remains in the grip of frost, and flocks are put to grass only between the months of May and November.[68]

It is to be kept in mind that the advent of Jesus in this world occurred under abnormal or supernatural conditions. Mary was impregnated in the month of December and Jesus was born in June, after a span of seven months. It is to be noted that the calculation from June to December or December to June comes to seven. The appearance of the Star of the Magi derives its origin from the number 17, and, as such, the advent of Jesus Christ can be fixed on the 17th of June, 7 B.C. At the same time, it must be noted that, besides that Star of the Magi, two other stars, namely, the Star of Horus and the Star of Bethlehem are connected with the advent of Jesus Christ. The Star of Horus is also known as the Star of the Three Kings, which guided the wise men of the East to locate the newly born infant god. The Star of Bethlehem was the third comet, which appeared in 6 or 7 B.C.

Comets, stars and fiery beams have not only impressed human beings but have special significance for astrologers and astronomers. Their appearances have been connected with important occurrences in the world, and are recorded in the works of Indian, Egyptian, Greek, Tibetan and Chinese astronomers. If the position of the stars is calculated backward with equal precision, it is possible exactly to locate the time of the appearance or conjunction of various stars, known and unknown. Observations recorded by the ancient Chinese astronomers have come to light which speak of appearances of comets and conjunctions of the known stars.

The wise men from the East had seen the star and received a signal about the birth of their incarnate Buddha. For centuries, information provided by Matthew about this extraordinary star has attracted the attention of astronomers. It was Johannes Kepler who for the first time observed in 1603 a conjunction of Saturn and Jupiter in the constellation of Pisces. After making astronomical calculations, he recorded the same event in the year 6 B.C. and thus dated the birth

of Jesus in 7 B.C. But it goes to the credit of the German scholar Schna-
bel to have discovered a note about the position of the planets in the
constellation of Pisces which reckons the year as 7 B.C. It was further
discovered that this conjunction of the stars occurs three times in a
given year. It was seen in Palestine on the 29th of May, 7 B.C.[69] This
star is designated as Haley's comet, which reappears always after an
interval of 76 years, and it was seen in 1986 also.

The Visit of the Wise Men

Matthew connects the birth of Jesus with the visit of the wise
men from the East to Jerusalem. For the first time a connection is
established between Jesus and the East and this connection had far-
reaching effects on his life. This would be examined in subsequent
pages and for the time being, let us revert to Matthew:

> Now when Jesus was born in the days of Herod,
> Behold, there came
> Wise men from the East to Jerusalem,
> Saying:
> Where is he that is born king,
> For we have seen his star in the East,
> And are come to worship him.[70]

When Herod heard these reports, he felt distressed. The an-
nouncement of a born king brought his sovereignty into peril. He
gathered all his chief priests and demanded of them to give him the
name of the place where the future Redeemer could have been born.
Then he called for the wise men from the East and directed them to
search for the baby and inform him accordingly.

After this interview, these wise men started out again, and
when they saw the star standing over Bethlehem, their joy knew no
bounds. Entering the house where the baby and his mother were,
they threw themselves down before him, worshipping. Then, they
opened their presents and gave him gold, frankincense and myrrh.
But they returned to their own land; they did not go through Jerusalem to report to Herod. These astrologers of the East have been
termed as wise men from the East.

Visit of the Wise men from Zadar, Yugoslavia, 10th century
(Museum of Archeology)

Wise men of Tibet

Wise men
from Ladakh

Who were these wise men who, after worshipping the baby, departed to their own country another way? Some scholars have raised objections regarding the Magi and the star. Some have even denied the existence of the people, known as the Moon or star-gazers. Archaeology has proved that there were people who were Moon or star-gazers. Many relics of tablets and other antiquities carved by them have been unearthed in the East. Tiles showing the moons, the Sun and stars have been dug out from Kashmir, Sumer, Central Asia and China. As such, the existence of the Magi is beyond doubt. The Japanese are star-gazers and they feel special pleasure in gazing at the Moon and stars for hours together. It is interesting to note that the Magi have been mentioned in the *Bhavishya-maha-purana,* a second-century manuscript of Kashmir. The Magi as a prominent sect did exist in China, Central Asia, Kashmir, Iran and Sumer, during prehistoric times. The tiles located at Harwan in Kashmir with the Moon motifs are preserved in the Government Museum, Srinagar. Again, the travel of a star from east to west has been questioned. Did the wise men travel during night only, when the stars are visible? Such questions are irrelevant, which will be explained in subsequent paragraphs.

> Where is he that is born King of the Jews?
> For we have seen his star in the East,
> And are come to worship him.[71]

The above would show that the wise men of the East came in search of the baby, for they had seen his star in the sky.

> And when they were come into the house,
> They saw the young child with Mary his mother,
> And fell down,
> And worshipped him:
> And when they had opened their treasures,
> They presented unto him gifts;
> Gold,
> And frankincense,
> And myrrh.[72]

The above would make it clear that the wise men of the East were either Hindus or Buddhists, who worshipped Jesus as their *Avatara*, or god. Secondly, they made offerings to him, as per their custom.

> And being warned in a dream
> That they should not return to Herod,
> They departed into their own country
> Another way.[73]

It is significant that these wise men kept the secret and departed through another highway to their country. It is clear that during the days of Herod there existed many communication links between the east and the west. These people had come from a faraway country.

It is to be remembered that Buddhism had made inroads into Iran, Syria, Jordan and Egypt, long before the advent of Christianity. They had collected small groups of followers in these regions and built small monasteries, known as *"Navviharas,"* or the new *viharas*. These places later came to be known as *Nav-bahars*. It is also a historical fact that a Buddhist mission from the East found a welcome at the court of Ptolemy Philadephus, some time in the third century B.C.[74]

The above statement clearly reveals that long before the birth of Jesus Christ, the Buddhists of India lived in the region. From its advent, Buddhism began to influence both the East and West. Not only did it become popular in the East, it started its triumphant march toward the West through Alexander the Great, who had consolidated the whole vast region of the globe from Greece to the Punjab. After his demise, Buddhism penetrated into the region, step by step. During the reign of Ashoka, the whole of Afghanistan, Bluchistan and southern Iran had been converted to Buddhism. The missionary zeal of the Buddhist monks took this religion right up to Alexandria, covering Iran, Mesopotamia and Judah. Archaeological remains of the Buddhist civilization have been located at various places in the region.

The Future Buddha

Worshipping of the *devas* and the *Bodhisattvas* is a favorite religious ceremony with the Hindus and the Buddhists. The *devas* or the *devatas* is equivalent to the gods or the gods incarnate, while the term Bodhisattva stands for the coming Buddhas. They believe in the incarnation of gods and in the advent of future Buddhas or the enlightened ones. The Hindus are renowned throughout the world for their proficiency in astrology since ancient times, and their astrologers can predict the future. The Buddhists await the future Buddha, and always make a search for him.

The Buddhists of Tibet and Ladakh make use of *Tantra* for searching future Buddhas. For this purpose, a minute study of cosmic signs is conducted by their priests. The succession of the incarnate lama is a complicated affair, and rests on the belief in the transmigration of

souls. Sometime after the demise of the lama, a complicated search in all directions is conducted for the newly born baby by a special band of priests. The newborn baby is to be examined in detail. Personal belongings of the departed lama, such as incense, holy water and a cup are placed before the newborn baby, along with presents. These articles are mixed with other articles, and if the baby touches the belongings of the deceased lama, then the priests declare the baby as the incarnate lama, and worship him. Much rejoicing is done on this auspicious occasion. For searching out the incarnate lama, besides consultation of astrological works, the occult science of numbers is used by the priests.

According to Buddhist mythology, when a lama dies, his soul is infused in another baby, and such incarnation is perpetuated involuntarily, through the force of *karma*. The position of the incarnate baby is very high, holy, and esteemed.[75] He is termed as the *Bodhisattva* or the future Buddha.

The above would amply clarify the hypothesis that the Buddhists had already studied the stars, come to know about the birth of Jesus, and had come from far-off Eastern lands to worship him. Seeing the baby, they threw themselves down before him, and worshipped him like the Buddhists. They also offered presents and other articles, such as gold, incense, and myrrh.[76] After having established his identity as the future Buddha, they went to their own country by another way. As is the custom with the Buddhist lamas, they would come again to take the child for worship. It is now possible to reconstruct the gaps in the life of Jesus Christ. Suffice to say that after his return from Egypt, they came and took him away to India, wherefrom he returned after many years and proclaimed his ministry in Palestine. We will discuss this issue at length, later on.

The Buddhist Version

It is interesting to give the Buddhist version regarding the birth of Jesus Christ. Hereafter we quote:

> At this time came the moment when the all-merciful Judge elected to become incarnate in a human being. And the eternal Spirit, dwelling

in a state of complete inaction and of supreme beatitude, awoke and detached itself for an indefinite period from the Eternal Being, so as to show forth in the guise of humanity the means of self-identification with divinity and of attaining to eternal felicity. And to demonstrate by example how man may attain moral purity, and by separating his soul from its mortal coil the degrees of perfection necessary to enter into the kingdom of heaven, which is unchangeable, and where happiness reigns eternal. Soon after, a marvellous child was born in the land of Israel, God Himself speaking by the mouth of this infant of the frailty of the body and the grandeur of the soul. The divine child began from his earliest years to speak of the one and indivisible God, exhorting the souls of those gone astray to repentance and the purification of the sins of which they were capable. People came from all parts to hear him, and they marvelled at the discourses proceeding from his childish mouth. All the Israelites were of one accord in saying that the Eternal Spirit dwelt in this child.[77]

Protection by the Essene Order

During the life of Moses, a distinct Order arose among his followers who claimed that they loved and worshipped God in purity of heart. They believed that the soul was immortal and nothing happened in this world without the will of God. They lived in wilderness and aspired to lead a righteous and honest life. They were most esteemed among the people, for they showed great kindness to children, held them dear, and taught them all kinds of knowledge and science, morals and religion. After his birth, Jesus was put under the protection of the Essene Order by a member of this sect. It was these people who gave protection to Joseph and Mary.[78]

In the Temple

Jesus' circumcision ceremony took place after eight days. At the expiration of the days of purification, his parents went to the temple in Jerusalem. They also took him to the temple where Simeon the priest, seeing him, declared that he was the promised Messiah. When his parents felt amazed, Simeon blessed them and said:

Jesus admitted in an Essene school

Behold,
This child is set for the fall
And rising again of many in Israel;
And for a sign,
Which shall be spoken against;
Yea,
A sword shall pierce,
Through thy own soul also;
That the thoughts of many hearts,
May be revealed.[79]

In that instant, Anna, a prophetess, came into that place and gave thanks likewise unto the baby.

The Massacre

Jesus was born at the time when the Messianic fervor was rampant. The land in which he was born had been subjugated by the Romans, and the Jews wanted to get rid of them. They believed that God might intervene on their behalf, and depute the Messiah for their salvation.

> In this extreme distress,
> The people remembered their great God;
> They implored his grace
> And besought Him to forgive them;
> And our Father in His inexhaustible mercy
> Heard their prayer.[80]

The Jews had eagerly awaited the birth of the promised Messiah, and lived on prophesies. Many soothsayers had declared that the promised "holy one" should rule the people of Israel, and that he would be the king of the Jews. Naturally, the rulers were anxious to find the child and kill him.

This was the situation prevailing at the time of the birth of Jesus. The prophecy claimed that the next king of the Jews would be born at Bethlehem. Herod set his spies on every hearth and home, and tried his best to find the miraculous child.

Joseph had a disturbing dream about his son being taken to the court of Herod. He felt very much alarmed and departed for Egypt during the night.[81] Jesus was hardly two years old at that time. Herod felt mocked, and in anger ordered that all children who were two years old be killed. This resulted in the wholesale killings of innocent children. It was a day of great mourning for the parents whose children had been killed. They wept and lamented, and some of them fled away to different lands. At that time, there lived many members of the Essene Order on the borders of Egypt, and one of them gave refuge to Joseph and Mary during their flight.[82]

The Flight to Egypt

The Gospels provide no information about the sojourn of the Holy Family in Egypt. However, Apocryphal records point to nu-

Entry into Egypt

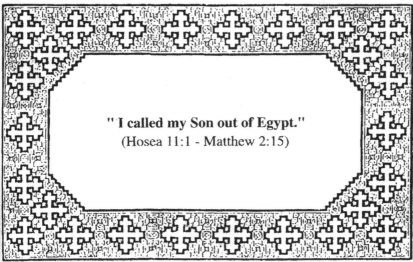

" I called my Son out of Egypt."
(Hosea 11:1 - Matthew 2:15)

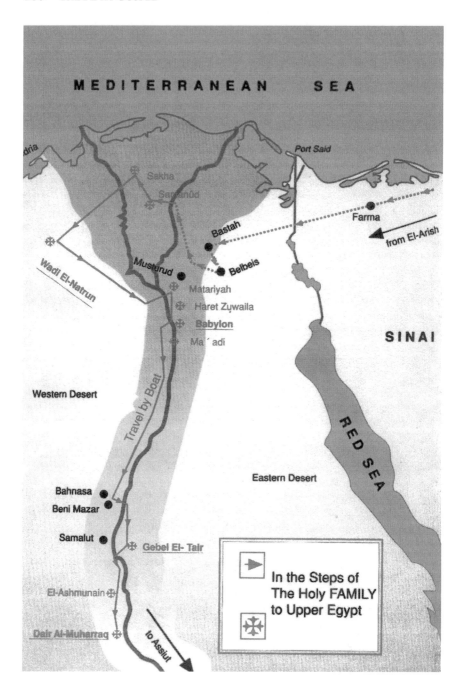

MEDITERRANEAN   SEA

Port Said

dría

Sakha

Samanûd

Farma

Bastah

from El-Arish

Musturud

Belbeis

Wadi El-Natrun

Matariyah

Haret Zuwaila

Babylon

Ma´adi

SINAI

Western Desert

Travel by Boat

Eastern Desert

RED SEA

Bahnasa

Beni Mazar

Samalut

Gebel El- Tair

In the Steps of
The Holy FAMILY
to Upper Egypt

El-Ashmunain

Dair Al-Muharraq

to Assiut

merous places where Jesus stayed with his parents in Egypt. According to earlier Coptic traditions, they stayed in the monasteries of Wadi-el-Natrun, Mataria and Al Moharrak.[83] In the Middle Ages, the garden at Mataria was famous for its fruits and flowers, which were not found anywhere else in Egypt. This garden was also known as the "Herbal Garden."[84] In these monasteries lived members of the Essene Order who, according to Philo of Alexandria, totaled four thousand souls.[85] They led simple lives as mystics, and investigated the healing virtues of herbs, roots and stones.[86] The village of Mataria lies on the right bank of the Nile and it was here that the Holy Family obtained a refuge under the protection of the Essenes. At present, the Church of the Holy Family exists in the Herbal Garden, which also has the fig tree with its hollow trunk. According to a Coptic legend, Jesus and his parents hid themselves in this hollow trunk to save themselves from their pursuers. The information provided by the Essenes about the sojourn of the Holy Family is reproduced below:

During their flight to Egypt, Joseph, Mary, and Jesus were protected and guided by the Essenes. They were first conducted as guests to their dwellings near the slopes of the mountain, where the Romans had built a temple dedicated to Jupiter. Having been introduced to the Essene congregations, they learned their way of worship as well as the ceremony of the eating of consecrated bread and drinking of holy wine. At the time of introduction, Joseph was placed among the half-circle of men on the right hand, and Mary, among the women on the left hand. All of them ate the bread, drank the holy wine and sang the holy hymns. Here for the first time, after the ceremony, Joseph renounced forever any claim on Jesus. After that he was made acquainted with secret signs of the Order by which he could make himself known to other members during his travels. Now, Joseph and Mary freely mixed with the members of the Order at various settlements. Both Joseph and Mary instructed Jesus in knowledge and wisdom. The elders among the Essenes loved and protected Jesus, and he became well-versed in scriptures. When the peril of the Romans was over in Galilee, Joseph went to Nazareth and from that place returned to Jerusalem.[87]

Return from Egypt

Herod died in 4 B.C. and Archelaus came to power as the next king of the Jews. Joseph decided to return to his native place, with his wife and Jesus. By now, Jesus was literate, wise and skilled in his father's profession. He had learned the trade of his father and could make wooden tools for agriculture.[88]

It was customary to visit Jerusalem every year with his parents. As such, on their return from Egypt, the first thing they did was to pay a pilgrimage to the holy temple at Jerusalem. Jesus felt astonished to participate in the Feast of the Passover as well as in rituals performed by the priests. Being mature in wisdom and knowledge, he absorbed himself in religious discussions and also studied the scribes.

The Essenes

An old parchment was found in a house in Alexandria which belonged to the Essenes, giving details about the crucifixion of Jesus Christ. This document first appeared in America in 1873, under the title *Eye-witness*.

Since then much interest has been shown in the Essenes, enabling us to learn more about them. Josephus has described this sect as a secret brotherhood which was opposed to the Pharisees and the Sadducees. They held their meetings away from the cities in their monasteries, known as the white houses. They wore white garments and were interested in the healing properties of herbs and stones. A wing among them was known as the Therapentees, who lived in mixed communities but observed celibacy. The monks and the nuns of this order lived separately but mixed every seventh week after supper, singing hymns, and dancing until dawn.[89] Another wing of the Essenes was known as the Sampsaeans or the sun-worshippers, who mostly lived by the Eastern shores of the Dead Sea.[90]

Josephus Flavius makes mention of three sects of Pharisees, Sadducees and Essenes living in Egypt, Syria and Palestine during ancient times. He calls the Essenes "the most perfect of all the sects in Palestine." The members of this Order embraced the teachings of nonviolence and enjoyed a high moral reputation among the Jews.

They were not meat-eaters and did not believe in the sacrifice of living animals. All these facts lead us to believe that the Essenes were the Buddhists of Western stock, who maintained secrecy about their identity. It is a historical fact that soon after the advent of Alexander the Great on Indian soil, the Buddhist missionaries made their appearance in Egypt.[91] We are also informed that a section of the Essenes were known as "Therapentees." We know that two hundred years after the passing away of the Buddha, the first major split appeared among the Buddhists, and they divided themselves into two sects: the Theravadins and the Sarvastivadins.[92]

Both Eusebius and Allegro speak about the two wings among the Essenes and name them: the Therapentees and the Sampsaeans, which can be identified with the *Theravadins* and the *Sarvastivadins*, among the Buddhists.

We have stated earlier that during their long stay in Egypt, the Holy Family remained under the protection of the Essenes. Jesus grew up as a normal child among the balsam bushes of the Herbal Garden at Mataria. Besides receiving much love from his fugitive parents, be received the care and attention of the Essenes. The "saints," as they were called, absorbed themselves in study, contemplation and meditation. During his formative years, Jesus followed their example. He read and reflected on the sacred literature and mystical practices of these persons. He felt delighted in the Jewish festivals of Passover, Pentecost and tabernacle.

The only story Luke tells us about Jesus is that at the age of twelve, he was so lost in his thoughts that he could not visualize the anxiety of his parents.[93] Before we proceed with the examination of this Gospel story, we must record that Jesus greatly loved to read the Psalms of David and the pungent words of Solomon. When he reached his seventh year, he had studied all the scriptures and fixed in memory every word.[94]

Jesus Lost and Found

The only account of the intervening years is given by Luke when he tells us how Jesus was lost and found by Joseph and Mary. He says:

And when he was twelve years old,
They went up to Jerusalem,
After the custom of the feast.
And when they had fulfilled the days,
As they returned,
The child Jesus tarried behind in Jerusalem,
And Joseph and his mother knew not of it.
But they,
Supposing him to have been in the company,
Went a day's journey;
And they sought him,
Among their kinsfolk and acquaintance.
And when they found him not,
They turned back again to Jerusalem,
Seeking him.
And it came to pass,
That after three days,
They found him in the temple,
Sitting in the midst of the doctors,
Both hearing them
And asking them questions.
And all that heard him were astonished
At his understanding and answers.[95]

The above would show that Jesus was lost by his parents at the age of twelve. No information is available from the Bible about Jesus from then on, up to the age of twenty-nine. Where he spent these seventeen years of his life is a puzzle which requires to be solved.

Jesus Protected

The Essenes have given a different version of the incident in the temple, which is given below:

When Jesus spoke with the scribes concerning holy things, his doctrines gave deep offence to the Pharisees in Jerusalem. They knew him to be from Galilee, and they despised him as they despised the whole people of Galilee. When the divine child had spoken publicly in the temple, the Essenes were apprehensive of the dangers that threatened him. They knew that the Pharisees were in private council fully determined to banish him from the synagogue of Sopherim. Thus it came to pass that Jesus became separated from his parents in the large city, which at that time was full of people from all over the country because of Passover. At last, on the fourth day, Jesus was again found by his parents, according to information given by the Essenes.[96]

Later Events

Joseph and Mary returned with their other children to Nazareth. They felt disturbed, but he had told them that he was not interested in the profession of carpentry and that instead, he would like to take up the profession of a priest and serve God.[97] The above reveals that already, at the age of twelve, Jesus was fully conversant with the scriptures and had committed some to memory. Where had he learned all this? The answer, as we have suggested above, is that his parents had lived with him in Egypt, where the boy had been taught by Essene teachers. Later, it is likely that he studied at Qumran, where the Essenic centers of learning were already available for seekers. It is a fact of history that Jesus was hostile to the Pharisees. But why? This may relate him to the Essenes.

Like the Pharisees, the Essenes meticulously observed the law of Moses, the Sabbath, and ritual purity. They also professed belief in divine punishment for immorality and sin. But, unlike the Pharisees, the Essenes denied the resurrection of the body and refused to immerse themselves in public life. With few exceptions, they shunned temple worship, content to live ascetic lives of manual labor in seclusion. The Sabbath was reserved for day-long prayer and meditation on the Torah. Those who qualified for membership were called upon to swear piety to God, justice toward men, hatred of falsehood, love of truth and faithful observance of all other tenets of the Essene sect.[98]

Jesus spent most of his time in Jerusalem, which is less than twenty miles away from Qumran. He would occasionally visit the ascetics there and discuss philosophical issues with them. Josephus records that Jesus was noted as a boy for his learning, and when he was only fourteen, was often consulted by the chief priests and doctors of Jerusalem. People came from all parts to hear him, and they marvelled at the discourses proceeding from his childish month.[99] It is certain that he was taken up by the Essenes, while still pliable and teachable, who trained him in traditional Jewish scriptures.

The Essenes hated the Roman subjugators, and, in order to provide moral support for the movement, trained a batch of preachers including John who often predicted:

> There cometh one mightier than I after me
> The latchet of whose shoes
> I am not worthy
> To stoop down and unloose.
> I indeed have baptized you with water;
> But he shall baptize you
> With the Holy Ghost.

They had prepared him for the establishment of the Messianic kingdom.

The Gospels are silent about the later life of Jesus Christ prior to his ministry.

Initiation

The Essenes told Jesus to tell Joseph that the time had come for him to fulfill the vow he had made in Egypt regarding renouncing his claim on Jesus. When he returned to his home, he told Joseph all about it. At the appointed time in the evening, they saw the fire signal ascend from the mountain. Immediately, they set forth towards the mountain, where they were met by the white-robed messengers from the Essenes. Jesus remained with the Essenes for one year, during which period he was initiated into their Order. At the first ceremony, Jesus was shown the way to enter into the assembly, where the Essenes were seated in four separated groups. While he made the first vow, all placed their right hands upon their chests, with the left hand hanging down at the side. It meant that only the pure in heart shall see that which was sacred and holy. He then vowed indifference to the treasures of earth, to worldly power or name, and agreed to keep secrecy.

After the vow, he was led into a lonely cavern, where he had to remain for three days and three nights. After the third day, he was clothed in white robes. After this, he was instructed concerning the trials and the disciplines through which he had to pass. After one year, when the period of trial and self-examination had passed, the final ceremony of initiation was performed. He was then conducted to the secret chamber of worship and admitted as a member of the Order. Now he was free to go out into the world, to preach or heal.[100]

Joseph and Jesus

The New Testament informs us about the two personalities bearing the same name of Joseph; one is Joseph of Arimathea, and the other is Joseph, the husband of Mary.

The genealogy of Joseph is given as under:

> Abraham begat Isaac;
> Isaac begat Jacob;
> And Jesse begat David the king;
> David begat Solomon;
> Azor begat Zadok;
> Zadok begat Achim;
> Matthan begat Jacob;
> Jacob begat Joseph, the husband of Mary.[101]

Joseph was a carpenter by profession, and he worked at Jerusalem.[102] He was betrothed to Mary, and had promised to take her as his wife at the proper time. According to Matthew, Mary was espoused to Joseph, when she already had conceived Jesus.[103] Joseph was then married to Mary, and after some time took her up to his house. When he found her with child, he thought of putting her away. Subsequently, the angel of the Lord appeared unto him in a dream, saying:

> Fear not to take unto thee Mary thy wife:
> For that which is conceived in her is of the Holy Ghost.[104]

After being married with Joseph, Mary gave birth to other children, who were considered as the brothers and sisters of Jesus.[105]

The people of Nazareth considered the following as the brothers of Jesus:

James
Joses

Juda
Simon[106]

All the Gospels speak about the brothers of Jesus Christ, but the names of his sisters are not given. Mark refers to his sisters thus:

And are not his sisters also with us.[107]

It may also be pointed out that Jesus had a twin brother, Judas Thomas, who is also called Didymus.[108]

According to the Gospel, Joseph fled into Egypt with his wife and Jesus. After the death of Herod, an angel approached in a dream to Joseph, and told him to take the child and his mother into the land of Israel.[109] Accordingly, he returned to Nazareth along with Mary and Jesus. From this stage, Joseph is not mentioned anywhere in

The Carpenter's Son
(from the painting exhibited at the Church at Nazareth)
Joseph, the husband of Mary was a carpenter.
Jesus, the son of Joseph, had to learn carpentry during his early years.

any significant manner. It is also significant that Joseph never mentions Jesus as his son, and Mary only describes Joseph as the father of Jesus.[110] It cannot be denied that Jesus himself never addresses Joseph as his father.

Only at the death of Joseph, Jesus is said to have uttered the following lamentation:

> Not a single limb of it shall be broken,
> Nor shall any hair of thy head be changed,
> Nothing of thy body shall perish:
> O! my father Joseph.[111]

There is another important point which cannot be overlooked. It has been stated earlier that it can also be presumed that Jesus was in reality the son of an Essene, and was to be handed over to the Order at the age of twelve. When he visited Jerusalem with his parents, the Essene priest recognized him, and Jesus stayed with his real father in the temple. When his mother said unto him:

> Son,
> Why hast thou thus dealt with us?
> Behold,
> Thy father and I have sought thee sorrowing,

he replied:

> How is it that ye sought me?
> Wist ye not that I must be about my Father's business?
> And they understood not the saying,
> Which he spake unto them.
> But his mother kept all
> These sayings in her heart.[112]

The above can be explained in this way: that Jesus had found his real earthly father. When his mother told him that she and his father were searching for him, he told them, as to why they were searching for him, did they not wish that he should do the work of his real father? When Jesus spoke to them like this, they did not understand him. No one understood him except his mother, who kept the meaning of his words a secret. This means, he was not to do the work of a carpenter, which was the profession of Joseph, but Jesus had to be a preacher.

Travelogue

One of the most important and most interesting episodes in the life of Jesus Christ is the account of his thirst for travel. After the Passover, why did he abandon the house of his parents? Was it the spirit of adventure which drove him out of Jerusalem, or did he go in search of the Buddhist monks? He already knew that it was the wise men of the East who had come to search for him when he was a baby. As such, there is no wonder that in his heart he had a yearning to move from one place to another.

It is a historical fact that during the period under view, the members of the Buddhist *Sangha,* or Order, had penetrated as far as Alexandria for missionary activities. It is also an established fact that the Essenes had established close contacts with the Sun-worshippers of Iran and Central Asia. Jesus had been a member of the Essene Order, and had already come into contact with mystics and monks of the west Asian region. It is in the light of the above facts that we would try to find out the details of his early travels in neighboring countries. Unfortunately, no sufficient material is available to us to reconstruct the whole story.

Jesus grew and waxed strong in spirit, filled with wisdom, and the grace of God was upon him.[113] When he was thirteen, many rich and noble people were desirous of having him as a son-in-law.[114] His parents used to visit Jerusalem every year at the Feast of Passover. When they had fulfilled the days, they returned, but Jesus tarried behind in Jerusalem. They went a day's journey, and sought him among their relatives and acquaintances, but they could not find him there.[115]

After mentioning this incident, the Gospels are silent about the life of Jesus Christ, up till his twenty-ninth year. What happened to him for nearly seventeen years is shrouded in mystery. In order to complete the life story of Jesus Christ, we have to search information from other sources. In the old edition of the Bible, Luke says:

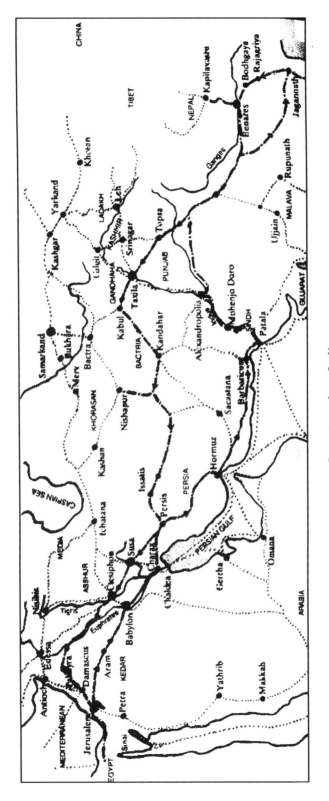

Jesus travels to India

And the child grew,
And waxed strong in spirit,
And was in the desert.
Till the day of his showing in Israel.

But in the new edition of the Bible, Luke is made to say

And the child grew,
And waxed strong in spirit,
Filled with wisdom,
And the grace of God was upon him.

It is clear that the sentence: "was in the desert till the day he came back into Israel," has been changed into: "filled with wisdom, and the grace of God was upon him." The statement that Jesus was in the desert till his return clearly indicates that he left the country at that time.

Jesus in India

Jesus secretly left his parents and, together with the merchants of Jerusalem, turned towards India "to become perfected in the Divine Word." He passed from place to place and dwelt in peace with the low caste people. When the high caste people wanted to teach him, he refused to listen to their speeches. He believed that those "who deprive their brothers of the common blessings shall be themselves stripped of them." Jesus went into the Himalayan mountains and, when he was twenty-nine, he returned to Israel.[116] This information is available about his temporary stay in India from the Tibetan scrolls found by Nicolas Roerich in 1925.

Another Oriental work of importance gives us the exact age of Jesus when he first travelled towards the East. It says:

Jesus was thirteen years old when he left for the eastern countries.[117]

We feel that Jesus travelled between India and Palestine twice, before and after the crucifixion. In the Gospel of the Hebrews we are informed that Jesus went to Assyria and from that country proceeded to the country of the Chaldeans and then to India. He performed many miracles in these countries.[118] At that time, Assyria was under the royal house of Adiabene and its king Ezad had extended his sway right from Nisibis to Kharax on the Persian Gulf. Josephus fixes the date of his ascension to the throne of Adiabene at 36 A.D. He was therefore a contemporary of Jesus. It may also be mentioned that both Ezad and his mother Helena were buried at Jerusalem after their death. Now, at that time, the trade route to India passed from Babylon to Kharax, which was a meeting place of merchants from the Far East. It is probable that Jesus, after his departure from Jerusalem, may have reached Damascus, wherefrom the route lay to Babylon and then to Kharax on the confluence of the rivers Tigris and Euphrates. In the Hymn of the Soul of the Acts of Thomas, the prince declares that he passed Babylon on the left and came to Mesene which is a meeting place of the merchants of the East and sits on the shore of the sea.[119] We feel that Jesus also followed this very route on his first journey to India.

According to Hindu legends, the Jewish race originated in India centuries ago. After departing from India they migrated towards the west. The extraordinary persistence of the Jewish race as the chosen race may have had its basis in the Hindu caste system. Just as the Brahmanas of India consider themselves as superior to the other castes, the Jews also consider themselves as the chosen people. The present-day Jews of India also do not mix with other peoples—and the reason may be their subconscious memory of the caste system in the country of their origin. This legend ties in with the legend that Jesus also came to visit India after he was lost in the Temple at the age of about thirteen. Though he remained at one place for a very short period, yet he learned about the reincarnation theory of the Hindus, and after his return to the country of his birth, he asserted that he was the Son of God. The Sutra known as *Natha Namavali* also asserts that Jesus, who is called as Isha Natha, came to India at the age of fourteen, and after great concentration understood that Shiva was a great god.[120]

Return of Jesus

Jesus was twenty-nine years old when he arrived in the land of Israel. During his absence, the Pagans had caused the Israelites to endure more atrocious sufferings, and they were filled with despair.[121] In order to understand their condition, we have to go back to 63 B.C. when the spiritual and political independence of Israel came to an abrupt end. It was in this year that Pompey, the Roman general, marched into Palestine with his army.[122] Pompey stormed Jerusalem and broke into the Temple, being welcomed as a deliverer by the Pharisees. But later, all felt disillusion, and there followed several vain revolts. In 37 B.C. the Romans placed Herod of Idumea on the throne. He was a tyrant, but he beautified the Temple and built many fine buildings. The last part of his reign was made miserable by family disloyalty. These conflicts continued even after his death with the result that the Romans adopted the practice of putting in military governors.[123]

During the period, the Jews were divided into many sects such as the Pharisees, the Sadducees and the Essenes. Their priests kept them in a fever of an expected Messiah, who could restore their political power. It was in these days that John the prophet started preaching in the wilderness of Judas, saying:

> Repent ye:
> For the kingdom of heaven is at hand.
> For this is he that was spoken of,
> By the prophet Isaiah,
> Saying,
> Prepare ye the way of the Lord.[124]

Birth of John

Little is known about John the Baptist, except that he was the son of a priest called Zechariah, born to Elizabeth in a miraculous way. Elizabeth, we know already, was the cousin of Mary and both confided in each other. Zechariah had been informed by the angel:

> Fear not, Zechariah,
> For thy prayer is heard;
> And thy wife shalt bear thee a son,
> And thou shalt call his name John.
> And thou shalt have joy and gladness;
> And many shall rejoice at his birth.
> For he shall be great,

In the sight of the Lord,
And shall be filled with the Holy Ghost,
Even from his mother's womb.

Zechariah being an old man, wondered how Elizabeth could conceive. But the angel assured him that he was sent by God to speak unto him, and he should keep it a secret.[125]

The Sons of God

As willed by God, the same angel impregnated Mary, during her stay within the house of Zechariah, in a city of Judah. He also informed her that her cousin Elizabeth had also conceived a son in old age in the same way, and this was the sixth month with her. Accordingly, Mary went to confide in Elizabeth, who congratulated her, saying:

Blessed art thou among women,
and blessed is the fruit of thy womb.[126]

At the request of Elizabeth, she remained in the house of Zechariah for three months, after which she was married to Joseph. From the above account, the following similarities can be established between Jesus and John:

a) both of them were conceived by their mothers through the will of God.
b) the Holy Ghost had come upon both Elizabeth and Mary.
c) the power of the Highest overshadowed both of them.

It is clear that both Jesus and John were the Sons of God, and both had to perform the mission assigned to them by divine will.

Education

After his advent on this earth, on the first day, John praised God and all felt amazed. He grew up under the care of Elizabeth and Zechariah who, being a priest, provided good education to his son. As he had to follow the priestly trade, he received training in the temple ceremonies from his parents, and Zechariah taught him the scriptures. John also came into contact with the group of the saints known as the Essenes, who also taught him their scribes. He was admitted into the Order of the Essenes, along with Jesus in their years of early manhood, at Jutha, which was close to the castle Masada.[127] As time passed, he grew into a pious personality, intelligent, and destined to fulfill a mission.

John the Baptist preaching
(from an old print)

He grew, and waxed strong in spirit, and was in the deserts till the day he started preaching.[128]

Prophecy

Zechariah made a prophecy that in the person of John, the Lord God had created a redeemer for the people of Israel, so that they could be saved from their enemies.

Addressing the child, he said:

> And thou,
> Child, shall be called,
> The prophet of the Highest;
> For thou shalt go
> Before the face of the Lord,
> To prepare his ways.[129]

The people were full of expectations that the Messiah would come at any time, and his advent would be preceded by the Prophet Elijah. As such, everyone sincerely believed that Elijah had come in the person of John.

Preaching of Elijah

The words "was in the deserts" can be interpreted to mean that John went to the saints for spiritual guidance. The saints could be no persons other than the Essenes, who had established small colonies in the desert with their headquarters in the caves of Qumran. It was during this period that the word of God came unto John, and he started his mission from Jordan. He preached the baptism of repentance for the remission of sins.[130] He preached in the wilderness saying:

> Repent ye;
> For the kingdom of heaven
> Is at hand.[131]

John the Prophet preached among the people, the publicans, and the soldiers. To the people he asked them to share their belongings, saying, he that has two coats, let him bestow one to him that is without it. Of the publicans, he wished that they should exact no more than what is authorized. He told the soldiers not to do violence to any man, nor accuse anyone of false charges, and be content with their salaries.[132]

The above clearly reveals that John the Prophet demanded repentance from all, whether high or low, in the name of God. He warned that if they refused to obey, the wrath of God was sure to come. He told them that to be the children of Abraham was no guarantee for their salvation. The people had to mend their ways, and wash their sins through baptism.

He declared:

> I indeed baptize you with water;
> But one mightier than I cometh,
> He shall baptize you,
> With the Holy Ghost,
> And with Fire.[133]

Journey to Jordan

Jesus was aware of the activities of John, and his cry in the wilderness that he had prepared the way for the Lord. He had also heard about the huge crowds which flocked to hear John, declaring that one mightier than he was expected any time. Now, when all the people were baptized, Jesus himself went to John for baptism.

When John saw Jesus coming towards him, he told the gathering;

> Behold the Lamb of God,
> Which taketh away the sin
> Of the world.
> This is he of whom I said;
> After me cometh a man,
> Which is preferred before me;
> For he was before me.
> And I knew him not;
> But that he should be made
> Manifest to Israel,
> Therefore am I come baptizing
> With water.[134]

When Jesus came out of the water, the Holy Ghost descended upon him like a dove, and a voice came from heaven:

> Thou art my beloved son.
> In thee I am well pleased.[135]

There could be no need of baptism for the Son of God. As he had come to be a pattern for the sons of man, baptism was a symbol for cleansing of the soul.[136] Jesus was very much occupied with spiritual thinking; he needed time for meditation.

The Mystical Test

Now Jesus had to undergo a mystical test in the wilderness, for forty days, which is a symbolic period. In the East, the mystics undergo such tests, which include meditation and recitations for a period of forty days, after which the devotee attains complete spiritual power. During the period, the devotee has to fight with temptations. Now, when the spirit of God was upon Jesus, he fasted for forty days, and succeeded in avoiding the temptations, with the result that angels came to him, and ministered unto him.[137] Jesus would often go to the valley of Qumran in the Dead Sea, and visit monasteries as well as sanctuaries of the Essenes. Both the Buddhists and the Essenes displayed extraordinary interest in ancient scriptures, meditation and yoga. The Essenes were more interested in ancient writings pertaining to the welfare of the body, investigations of medicinal plants, and the treatment of diseases.[138] The Essenes were the masters of pharmaceutical and medical sciences, and a Dead Sea scroll testifies to this fact. Thus, Jesus learned *Yoga* and medicine from the Essenes.

Jesus in Greece

As Jesus longed to study with masters in Greece, he crossed the Carmel hills, at the port took ship and reached Athens. Once in the amphitheater he stood, and when the Greek masters bade him to speak, he said:

Athenian masters,
I come not here to speak of philosophy;
But I would tell you of a life beyond,
Within;
A real life that cannot pass away.
Return,
O mystic stream of Grecian thought,
And mingle your clear waters with the flood of Spirit life;
And then the spirit consciousness will sleep no more,
And man will know,
And God will bless.

Having spoken thus, he stepped aside. The Grecian masters were astonished at the wisdom of his words.[139] When there was a storm on the sea, he rescued many a helpless one with a mighty power. He told the crowd that the most efficient prayer that man can offer is helpfulness to those in need of help; "for what you do for other men, the Holy One will do for you."

John the Prophet

John the Prophet is better known in the Bible as John the Baptist. "He preached and baptized in the Jordan valley south of Jericho, where the river is crossed by the well-known ford." He urged the Jews to strive towards perfection by strictly following the law. He asked them to present themselves for baptism, and a great multitude became his followers. Herod Antipas received a report of his activities and came to the conclusion that this man was dangerous.[140]

It was John the Prophet who introduced Jesus to his followers. One day, in the presence of his two disciples, he pointed towards him and said that Jesus was the Lamb of God.[141] These two followed Jesus and became his disciples. One of them was Andrew, brother of Simon Peter. They spent a day with him in his abode. The next day, Simon also came to him and became his disciple. Later on, Philip also followed him. In subsequent days, Nathanael also accepted Jesus as the Son of God.[142]

The Temptation

Jesus being full of the Holy Ghost returned from Jordan, and was led by the Spirit into the wilderness.[143] Why was the Lord led into the wilderness? The answer to this question could be that he went there to contemplate the liberation of mankind. Contemplation as a basis for liberation is based on Eastern philosophy and is a way of wisdom initiated in India more than a thousand years before Christ. Besides the Hindu formula, known as *moksha* or the liberation of man from the bonds of *karma,* this way of salvation took various forms in the mysticism of Tao and the enlightenment of Buddha.[144]

Besides contemplation what did he do in the wilderness? He fasted for forty days and forty nights, and afterwards hungered like Buddha. Then temptations came to him as it had come to Buddha. Here is a parallel between him and the Buddha, for both of them went into the wilderness, fasted unto death, and tried to find the way for the liberation of mankind. When the first temptation came to him, and asked:

> If thou be the Son of God,
> Command that these stones be made bread.
> But he answered and said:
> It is written,
> Man shall not live by bread alone.[145]

Jesus was then taken up into a high mountain and shown all the kingdoms of the world in a moment of time. The second temptation said:

> All this power will I give thee,
> If thou therefore will worship me.
> And Jesus answered:
> It is written,
> Thou shalt worship the Lord thy God,
> And him only shalt thou serve.[146]

Jesus was then taken up into the holy city and placed on the pinnacle of the temple. The third temptation said:

If thou be the Son of God,
Cast thyself down.
But Jesus said:
It is written again,
Thou shalt not tempt the Lord thy God.[147]

Jesus rejected all the above-mentioned three temptations. Subsequently, he declared in Nazareth on the Sabbath day:

The Spirit of the Lord is upon me,
Because he hath anointed me,
To preach the gospel to the poor;
He hath sent me
To heal the brokenhearted,
To preach deliverance to the captives,
And recovering of sight to the blind,
To set at liberty them that are bruised,
To preach the acceptable year of the Lord.[148]

The conclusion from the above can be drawn in the words that Jesus proclaimed absolute freedom for the oppressed. It had been the dream of all the prophets to bring good news to the poor and to enable mankind to live together in peace and love. But Jesus boldly announced that the fulfillment of what he had said was not in some remote future, but then and there.[149]

Jesus in Egypt

Jesus came to Egypt to meet the Essene saints. He told the aged teachers all about his life. They convened the council of brotherhood and Jesus stood before the hierophant, who said:

Your wisdom is the wisdom of gods,
Why seek for wisdom in the halls of men?

Jesus replied that in order to gain the heights, he was ready to pass the hardest test. After receiving his mystic name and number from the hierophant, Jesus passed the first test and received a scroll, on which was written just one word, sincerity. After this, Jesus passed the second test and the hierophant placed a scroll in his hands, on which was inscribed, justice. Then Jesus passed the third test and received a scroll, on which was written, faith. Then he passed the fourth test and the hierophant placed in his hands a scroll, on which was written, philanthropy. Jesus spent forty days in the monastery in deep meditation. He had conquered self and could talk with nature. He passed the fifth test, and the hierophant placed in Jesus' hand another scroll, and on this one was written, heroism. After this, Jesus passed the sixth test and the hierophant placed a scroll in his hand on which was written, love divine. And when Jesus passed the seventh test the hierophant placed a diadem on his brow and said, "You are the Christ." Then a voice that shook the very monastery was heard and it said: "This is the Christ," and every living creature said, Ameen.[150]

In every age since time began have seven sages lived. At the beginning of every age these sages meet to note the course of nations, peoples, tribes and tongues. An age had passed, and so the sages met in Egypt. Jesus addressed the sages and said:

> The history of life is well condensed in these immortal postulates. These are seven hills on which the holy city shall be built. These are seven sure foundation stones on which the universal church shall stand. The words I speak are not my own; they are the words of him whose will I do. And from the men of low estate I will select twelve men, who represent the twelve immortal thoughts, and these will be the model church. And when the better age shall come, the universal church will stand upon the seven postulates. And in the name of God, our father God, the kingdom of the soul shall be established on the seven hills. And all the peoples, tribes and tongues of earth shall enter in. The Prince of Peace will take his seat upon the throne of power; the Triune God will then be All in All.

With these words Jesus finished his discourse and all the sages said, Ameen! After this no word was said and Jesus went his way and reached Jerusalem.

The Call

In Galilee, when Jesus was among his early disciples, he gave the following call;

Verily, verily, I say unto you,
Hereafter ye shall see heaven open,
And the angels of God ascending and descending
Upon the Son of man.[151]

When many people came to him for blessings, he came down with them, and stood in the plain. He lifted his eyes upon his disciples, and said:

Blessed be ye poor:
For yours is the kingdom of God.
Blessed are ye that hunger now:
For ye shall be filled.
Blessed are ye that weep now:
For ye shall laugh.[152]

Many disciples collected around him, and he manifested many miracles in different parts of Israel. Jesus declared:

And this is the condemnation,
That light is come into the world,
And men loved darkness rather than light,
Because their deeds were evil,
For every one that doeth evil,
Hateth the light, neither cometh to the light,
Lest his deeds should be reproved.
But he that doeth truth cometh to the light,
That his deeds may be made manifest,
That they are wrought in God.[153]

His fame spread in the whole of the country. Some who were God-fearing came to his fold, while those who had misgivings came to argue with him. God had given ten Commandments unto men through Moses, and Jesus unfolded the spiritual aspects of some of the Commandments. He declared:

The Lord our God is one Lord:
And thou shalt love the Lord thy God,
With all thy heart,
And with all thy soul,
And with all thy mind,

And with all thy strength.
This is the first commandment.
And the second is namely this;
Thou shalt love thy neighbor as thyself.
There is none other commandment greater than these.[154]

Opposition

The preaching of Jesus antagonized the local Pharisees, who, being communal in outlook and thinking, demanded strict observance of the Commandments according to Torah. But Jesus wanted to make them free from rituals, superstition and ignorance. By nature, he was sociable, and did not believe in caste distinctions. As such, the Pharisees campaigned against him and quoted his disciples as saying that Jesus claimed heavenly descent. But he had told them that he was sent by God to be their teacher. The priests also became his enemy, for they saw in his preaching the seeds of their ruin as a class. As such, they started wild propaganda against him, and charged him as saying that he had claimed to be the Son of God. They pronounced that the demon had possessed Jesus. They made people throw stones at him and disturb his religious gatherings.[155] They even alleged that he was declaring himself to be God, and this was blasphemy.[156] An enquiry was instituted to find if Jesus was guilty of the charge of blasphemy, but they could not find a single witness to prove this allegation. Thus his fame spread far and wide and his name became a legend overnight.[157]

Now they took another line, and that was to make an allegation of a political nature against him. The priests claimed that Jesus had political motives in claiming that he was the king of the Jews. Pilate, who tried this case, came to the conclusion that it was simply to involve Jesus. He told priests and the people that he found no fault in Jesus or his sermons.

Persecutions

The authorities in power started persecution of his followers. The first to be arrested was John the Prophet. When Jesus heard about this, he and his followers started their journey toward the city

Mary Magdalene

of Samaria, because the people there had no dealings with the Jews. Many came to see him and hear his sermons.

Jesus felt disgusted with the people and thought of migrating to some other place. He went to Galilee and many disciples followed in his footsteps. He went to Nazareth to preach, and there met his mother Mary and his brothers James and Judas. The people of Nazareth made sarcastic remarks about him but he declared:

> Verily I say unto you,
> No prophet is accepted in his own country.[158]
> And among his own kin,
> And in his own house.[159]

Jesus reminded his disciples that they would be persecuted for righteousness. They would have to separate from their kith and kin. He told them that prophets in the past had been persecuted and that this might happen again. As such, they should be prepared for sufferings, for theirs was the kingdom of heaven. He told them he had not come to destroy the sacred law, nor was he against any prophet who had come before him. He had only come to fulfill his mission, and to exhort the people from breaking any commandment.[160]

Mary Magdalene

Jesus went to several cities and villages for preaching. During his travels, he was accompanied by his disciples and certain women who had been healed of evil spirits and infirmities. Notable among these women were his mother and Mary Magdalene. Then there were other women like Joanna and Susanna.[161] Out of all the women, Mary Magdalene loved Jesus, and he, in his heart, returned her love.[162] According to Jewish law, it was incumbent on him to marry because "an unmarried man could not be a teacher." But according to the pledge taken as an Essene, he was required to practice celibacy, so as to preserve his vital energy for mental development. The Gospel of Philip contains the following information on this issue:

> And the consort of the Saviour is Mary Magdalene and he loved her more than all his disciples and used to kiss her lips. His disciples

said to him, "Why do thee love her more?" The Savior said to them, "Why do I not love thee like her?"[163]

The members of the Essene Order prevailed upon Jesus to overcome his love for this woman, so that sacred work be not retarded. It was very hard for him, but he agreed to remain dutiful to the service of the Brotherhood. Both Jesus and Mary wept bitterly and agreed to part.[164] Perhaps the situation at that time was most unfavorable. Herod Antipas had let loose a reign of terror on the people. Every day clashes occurred between the masses and the Roman soldiers. John and his disciples were rotting in jails. Josephus, the contemporary historian, recorded that Herod felt alarmed at the popularity of John and believed that baptism and preaching were the main cause of disturbances in his kingdom.[165]

Contact with the Persecuted

Jesus maintained close contact with the persecuted public and those who had been put in prison. John the Prophet heard in prison about the works of Jesus, and sent two of his disciples to him.[166] The secret message, "Art thou he that should come or are we to look for another?" meant: "Are you our deliverer or have we to search for him elsewhere?" Jesus told them to go their way and tell John what things they had seen and heard.[167] When the disciples had departed, Jesus told the multitude that John was not only a Prophet but more than a Prophet, for he had come to prepare the way for him.[168]

The time was one of intense messianic expectation, and Jesus for the first time gave a clear indication that John the Prophet had come to prepare the way for his advent. All those that heard him began to discuss the issue between themselves. While the publicans believed in the declaration of Jesus, the Pharisees rejected his claim to be their redeemer. Jesus had declared that he was the promised Messiah, and that he had to perform the role of the Messiah, as ordained by God. But the Pharisees wondered how the Son of man, who eats and drinks, could be their redeemer.[169]

John the Prophet Killed

From the Bible we learn that John the Prophet was imprisoned and killed for the sake of Herodias. We also learn from an account given by Josephus that Herod Antipas fell in love with Herodias, his brother's wife, in the course of his trip to Rome.[170] This lady had a beautiful grown-up daughter named Salome. Perhaps Herod had an extravagant passion both for the mother and the daughter. Salome would sit with Herod and please him with her dancing.[171] It was John the Prophet who had stood in the temple and spoken against Herod, saying;

> Lo, you have lived in sin,
> Your rulers are adulterers.[172]

It is clear that the main cause for the arrest of John the Prophet was that he had denounced relations of Herod with Herodias and her daughter Salome. Herod had to face a political problem also, for his first wife was the daughter of Aretas, the king of Arabia. In order to avenge this insult to his daughter, Aretas prepared for war and Herod had to defend himself.[173] Secondly, according to Jewish tradition, marriage with a sister-in-law or her daughter was forbidden.

John had been kept as a prisoner in the fortress of Machaerus, which existed on the east side of the Dead Sea. It was Herodias and Salome who demanded beheading of John. Herod, having agreed, sent for an executioner, who beheaded John the Prophet and brought his head on a charger to be seen both by the mother and her daughter.[174]

After having procured the execution of John the Prophet, Herodias exclaimed:

> This is the fate of every man who dares to scorn, or criticize, the acts of him who reigns.

The head of John the Prophet was thrown away to his disciples. They took away the corpse, and informed Jesus about this tragedy. They carried his coffin to a graveyard near Hebron, and buried it.[175] John was beheaded in about 34 A.D., shortly before the battle between Herod Antipas and Aretas.

Jesus departed in a ship for the place, so as to pay homage to the fallen hero. After the event, he went into a desert, near the city of Bethsaida. A great multitude of people followed him. When he perceived that these people were bent upon declaring him as their king, he ran away towards a mountain. All the above would show that the people wanted to throw out the Romans, and wanted to have a leader bold enough to lead them. Jesus felt that he could not trust these people, for they were not sincere. He wanted to raise them both spiritually, and morally. Accordingly, he told them:

> Spend no more time than is necessary,
> worrying about material things.
> When you are busy telling other people
> what is wrong with them, pause occasionally,
> and take a look at yourself.
> Try to understand what God wants from you.
> Return good for evil and love your enemies.

Naming of Apostles

Jesus felt very unhappy at the tragic end of John the Prophet and left Nazareth, because the people inhabiting this city were unruly, and there was every apprehension of the outbreak of violence.

He moved down to Capernaum, a small town on the shores of the Sea of Galilee. He had two reasons to select this place. In the first place, he wanted peace of mind, for he had suffered bereavement in losing his forerunner and friend in the person of John. The seashore, its calm and cool atmosphere, would provide a soothing environment suitable under such circumstances. Secondly, the place, being a seaport, had a mixed population, progressive in outlook and secular in thinking. His message of peace could be well received in the region, and he would not be bothered with arguments and the opposition of the Pharisees. He travelled in the countryside, and spoke in parables. One day, he saw two ships standing by the lake. He entered into one and sat down. He said:

> I say unto you,
> He that entereth not by door into the sheepfold,

But climbeth up some other way,
The same is a thief,
And a robber.
But he that entereth in by the door,
Is the shepherd of the sheep.
To him the porter openeth;
And the sheep hear his voice,
And he calleth his own sheep by name,
And leadeth them out.
And when he putteth forth his own sheep,
He goeth before them,
And the sheep follow him,
For they know his voice.[176]

Jesus wanted to choose a band of trusted workers to spread his message. He went out into a mountain to pray.[177] Possibly he had to consult the Essenes. After a night's stay, he came back among his disciples, and selected thirteen lieutenants, out of which twelve were most trustworthy, loyal and faithful. They are:

1.   Simon, who is called Peter.
2.   Andrew, the brother of Simon.
3.   James, the son of Zebedee.
4.   John, the brother of James.
5.   Philip.
6.   Bartholomew.
7.   Thomas, the publican.
8.   Matthew, the publican.
9.   James, the son of Alpheus.
10.   Lebbeus, whose surname was Thaddeus.
11.   Simon, the Canaanite.
12.   Judas Iscariot.[178]
13.   Judas, the brother of James.[179]

In order to camouflage their identity, Jesus surnamed and nick-named some of them. Simon was surnamed Peter, while James and John were nicknamed as Boanerges or the sons of thunder.[180]

It seems that there exists some confusion about the number of disciples. While Judas Iscariot has been mentioned in all the Gospels,

Luke and John have named Judas, the brother of James, in addition to Judas Iscariot.[181]

Jesus desired of his disciples to remain with him so that he might send them forth to preach and to have power to heal sickness. They constituted his well-trusted followers and personal bodyguards. He told them:

> Follow me into the path of true discipleship,
> For this is the path that leads to life.

They also had boats in case of danger and the boats could be utilized for voyages to other lands.[182]

Common people gathered around Jesus Christ and he mixed with them freely and lived with them. But the priests had sent adverse reports against him to the authorities. They spread propaganda that he was possessed by a devil. They said: "This fellow hatcheth Beelzebub, and by the price of the devils casteth he out devils."

Go to the Lost Sheep

Jesus commanded his apostles to preach among the common people rather than among the upper classes. He told them to go to the lost sheep of the House of Israel.[183] He advised them to take nothing for their journey in the shape of clothing, food or money, but remain ready always for their pedestrian march into different lands.[184] Everyone was directed to have a staff, and be shod with sandals.[185] He told them that he was sending them into hazards, and that their position was just like sheep in the midst of wolves. He cautioned them that they would be caught, and charged before councils and synagogues. He also cautioned them that, as his mission was universal, his disciples would be brought before governors and kings, and put to death. He told them that "when they persecute you in the cities, you flee into another."[186]

As Jesus had himself travelled in far-off lands, he gave full guidance, and explained minute details of hazards in long journeys. At the same time, elaborate instructions were given and a code of conduct was prescribed for them. Some of the instructions quoted below are ample proof of the fact that Jesus forewarned them about travel hazards:

> And as ye go, preach, saying,
> The kingdom of heaven is at hand.
> Provide neither gold,
> Nor silver, nor brass in your purses;
> Nor scrip for your journey,
> Neither two coats,
> Neither shoes,
> Nor yet slaves;
> For the workman is worthy of his hire.[187]
> And into whatever city or town,
> Ye shall enter,
> Inquire who in it is worthy:
> And with these abide till ye go thence;
> Behold,
> I send you forth as sheep,
> In the midst of wolves;
> Be ye therefore wise as serpents,
> And harmless as doves.
> But when they persecute you,
> In this city,
> Flee ye into another.
> And fear not them which kill the body,
> But are not able to kill the soul.[188]

After having given these instructions, he told them:

> Think not
> That I am come to send peace on earth;
> I am come not to send peace
> But a sword.
> For I am come to set a man,
> At variance against his father,
> And the daughter against her mother,
> And the daughter-in-law against her mother-in-law
> And a man's foe shall be
> They of his own household.[189]

The above reveals that Jesus was not happy about the conditions prevailing at that time in Palestine. At the moment, when Jesus spoke of the sword, the Jewish people were an occupied nation under the garrison of imperial Rome. It is probable that he was tempted to take up the sword against the imperial forces, and attempt to seize all power for the people.[190]

Intelligence Report

The whole country was in an agitated mood. The people were divided in their opinion about Jesus and his mission. While the common people had great reverence for him and admitted him as the Messiah, the rich and the upper classes rejected him and became his enemies. The priests exercised great influence upon the authorities, and they had exhibited their enmity towards Jesus in the past also. Now, when some reports about the popularity of Jesus reached Pontius Pilate, his advisors, who were mostly priests, cautioned him about the upheaval which was at hand. Jesus was charged with sedition for having declared himself the King of the Jews. Pilate was not a person to tolerate challenge to his authority, and he began to think seriously about Jesus and his followers. It had been reported that Jesus had declared that he had not come to bring peace but to send a sword. Pilate became perturbed over such a possibility, and set his spies to bring him intelligence about the activities of Jesus. What he found about Jesus is given in his letter written in 32 A.D. to Tiberius Caesar, which is quoted below.[191]

A young man appeared in Galilee and, in the name of God who sent him, preached a new law, humility. At first I thought that his intention was to stir up a revolt among the people against the Romans.

My suspicions were soon dispelled. Jesus of Nazareth spoke more as a friend of the Romans then as a friend of the Jews.

One day I observed a young man among a group of people leaning against the trunk of a tree, and speaking quietly to the crowd that surrounded him. They told me that he was Jesus. This was obvious because of the great difference between him and those around him. His fair hair and beard gave him a divine appearance. He was about thirty years old and never before had I seen such a pleasant, kind face. What a vast difference there was between him, with his fair complexion, and those wearing black beards who were listening to him. As I did not want to disturb him, I went on my way, telling my secretary, however, to join the group and listen.

Later my secretary told me that he had never read in the works of the philosophers anything that could be compared with the teachings of Jesus, and that he was neither leading the people astray nor an agitator. That is why he decided to protect him. He was free to act, to talk, and to call a gathering of the people. This unlimited liberty provoked the Jews, who were indignant; it did not upset the poor, but it irritated the rich and powerful.

Later I wrote a letter to Jesus asking for an interview at the Forum. He came. When the Nazarene appeared, I was transfixed. My feet seemed fettered with iron chains to the marble floor. I was trembling all over as a guilty person would, although he was calm.

Without moving I appraised this exceptional man for some time. There was nothing unpleasant about his appearance or character. In his presence I felt a profound respect for him.

I told him that he had an aura around him, and his personality had an infectious simplicity that set him above the present-day philosophers and masters. He made a deep impression on all of us, owing to his pleasant manner, simplicity, humility and love.

These, worthy sovereign, are the deeds that concern Jesus of Nazareth, and I have taken time to inform you in detail about this affair.

After having selected his apostles, Jesus appointed another seventy also, and sent them in groups of two and two into other cities and places. He expected to visit all these in the near future.[192] He assigned different duties for his apostles and for his seventy disciples. The following are the commands for the apostles.

> Go not into the way of the Gentiles.
> And into any city of the Samaritans,
> Enter ye not:
> But go rather to the lost sheep,
> Of the House of Israel.
> And as ye go,
> Preach saying:
> The kingdom of heaven is at hand.[193]

After having commanded the apostles to carry out his instructions, he fixed the following mission for the seventy disciples:

> Go your ways:
> Behold,
> I send you forth as lambs among wolves.

Carry neither purse,
Nor scrip,
Nor hoes
And salute no man by the way.
And into whatsoever house ye enter,
First say.
Peace be to this house.[194]

Jesus spoke about the Kingdom of God, and the kingdom of heaven, which embodies the same idea. The nature of the kingdom as a spiritual society is clearly indicated in his teachings. It is neither synonymous with the Jewish theocracy, nor with an earthly empire. [195] The Kingdom of God is within us, he declared to his disciples, and through them to humanity.

CHAPTER FOUR

Ministry and Crucifixion

I am the Way, and the Truth and the Life.
St. John

CAPERNAUM, NOW KNOWN AS KEFAR NAHUM, stood on the highway linking the lands beyond Jordan with the Mediterranean and was the hub of busy life of the lakeside during the ministry of Jesus. It was a city of fishermen, who were the first people to hear Jesus and accept his teachings. As such, Capernaum had a special fascination for him. During the course of his ministry, this city remained the main center of his mission. He would go to many towns and villages for preaching, but would always return to Capernaum.[1] Andrew, John and James would prevail on Jesus and his mother to rest by the sea in Peter's home. Once when he had gone there, the news spread along the shore and many came to press his hand. Jesus taught the people many lessons as he walked with them beside the lake.[2] They brought unto him all sick people and those which were possessed with devils. He healed them all, and thus his fame went throughout all Syria.[3]

The Gospels do not provide us with information according to the chronological order about the ministry of Jesus. Hence, we cannot be sure about the sequence of events leading to his crucifixion. However, we can say that his ministry began in about 34 A.D. Subsequently, Jesus went to Jerusalem on the occasion when the Jews were to observe the Feast of Passover.

Finding Jesus among them, they conspired to kill him. There were arguments between him and the priests. He declared:

Lepers by the roadside
(from a photograph by Wilson)

My doctrine is not mine,
But his that sent me.
If any man will do his will,
He shall know of the doctrine,
Whether it be of God,
Or whether I speak of myself.
He that speaketh of himself,
Seeketh his own glory;
But he that seeketh his glory that sent him,
The same is true.
And no unrighteousness is in him,
Did not the Moses give you the Law,
And yet none of you keep the Law?
Why go ye about to kill me?[4]

The question arises as to why he went to Jerusalem to declare that his mission was "not to destroy but to fulfill the Mosaic Law." The answer is quite clear when we admit that Jerusalem, the holy city, had been the spiritual as well as temporal headquarters of the nation.

Secondly, the occasion coincided with the Feast of Passover as well as the Feast of Tabernacles, in which the Jews from all villages and cities of the region would participate. Both the place and the occasion were suitable for an important declaration, which Jesus wanted to make to the multitude. He had also been requested by his brethren to declare his mission at this important occasion.

After he declared his mission, the Pharisees, the Sanhedrin, along with their chief priests, opposed him.

Sermon on the Mount

One day, as the crowds were gathering, he went onto a mountain with his disciples and taught.

> Blessed are the poor in spirit.
> For theirs is the kingdom of heaven.
> Blessed are they that mourn:
> For they shall be comforted.
> Blessed are the meek:
> For they shall inherit the earth.
> Blessed are they who do hunger
> and thirst after righteousness:

The Sermon on the Mount (Bida)

For they shall be filled.
Blessed are the merciful:
For they shall obtain mercy.
Blessed are the pure in heart:
For they shall see God.
Blessed are the peacemakers:
For they shall be called the children of God.
Blessed are they which are persecuted
for righteousness' sake;
For theirs is the kingdom of heaven.[5]

Tense Atmosphere

The sermons of Jesus had created a furor among the people who surrounded him and sought his blessings. They ran after him, and struggled to touch his feet. To them he was the Messiah, destined to deliver them from misery, misrule and suppression. The whole atmosphere became tense. There also occurred a demonstration against the Romans, and Pilate ordered general stabbings of the masses. Some people went to Jesus to complain against the atrocities of Pilate.[6] He told them to repent so as to save themselves from utter destruction. In order to achieve their ulterior motives, they started propaganda that Jesus was an anti-Moses who wanted to destroy the law and the prophets. They even engaged assassins to kill him. Jesus was reviled and persecuted. Many lies were spread about him and his disciples. In order to clear these misrepresentations, one day Jesus declared to the audience not to misunderstand him, for he had not come to cancel or destroy the Law of Moses. He assured them that every Law in the scriptures will continue till its purpose is achieved. He told them that the Pharisees and their priests wanted to mislead them. While explaining his position he declared:

Under the Laws of Moses the rule was, if you kill, you must die. But I have added to that rule, and tell you that if you are only angry, even in your own home, you are in danger of judgment. If you call your friend an idiot, you are in danger of being brought before the court. And if you curse him, you are in danger of the fires of hell.

So if you are standing before the altar in the temple offering a sacrifice to God, and suddenly remember that a friend has something against you, leave your sacrifice there beside the altar and go and apologize and be reconciled to him, and then come and offer your sacrifice to God. The Law of Moses said, you shall not commit adultery. But I say: whosoever even looks at a woman with lust in his eye has already committed adultery with her in his heart.

Again the Law of Moses says, you shall not break your vows to God, but must fulfill them all. But I say: do not make any vows.

The Law of Moses says, if a man gouges out another's eye, he must pay with his own eye. But I say: do not resist violence. If you are slapped on one cheek, turn the other too. If you are ordered to court and your shirt is taken from you, give your coat too. If the military demand that you carry their gear for a mile, carry it two. Give to those who ask, and do not turn away from those who want to borrow.

There is a saying, "Love your friends and hate your enemies." But I say: love your enemies, and pray for those who persecute you. In that way you will be acting as true sons of your Father in heaven. For he gives his sunlight to both the evil and the good, and sends rain on the just and on the unjust too. If you love only those who love you, what good is that? Even scoundrels do that much. If you are friendly only to your friend, how are you different from any one else? Even the publicans do that.[7]

Jesus had explained his position in clear terms, but the priests challenged his authority. He denounced them, and they became his enemies.

Jesus went to Galilee, fearing that the Jews might kill him.[8] From that place he departed into the coasts of Tyre and Sidon.[9] He felt unhappy about these people and their dogmatic thinking. He felt restless, and again thought of going to Galilee. He went up into a mountain, and sat down there in meditation. These ungrateful people had made his life miserable. He took a ship, and came into the coasts of Magdala, but the Pharisees shadowed him there also. They desired of him to prove his credentials as a prophet, and asked him to show a divine sign. He sighed and felt sorry for these wicked people.

Consort of Jesus

During his wandering Jesus entered into a village known as Bethany, on the far side of the Mount of Olives near Jerusalem. There lived a family consisting of Martha, her sister Mary and their brother Lazarus. One of the Pharisees invited him to his house. His name is given as Simon the Leper.[10] The woman, who was a sinner, brought an alabaster box of ointment and stood at his feet weeping. She began to wash his feet with her tears, and did wipe them with hairs of her head. She kissed his feet, and anointed them with the ointment.[11] Jesus felt much moved and showed much affection for her. According to the rules of the Essene Order, Jesus had taken a vow not to take unto himself a wife. But Mary, the sister of Lazarus, loved him and he too in his heart returned her love. He proved gloriously his virtue by refusing to adopt a family life. He was sent of God, chosen by the Almighty, beloved of all and inspired both in teaching and in the knowledge of nature and its elements.[12]

Jesus left the multitudes and went with his disciples up to Mary Magdalene's home. Martha and other women engaged themselves to prepare food for the master and others, but Mary stayed with Jesus. When all sat about to dine, Jesus said,

> My little flock, fear not; it is your Father's will that you shall rule the kingdom of the soul. A ruler in the house of God is the servant of the Lord, and man cannot serve God except by serving mankind. A servant in the house of God cannot be servant in the house of wealth; nor in the synagogue of sense. If you are tied to lands, or bonds, or wealth of earth; where your treasures are, there are your hearts. Dispose of all your wealth, distribute it among the poor, and put your trust in God, and you nor yours will ever come to want. This is a test of faith, and God will not accept the service of a faithless one. The time is ripe; your Master comes upon the clouds; the eastern sky is glowing with his presence now. Put on reception robes; gird up your loins; trim up your lamps and fill them well with oil, and be prepared to meet your Lord; when you are ready, he will come. Thrice blessed are the servants who are ready to receive their Lord.[13]

The Gospel of John informs us that Jesus loved both the sisters of Lazarus and would often stay in their house.[14] Cana is a small village near Nazareth. The Gospel of John has given an interesting account of a marriage party at Cana without mentioning the names of the bride and the bridegroom. Not only is Jesus present at Cana but also his mother, his brothers and his disciples. The servants present at the function obey the orders of Jesus and his mother, indicating that they are hosts. For the guests, Jesus procures six hundred liters of good wine. We are inclined to believe that this function was a spiritual convention summoned by Jesus, which also served as his marriage function with Mary Magdalene. If the marriage had not been his own, there would have been no necessity for him or his mother to procure wine for the guests.[15] We have earlier hinted to the love affair between the two and their separation under the rules of the Essene Order. Although they discarded a husband and wife relationship, they continued to live and travel jointly. However, Mary Magdalene continued to behave as the consort of Jesus. In the Gospel of Mary, Simon addresses her:

> Sister, we know that the Saviour loved you more than rest of women. Tell us the words of the Master, which you know but we do not.[16]

Jesus and Mary Magdalene

The Gospel of Philip throws further light on their relationship in this statement:

> Mary Magdalene being the spouse of the Saviour, he loved her more than all the disciples. He used to kiss her often on her lips.[17]

In Hindu mythology, every God has a consort, which represents his creative energy or power and is termed *"Shakti."* These wives of the Gods are declared to be the source and support of all things. Together these consorts represent the active and passive poles of universal manifestation. As such, their sexual union, which is termed *Mythuna*, is symbolic. When we speak of Mary Magdalene as the chief consort of Jesus, we are using Hindu *Tantric* terminology.

It appears that among the women, Mary of Bethany, Mary Magdalene and even Martha took a deep, loving, and personal interest in the affairs of Jesus. These women loved him, and served as his beloveds. As he had taken a vow not to marry, he refused to take them as his wives. At the most, they were his consorts, and out of all of them, Mary Magdalene remained faithful to him to the last. The Gospel of Philip informs us that Mary Magdalene was Jesus' consort.[18]

Now, before his participation in the passion week, he entered the house of Martha who received him well. Both she and her sister Mary sat at the feet of Jesus.[19] Martha complained that Mary left her alone and did not help her. He said unto her:

> Martha, Martha,
> Thou are careful and troubled about many things,
> But one thing is needful;
> And Mary hath chosen that good part,
> Which shall not be taken away from her.[20]

As they sat about the board, a courtesan came uninvited to the feast. She came to Jesus, kissed his feet and her tears fell fast. She dried them with her hair and anointed his feet with balm. Simon did not like a sinner to touch Jesus and thought that Jesus was not a prophet.[21] Jesus understood the feeling of Simon and said:

Seeth thou this woman?
I entered into thine house,
Thou gavest me no water for my feet;
But she hath washed my feet with tears,
And wiped them with the hairs of her head,
Thou gavest me no kiss;
But this woman,
Since the time I came in,
Hath not ceased to kiss my feet.
My head with oil thou didst not anoint;
But this woman,
Hath anointed my feet with ointment,
Wherefore I say unto thee,
Her sins,
Which are many,
Are forgiven;
For she loved much;
But to whom little is forgiven,
The same loveth little.[22]

Jesus told Simon that sin is a monster of iniquity; it may be small or it may be large. One person leads a life of sin and when he repents, he is redeemed. But another person, who is in a careless mood, forgets the things that ought to be done to reform oneself. When a sinner seeks forgiveness, he finds it. Then Jesus said to the courtesan:

Your sins are all forgiven;
Your faith has saved you.[23]

Lazarus passed away after a brief sickness. Jesus, along with his disciples, went to console Martha and Mary Magdalene. Then Martha, as soon as she heard that Jesus was coming, went and met him; but Mary sat still in the house. She implored of Jesus to give life to her dead brother, and he consoled her saying that Lazarus will rise again. Then he called for Mary and she came to him. She fell down at his feet and wept. When Jesus saw her weeping, tears came to his eyes. Then Mary said,

Lord, if thou hadst been here,
my brother would not have died.

After having said thus, she started wailing, and seeing her, all the Jews started weeping. Jesus felt sad and looked towards the heaven. He asked them to remove the stone of the sepulchre, where they had put Lazarus. Jesus lifted his eyes towards heaven and said:

> Father, I thank thee that thou hast heard me.
> And I know that thou hearest me always.

After saying this, Jesus called for Lazarus, who came out of the grave and stood alive before the multitude. Then many of the Jews, who came to Mary Magdalene and had seen the miracle, believed in Jesus.[24]

As time passed, many women who possessed wealth became his devotees and implored Jesus to heal them. Mary Magdalene, who was obsessed by spirits, had been healed earlier by Jesus. Now, Susanna, who owned an estate at Caesarea Philippi, Jehanna, wife of Chuza, and Rachel, who lived on the coast of Tyre, implored that Jesus and his disciples preach and heal others.[25]

Transfiguration

Now, Jesus wanted to be alone to think over the past events and chalk out his future program. He had received a message from one of his devotees that there were many dangers to his life, and he should leave that place. Accordingly, he went out of the territory of Herod and reached Caesarea Philippi, which existed in the territory of Philip. One day, when his disciples were with him, he declared that he would build his church. He enquired of them as to what rumors were afloat about him among the people.

When they told him that the masses believed that he was their redeemer, he told them not to reveal his identity to anyone.[26] His disciples got confused, and one of them named Peter began to rebuke him. Jesus got enraged and told him that he was an offense to him.[27] They began to discuss what they should do under the circumstances. Should they run away from danger or take his side? Jesus thought of his disciples, and the sufferings which were in store for them. He also thought of the authorities at Jerusalem, which were bent upon killing him in the name of God. He told his disciples:

If any man will come after me,
Let him deny himself,
And take up his cross,
And follow me.
For whosoever will save his life,
Shall lose it:
And whosoever will lose his life, for my sake:
Shall find it.[28]

He assured them that the Son of man shall come in the glory of his Father with his angels. The above would clearly reveal that Jesus assured his disciples that the angels would help him, and they should not feel afraid of any danger. His assurance had the desired effect, and none of his disciples left him.

Now, after six days Jesus took Peter and others up unto a high mountain and showed them a miracle. He meditated and was transfigured before their very eyes.[29] His raiment became shining, exceedingly white as snow, and it was difficult to recognize him. Two men came and talked with him.[30] His disciples became afraid, but he told them not to fear. These two men who had came to meet him talked about the trial of Jesus.[31] Peter suggested making a tabernacle for him at the top of this mountain, but Jesus told him not to feel afraid.[32] Now Peter had suggested that it was good for all of them to stay on the high mountain, and prepare hiding places for Jesus and his disciples. It is probable that they might have prepared such hiding dens, to be used in emergency. It is significant that at the time of transfiguration, Jesus prays, his countenance is altered, and his raiment becomes white. Then come the two men, and he seems to be talking with them. Then a cloud overshadows them, and a voice is heard:

This is my beloved Son;
Hear him.[33]

According to Matthew, Jesus was transfigured before his disciples, and his face did shine as the Sun. He then talked with Moses and Elijah. While they were talking, a bright cloud overshadowed them, and a voice was heard:

This is my beloved Son,
In whom I am well pleased;
Hear ye Him.[34]

Three facts emerge out of the above incident of transfiguration:

a) Jesus Christ had the power to change his countenance.
b) He had the power to call gods, angels and prophets.
c) He could make them disappear in the clouds.

Transfiguration is a *Tantric* feat, practiced in Tibet. Let it be re-corded that I have myself witnessed alteration of countenance prac-ticed by a Tibetan woman saint, named Chomo Ji, at Leh, Ladakh. Calling of spirits or souls is a common practice with mendicants in Kashmir and other hilly regions in the Himalayas. Disappearance is a *Yogic* feat or a *Tantric* manifestation recorded by travelers in Tibet. Hundreds of such incidents have been recorded as miracles of saints, ascetics, mendicants, and *fakirs* in the East. We would not rule out the possibility of transfiguration, because Jesus had already acquired such powers during his early travels in the East.

Who were the two men who came and talked with him on the top of the mount ? They have been named as Elijah and Moses, who appeared in glory, and talked with Jesus. Moses, as we know, gave Israel their first Laws, and during his last days departed in search of the site where he was ordered by God to die. Elijah the Prophet came from the desert across Jordan, and having defeated the false gods, disappeared in the wilderness, after having handed over his cloak to Elisha. Both Moses and Elijah had died centuries ago, and there was no reason for them to meet Jesus. It may have been a vision of his disciples who saw the scene, for they were asleep at the moment. As such, they named the two men Moses and Elijah, saints with whom Jesus used to meditate, in exercises he conducted whenever he went into the wilderness or the mountains.

It is also significant that, at the time of crucifixion, he calls these two men for help, terming them as glorious and praiseworthy. It is also strange that these very two men take him away from the sepul-chre. Thus one thing is clear—that these two men have always been his protectors. Were they angels of God, or were they Essene saints?

This question will be dealt with subsequently. It will suffice to say here that both these men were Essenes who were friends of Jesus and had come to meet him and prepare for his safety and survival.

Confrontation

Jesus Christ departed for Galilee again in secret and reached Capernaum.[35] He made a decision and chose to go to Jerusalem and openly face the heretics. Then he reached his ancestral house. His brothers, who were very much perturbed, asked him to go into Judea, and declare his mission openly to the people. They told him that if he was so great, he must prove it to the world.[36] He sent his messengers in advance to see the reaction of the people in the villages on the way to Jerusalem. When his disciples found that the people were hostile, James and John asked for his permission to burn these villages, but he rebuked them and sent them to other villages.[37] He deputized his seventy disciples and sent them ahead in groups to all the places he intended to visit later.[38]

The Jews had received information about his movements and sought him in Jerusalem. He came into the coasts of Judea from the other side of Jordan. This fact is important; for the shortest way to Jordan passes through the valley of Qumran. Since his childhood, Jesus had established contacts with the Essenes living there, and he would occasionally go to the hills to see them. This time also he went to them, maybe for further consultation and advice.

Jerusalem

Jesus went beyond Jordan and reached the territory of Herod. Someone advised him to leave the place so as to save his life. But he told them that it could not be that a prophet was to perish out of Jerusalem.[39]

In the meanwhile, Judas had betrayed him and conveyed his secret to the priests. He had informed them that Jesus had assumed the role of the promised Messiah and wanted to be the king of the Jews. This was the time when Jews from all parts of Palestine would come to Jerusalem to celebrate the feast. Jesus predicted the fate of Jerusalem in these verses:

O Jerusalem, Jerusalem,
Thou that killest the Prophets,
And stonest them
Which are sent unto thee,
How often would I have gathered
Thy children together,
Even as a hen gathered
Her chickens under her wings,
And ye would not;
Behold,
Your house is left unto you desolate.[40]

Council

Fearing that Jesus was planning a revolt against them at the coming Passover, the priests convened a Council under the chairmanship of Caiaphas, the high priest. They said:

What do we?
For this man doeth many miracles.
If we let him thus alone,
All men will believe on him;
And the Romans shall come
And take away
Both our place and nation.[41]

Hence they decided that Jesus must be killed, so that they might not perish. Nicodemus came before the Pharisees and defended Jesus by saying that it was illegal to sentence a man without hearing him first, but they refused to admit his plea.[42] While the orthodox desired to make an end of Jesus, the less conservative were well disposed towards him. The priests had decided to take Jesus by subtlety and kill him. But they feared that they could not do it, lest there be an uproar among the people who were devoted to Jesus.[43]

Ephraim

Jesus received information about the decision taken at the Council through Nicodemus. Therefore, he decided to take certain precautions. In the first place he stopped walking openly among the Jews.[44] Now Jesus did not remain in Bethany but in the hills of Ephraim, upon the borders of Samaria. He and his disciples found a home and abode there for many days.

Capernaum

Jesus now departed for Galilee, and at Capernaum he was asked to pay annual tribute of one half-shekel. He questioned:

> Of whom do the kings of this earth
> Take custom or tribute?
> Of their own children,
> Or of strangers?[45]

Thinking that he should not offend the tribute collectors, he asked his disciples to make payment of the tribute money under protest. His disciples had again started quarreling among themselves as to who was the greatest among them.

When he asked them what they were disputing among themselves, they kept quiet. He sat down and told them that all his disciples were equal, and if any one among them desired to attain the first position, he should be last of all and servant of all.[46]

Jericho

Many people who were on their way to Jerusalem to participate in the national festival came to pay their homage to Jesus, and most of them were from Galilee. As the number of devotees increased, Jesus decided to move on to Jericho. He stayed at the house of Zaccheus, who was the chief among the publicans. Jesus felt happy to see his chivalry and blessed him, saying:

> This day is salvation come to this house.[47]

Triumphal Entry

From Jericho, Jesus, along with his disciples and devotees, proceeded towards Bethphage and Bethany, at the hill called the Mount of Olives. An ass was brought by his two disciples, who cast their garments on the animal.[48] He mounted the ass and some of the disciples were given the honor of grasping the bridle. Then the whole procession moved towards the Temple. The people spread their clothes before him in the way, and the crowds raised slogans:

> Blessed be the King,
> That cometh in the name of the Lord;
> Peace in heaven,
> And glory in the highest.[49]

Some of the people took branches from palm trees and went forth to greet him, crying:

> Hosanna;
> Blessed is the King of Israel
> That cometh in the name of the Lord.[50]

The crowds shouted slogans; and when some of the Pharisees requested Jesus to stop them, he said:

> If these should hold their peace,
> The stones would immediately cry out.[51]

The procession moved on, and he rode into Jerusalem on Sunday, and entered the Temple in the evening.[52]

Destruction of the Temple

His entry into the Temple at Jerusalem proved to be eventful. He found that those who sold oxen, sheep and doves were sitting there. He also found that usurers were changing money before the altar.[53] Seeing all this, he became enraged, saying:

> My house is the house of prayer:
> But ye have made it a den of thieves.[54]

After this, the situation turned into a riot. He and his disciples overthrew the tables of the usurers and drove out the merchants along with their animals. The Pharisees questioned his right to do all these things, but he told them:

Destroy this temple,
And in three days
I will raise it up.[55]

He told them that he was not bound to tell them under whose authority he was doing all these things. And when he departed from the Temple, he told his disciples:

Verily I say unto you,
There shall not be left here
One stone upon another
That shall not be thrown down.[56]

When his disciples asked him privately when it should happen, he told them to be cautious of imposters acting in his name, and not to be troubled when they heard of wars. All this would show that, after the riot, Jesus anticipated further trouble. In the evening Jesus and his disciples went again to Bethany.[57]

Betrayal

From that day Jesus Christ taught daily in the Temple, and the devotees heard him with reverence. As he was always surrounded by his bodyguards and disciples, the priests could not kill him. This being so, they purchased one of his disciples, namely Judas Iscariot, who promised to betray him.[58] The traitor told them that the betrayal would be accomplished in the absence of the multitude, when Jesus would be alone.

The priests tried another stratagem, and that was to put him in a quandary by asking his opinion on vague and tricky questions. Their scheme failed, and now they depended on Judas only.

Prayer in the Garden

One day, late in the evening, Jesus Christ came out of the Temple and went into the garden of Gethsemane. His disciples followed him. On that occasion he was extremely sad, and gloomy. He kneeled down and prayed:

Judas accepting the thirty pieces of silver

Abba, Father,
All things are possible unto thee;
Take away this cup from me;
Nevertheless,
Not what I will,
But what thou wilt.[59]

While he made this moving prayer, he felt agony, and his sweat was, as it were, drops of blood falling down to the ground. As he implored God, an angel from heaven appeared before him, strengthening him. It is evident that his prayer had been heard, and he was assured of all help from God. Jesus had earnestly asked for deliverance from enemies, and it is utterly unbelievable that such an earnest prayer from the Son of God should go unanswered. He had to live long, for it was already predicted:

And hereafter,
Twelve mighty ones shall come forth,

And Jesus the Messiah,
Shall come of Thy seed of a virgin;
Whose name is Miriam,
And God shall abide upon him,
Till a hundred years be fulfilled.[60]

The priests and elders gathered a band of soldiers to arrest Jesus, and Judas Iscariot escorted them to the garden of Gethsemane. It was night, and they were holding lanterns, torches and weapons in their hands. As soon[61] as Judas Iscariot identified Jesus they moved to capture him. Then, Simon Peter having a sword, drew it and smote the servant of the high priest, but Jesus stopped him saying:

Thinkest thou that
I cannot now pray to my Father,
And he shall presently give me
More than twelve legions of angels.[62]

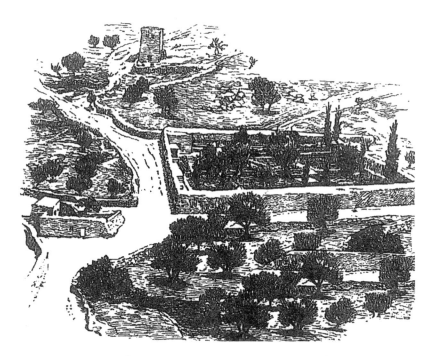

Garden of Gethsemane and road to Mount of Olives

He asked the multitude why they had come with swords and staves to take him as if he was a thief. If it was so, then they could have taken him when he was daily teaching in the Temple.[63] The above narrative given by Matthew and Mark clearly shows that Jesus was quite confident that no harm could be done to him, as God was with him and would provide help at the time of need. At that very moment, a young man arrived at the scene to inform Jesus, but it was too late. They tried to catch him also, but he ran away, leaving his linen cloth on the ground.

Before the Council

Leaving the Lord alone, his apostles and other disciples ran away. The soldiers laid hold on Jesus, and led him to the Council. Caiaphas sat there with his priests and other elders. Some among the crowd made false accusations against Jesus, saying that he had boasted of destroying the temple of God and rebuilding it in three days.[64] Then the chief priest asked him:

Thou tell us whether thou be the Christ?

Jesus replied: Thou hast said so: If I tell you, ye will not believe. Joseph ben Caiaphas had been appointed chief priest by the Roman procurator Valerius Gratus, who remained in office from 18 to 36 A.D. He was the person who gave counsel to the Jews.[65]

As soon as he heard Jesus, he cried that Jesus had been guilty of blasphemy and deserved to be killed. After taking this decision, they took him before the Governor, at the castle of Antonia.

Pontius Pilate

Having brought the prisoner before Pontius Pilate, they began to accuse him of inciting people against the established government. They also said that he claimed to be the king of the Jews. When Pilate asked him whether he was the king of the Jews, he replied, "Thou sayest."[66]

Pilate marveled, for Jesus did not refute accusations of the priests. Then Pilate told the priests that he found no fault with

Jesus.[67] The priests and the Jews became fierce and all of them began to make wild charges against Jesus and demanded his death. But Pilate refused to oblige them. He himself had earlier informed the authorities that Jesus was neither leading the people astray nor was he an agitator, and that he spoke more as a friend of the Romans than as a friend of the Jews.[68] Pilate was in a fix; on the one hand, he wanted to set Jesus free, but, on the other hand, he did not like to antagonize the priests, who could approach the higher authorities. After much thinking, he thought of a stratagem, and that was to carry out the wish of the Jews, and at the same time, try to save Jesus. How he achieved his aim will be discussed in subsequent pages. He ordered that, as Jesus belonged to Galilee, his case be heard by Herod.[69]

Verdict

Herod had heard a lot about Jesus and was eager to see him perform a miracle. The priests and others stated their accusations against Jesus. They informed him that Jesus had proclaimed himself as the king of the Jews and asked people not to pay taxes.

He was accused of leading a revolt against the Romans. Jesus was asked many questions, but he remained silent. The chief priests and scribes continued accusing Jesus, but Herod did not care and sent him back to Pilate.[70]

When Jesus was brought again before Pilate, he told the chief priests that, after examining Jesus, he had found no fault in him. He told them that even Herod could not find anything against Jesus. He informed them of his intention to release him.[71] However, the Jews warned him:

> If thou let this man go,
> Thou are not Caesar's friend;
> Whosoever maketh himself a king,
> Speaks against Caesar.[72]

Pilate was in a fix, for he could not afford to jeopardize his position and status. He felt afraid of the Jews, who could complain against him before Caesar and get him demoted.[73]

As it was a feast, and he had the authority to release a prisoner, he asked the Jews whom, between Jesus and Barabbas, he would release. They asked him to release Barabbas and demanded that Jesus be crucified. In the meanwhile his wife also approached him and implored him to do no harm to Jesus. He again questioned them saying, what evil has he done? They all cried; crucify him. He had to surrender before the chief priests and the mob. He took water, and washed his hands before them and declared:

> I am innocent of the blood of this just person;
> See ye to it.[74]

While the devotees of the Lord and the Essenes held councils with Nicodemus and Joseph of Arimathea, the Governor of Judea announced the verdict.

Death Warrant

During excavations in the ancient city of Aquila, in the kingdom of Naples, a copper plate was found in an antique marble vase. It was discovered by the Commissioner of Arts in the French Army. Written originally in Hebrew, it was translated into French and it came to light that it was the death warrant of Jesus. It is reproduced below:

In the year seventeen of the Emperor Tiberius Caesar and the 27th day
    of March, in the city of holy Jerusalem:
Annas and Caiaphas being priests;
Sacrificators of the people of God;
Pontius Pilate, the Governor of Lower Galilee;

    Sitting in the presidential chair of praetory, condemns Jesus of Nazareth to die on the cross between two thieves, the great and notorious evidence of the people, saying:

(a) Jesus is a seducer.
(b) He is seditious.
(c) He is the enemy of the law.
(d) He calls himself falsely the Son of God.
(e) He calls himself falsely the king of Israel.

(f)   *He entered into the Temple, followed by a multitude bearing palm branches in their hands.*

Orders the first Centurion, Quilius Cornelius, to lead him to the place of execution;
Forbids any person whomsoever, either poor or rich, to oppose the death of Jesus.
The witnesses who have signed the condemnation of Jesus are:

1. *Daniel Robani, a Pharisee.*
2. *Joannus Robani.*
3. *Raphael Robani*
4. *Capet, a citizen.*

Jesus shall go out of the city of Jerusalem by the gate of Struenus.[75]

The Crucifixion

Jesus was taken in a procession along with the two thieves to Golgotha, the place of execution.[76] He was followed by a great company of people, and of women, which also bewailed and lamented him.[77] They compelled Simon, a Cyrenian, to carry the cross meant for Jesus.[78] Having arrived at the barren mountain ridge named Gileon, they halted because Jesus fell to the ground from exhaustion.[79] Meanwhile the Roman soldiers had selected the place for erection of the crosses. Turning towards the wailing women, Jesus said:

> Daughters of Jerusalem,
> Weep not for me.
> But weep for yourselves,
> And for your children.
> For, Behold;
> The days are coming
> In the which they shall say,
> Blessed are the barren
> And the wombs that never bare,
> And the paps which never gave suck.[80]

In order to prove their sympathy with the sufferers by giving a drink that made them unconscious, the soldiers offered the drink made from sour wine mingled with wormwood to Jesus. As he did not wish to die for his faith and the truth as a drunkard, he refused to drink it.[81] The Gospels differ on the drink offered to Jesus at this moment.

According to Matthew, they gave him vinegar to drink mingled with gall, but he refused to drink after having tasted it.[82] According to Mark, they gave him to drink wine mingled with myrrh but he received it not.[83]

At the request of the servants of the Sanhedrin, the cross designed for Jesus was placed in the middle, between those for the two thieves. His cross was designed differently from the others. For while their crosses were constructed in such a manner that the perpendicular beam did not reach above the cross beam, the cross meant for him was of a different form; the perpendicular beam reached far above the cross beam. In front of the cross, a short stake was placed so that he may rest there while being tied.[84] Why a special type of cross and stake was prepared for Jesus is a mystery and it may be that its construction had a special purpose! Perhaps it was designed to save this precious life which was so dear to poor artisans, most of whom belonged to the order of Essenes.

There is a controversy about the exact time when Jesus was put on the cross. According to John, it was about the sixth hour when Jesus was handed over to the priests for crucifixion.[85] Since the place of execution, Golgotha, lay within a narrow compass, it would have taken nearly an hour to reach the place. On this assumption, we feel that Jesus was put on the cross at one P.M. He was lifted up and placed on a short stake in front of his cross so that he might rest there while being tied. They tied his arms and legs with strong cords.

The peculiar atrocity of crucifixion was that the victim did not die instantly but continued in this misery for two days and even longer. The victim was fixed to the cross with ropes or nails through the hands or the feet. On the vertical beam there was often a small support attached called a sedile, on which the victim sat as on a saddle. It was possible for the victim to ease his misery, from time to time, by supporting himself on this seat. The cross for Jesus was a special one, for besides the sedile, it had also a similar seat for his feet. The bleeding from the hands and feet soon stopped and could not have been fatal. From a medical point of view, the blood pressure of the victim would drop and the pulse rate would increase due to a disturbance of the blood circulation in the body. The victim would suffer pains in the head and the heart from insufficient blood circulation to the brain resulting in orthostatic collapse. The original idea behind this type of punishment was not directly to kill him but to expose him to this agony for many days. Ultimately, death would come from exhaustion and hunger.

When the torture of the crucified man was finally to be brought to an end, the crurifragium was carried out: his legs were broken below the knee with blows from a club. That meant that he could no longer ease his weight on the footrests, and heart failure quickly followed.[86]

Jesus suffered quietly, directing his gaze to the sky. Then he said: Father, forgive them, for they know not what they do. When Jesus was consumed with thirst, a soldier put a sponge dipped in vinegar, on a long cane of hyssop, and from this Jesus quenched his thirst.[87] It was customary with the Jewish women to prepare a kind of anaesthetic drink for those who were to be crucified. It was considered a pious act and the real object was to blunt susceptibility to pain among the victims.[88] Wine mixed with myrrh was given to Jesus to lessen the pain.

When it was the sixth hour, there was darkness all over the earth, and it continued up to the ninth hour.[89] This means that Jesus had remained on the cross for three hours. When darkness descended on the earth, people started returning to their homes. Only his relatives, including his mother, Mary Magdalene, and some of his disciples remained on Golgotha. His friends from the Essene Brotherhood had assembled in the nearby worshipping center. A soldier who was noble and compassionate permitted John to conduct Mary, the mother of Jesus, close to the cross. From the Dead Sea was observed to rise a thick, reddish fog. The mountain ridges shook violently and the head of Jesus sank down upon his breast.[90]

> At the ninth hour, Jesus cried with a loud voice:
> *Elo-i, Elo-i, Lama sabachthani.*[91]

Matthew has given the above cry as:

Eli, Eli, Lama sabachthani.[92]

Luke and John have not mentioned the above sentence. According to Luke, he cried aloud saying: Father into thy hands I commend my spirit.[93] According to John, he said, it is finished.[94] Jesus had spoken in Aramaic and the people felt bewildered. Since the day of crucifixion, the above sentence has created confusion, due to the fact that most of the commentators of the Bible have interpreted it to mean;

My God, my God: Why hast thou forsaken me? In fact, God had not forsaken him, because Jesus Christ in the Sermon on the Mount had declared:

> Ask and it shall be given you,
> Seek, and ye shall find,
> Knock, and it shall be opened unto you.
> For every one that asketh receiveth,
> For every one that seeketh findeth,
> And to him that knocketh it shall be opened.[95]

In fact he had already spoken of this with God:

> Abba, Father.
> All things are possible unto thee;
> Take away this cup from me;
> Nevertheless, not what I will,
> But what thou wilt.[96]

In view of the above, it is certain that his prayer could not have remained unanswered and unaccepted. Jesus was in deep meditation at that moment in the Garden, and his prayer was heard and an angel of God visited him at that very time, strengthening him.[97] It is a strange logic to say that God forsake him and he cried in anguish:

> Oh God, Oh God, Why have you forsaken me?

Jesus had received the word of God, because he had himself said:

Father,
I thank thee
That thou hast heard me,
And I know that thou hearest me,
Always.[98]

He had already declared that God heard him always and granted his prayers. The same divine will happened this time also, when he cried.

Interpretation

As stated earlier, the so-called cry on the cross has been interpreted differently in the first two Gospels. According to Matthew, the last words of Jesus Christ were:

Eli, Eli, Lama sabachthani?

According to Mark, the words were:

Elo-i, Elo-i, Lama sabachthani?

But in earlier editions of the New Testament these were given as:

Eli, Eli, Lamah shavahhtani!

A question arises as to why the words have been changed by the Gospel compilers from time to time. It may be pointed out at the outset that the words; *Eli, Eli, Lamah shavahhtani,* in the original Hebrew, mean:

God, God, how thou hast glorified me!

The verb *shavahh* means to bring peace, to glorify and to soothe.[99] If he had said,

Eli, Eli, Lamah azavtani?

Then it would mean:

Eli, Eli, why hast thou forsaken me?

These words were borrowed from the Psalms, and the passage, being of utmost importance and full of significance, needs to be reproduced here to show that the truth has been concealed by the compilers of the Gospels.

> My God, why hast thou forsaken me?
> Be not far from me;
> For the trouble is near;
> For there is none to help.
> But be not thou far from me.
> O Lord:
> O my strength,
> Haste thee to help me.
> For the kingdom is the Lord's.[100]

The question arises as to whether the correct rendering is *Lamah* or *Limah,* because that would change the whole meaning of these words. *Li* stands for affirmative, while *La* stands for negative. As such the above words when translated into English would mean:

> My God, thou hast not forsaken me!

Keeping the above in view, Jesus Christ may have cried:

> My God, my God, thou hast not forsaken me.

There is another point of significance which cannot be ignored. We have already hinted that the Psalms may be the actual words of Jesus Christ. Can we explain who was the person who was crucified here? Who was the personality, whose hands and feet were pierced? In order to explain the issue, let us quote from the Psalms:

> Why art thou so far from helping me,
> And from the words of my roaring?
> Our fathers trusted in thee;
> They trusted,
> And thou didst deliver them,
> They cried unto thee,
> And were delivered;

> They trusted in thee,
> And were not confounded.[101]

The above makes it clear that the person crying has full hope that his supplications will be rewarded by his deliverance. Then he speaks of his life as follows:

> But thou art he that took me out of the womb.
> Thou didst make me hope
> When I was upon my mother's breasts.
> Be not from me;
> For trouble is near;
> For there is none to help.[102]

The person again seeks help from God, giving the actual facts as follows:

> For dogs have compassed me;
> The assembly of the wicked have enclosed me;
> They pierced my hands,
> And my feet.
> I may tell all my bones;
> They look and stare upon me.
> They part my garments among them,
> And cast lots upon my vesture.[103]

A pertinent question can be asked as to who the person is whose garments are being parted? Who is this personality whose hands and feet have been pierced?

It will be seen from the above that either the whole act of crucifixion was foretold centuries before or the above Psalm may be the actual cry of anguish by Jesus Christ. There is a definite statement on his part that the wicked have encircled him and they have pierced his hands and feet. This cry cannot be of any personality other than Jesus Christ himself. He further implores:

> Deliver my soul from the sword;
> Save me from the lion's mouth;
> For thou hast heard me.
> I will declare thy name
> Unto my brethren;

In the midst of congregations:
Will I praise thee.[104]

A minute examination of these verses would show that Jesus implored God to save him. He tells God that it is he who took him out of the womb and made him a hope for nations. He implores that he is in trouble and there is none to help him. He further says that the wicked have enclosed him and pierced his hands and feet. They have distributed his garments among them. He further says that his strength is dried up and all his bones are out of joint. He further implores God not to remain away from him and haste to help him so that he can declare his name in the congregations. God on his part gives him a vow that "your heart shall live forever."

Sumerian Version

The Sumerian rendering would make it as: *Elauia, Elauia, Limasba (la) g-ants*, which translated would mean, No God except God, thou glorious and praised one sent forth. It is interesting to note that the following oath is taken at the time of conversion to Islam: "There is no God save God and Mohamad is sent forth by God." In Arabic, Mohamad means praised one or glorious.[105]

The word *"Eloi"* or *"Eli"* has been interpreted differently by various scholars. It has also been asserted that this word means the prophet or the saint which was to come after the Lord, and as such, does not mean God.[106] This word was also used by Krishna, during the war between the Kauravas and the Pandavas, when he cried *Elia, Elia.*[107] This word was found inscribed on a metal plate near Jerusalem by the British Brigade during the first World War.[108] Another plate, said to be on Noah's ark, was found in Central Asia bearing words in Aramaic, including this, along with the words of Mohamad and his family.[109] Buddha also recited the word *Elia* in his prayers, at a time when he was opposed by his people.[110]

The Kingdom of God

Jesus Christ was the only begotten Son of God, and as such could never be left to the mercy of human beings. His mission was to show us how human beings could live in order to please God. Accordingly, the hand of God came into action and a hissing sound was heard in the air. The people were seized by a great fear, thinking that the evil spirits were proceeding to punish them.[111] Soon the mountain began to shake and the walls of the temple gave way until the veil of the temple was rent in twain from top to bottom. The graves were opened and many bodies of the saints which slept arose and came out of the graves. The Jews regarded all this as extremely super-natural, and the Roman centurion came forward to comfort Mary, the mother of Jesus. There were other women at the spot, including Mary Magdalene, and the mother of Zebedee's children. Mark tells us that Mary, the mother of James the Less, and of Joses and Salome, also stood far off looking at the cross. Many people smote their chests and departed, but some devotees of Jesus Christ did not move. The Essenes remained at the spot, for they knew the cause of this phenomenon of nature.

Friends and Foe

A study of the Gospels reveals that among the enemies, which stood near the site of crucifixion, the prominent were:
1) The priests.
2) The soldiers.

Among the friends and devotees of Jesus Christ, the following may be mentioned:
1) Mary, the mother of Jesus.
2) His sister.
3) Mary, the wife of Cleophas.
4) Mary Magdalene.[112]
5) Joseph of Arimathea.[113]
6) Mary, the mother of James.
7) Salome.
8) Other women.[114]
9) Mother of Zebedee's children.[115]
10) Disciples and devotees.
11) The Essenes of Golgotha.[116]

Joseph of Arimathea

Joseph was a rich man of Arimathea, and was also a devoted disciple of Jesus. He is also spoken of as an honorable counselor, who waited for the kingdom of God. He is also said to be a good man and just, who had opposed the verdict. He, being a disciple of the Lord, had secret consultations with Pilate, so that he might take away the body of Jesus. As hardly a few hours had elapsed since Jesus was put on the stake, he wondered if he were already dead. He called one of the guards, who told him that Jesus was already dead. Pilate commanded the body to be delivered to Joseph. Both he and Nicodemus rushed to the scene.[117] While Joseph brought fine linen with him,[118] Nicodemus brought a mixture of myrrh and aloes—about a hundred pound weight.[119] He was a Pharisee known as the ruler of the Jews. He believed that Jesus Christ had come from God, and also used to meet the Lord in the darkness of night.[120] Both he and Joseph belonged to the Essene Order.[121]

The Essenes were the great healers of the ancient world. They investigated uses of herbs, plants and minerals. They knew the art of preparing anointing oils which, when rubbed on the body, could produce the strange psychological effect of self-omnipotence. They knew the secret herb which, when mixed with ointments and spices, could impart life and rebirth, even to the dead. The Lord himself was a great healer, and he had taught his disciples to heal the sick. He had himself learned yoga and practiced the healing craft. The Essenes had kept all first-aid material and other herbs ready at hand to save Jesus.[122]

Blood and Water

As soon as the priests heard that Joseph had been permitted to take away the body of Jesus, they went to Pilate and besought that, as the victims should not remain upon the stakes on the Sabbath, their legs be broken.[123]

Then came the soldiers, brought by the priests for breaking the legs of the victims. They broke away the legs of the first and of the other, but when they came to Jesus, they felt that he was already dead. This being so, they did not break his legs.[124] But one of the soldiers pierced his side and forthwith came out blood and water.[125] Jesus Christ was stabbed on the right side by a spear pointed upwards which could not reach the heart.

It appears that the Lord was in a state of coma at that time.[126] It is also probable that he only feigned death by putting himself into a cataleptic trance. The existence of blood and water still in the body of Jesus Christ would suggest, on medical grounds, that he was alive at the time when Joseph of Arimathea and Nicodemus, the ruler of the Pharisees, arrived at the spot.

The Essene Version

The letter sent by an Essene to their brethren is very interesting and informs us about their part in saving the life of Jesus Christ. Its summary is reproduced here:

Dear Brethren,

Two of our brethren, influential and experienced, did use all their influence with Pilate and the Jewish council in behalf of Jesus, but their efforts were frustrated in that Jesus himself requested that he might be permitted to suffer death for his faith.

Joseph, from Arimathea, and his friend Nicodemus, who belonged to our Order, prevailed upon Pilate to permit them to take Jesus' body from the cross that very night, and put it in the sepulchre, hewn in the rock, belonging to Joseph. The Jews had obtained orders regarding breaking away of the bones of the crucified so that they may be buried. As the Centurion was friendly, he ordered his soldiers not to break the bones of Jesus, for he was dead. To be more sure of it, one of the soldiers stuck his spear into the body in such manner that it passed over the hip, and into the side. The body showed no convulsions, and this was taken as a sure sign that he was actually dead. The Centurion hurriedly went away to make his report to Pilate. But from the insignificant wound flowed blood and water, at which our hope revived.

After this, they hurried to the cross, and according to the prescription of the medical art, they slowly untied his bonds, drew the spikes out from his bands, and with great care laid him on the ground. The body was then laid in the sepulchre.[127]

Concept of Time

Jesus Christ remained on the cross from the sixth hour to the ninth hour. The basic unit of computing time, in old times, was a day, which among the Jews was counted from sunset. It is evident that the day and night was composed of eight watches of about three hours each, so that day and night had twenty-four hours. The sixth hour in the day would come to about twelve noon and the ninth hour would come to about three p.m. The Sabbath started at sunset on Friday and terminated at sunset on Saturday. The Jews had to remember this day and keep it holy.[128] It was observed on the seventh day of the week. Similarly, the seventh month and the seventh year had also a special Sabbath. It was ordered that the believers should worship before the Lord was in the Sabbath, and in the new moons.[129] It was not lawful to keep bodies on the cross on Sabbath.[130] Thus it is clear that Jesus was put on the cross at twelve noon and was removed from it at three P.M.

The Hindu Version

An ancient Hindu *Sutra*, known as *Natha-namavali*, which is preserved among the Natha Yogis, has given a different version of the resurrection of Jesus Christ, whom they name as Isha Natha.

> Isha Natha came to India at the age of fourteen. After this he returned to his own country and began his preaching. Soon however, his brutish and materialistic countrymen conspired against him and had him crucified. After the crucifixion, or perhaps even before it, Isha Natha entered samadhi, or a profound trance, by means of yoga. Seeing him thus, the Jews presumed he was dead and buried him in a tomb. At that very moment, however, one of his gurus, or teachers, the great Chetan Natha, happened to be in profound meditation, in the lower reaches of the Himalayas, and he saw in a vision the tortures which Isha Natha was undergoing. He therefore made his body lighter than air and passed over to the land of Israel. The day of his arrival was marked with thunder and lightning, for the gods were angry with the Jews and the whole world trembled. When Chetan Natha arrived, he took the body of Isha Natha from the tomb and woke him from his samadhi, and later led him off to the sacred land of the Aryans. Isha

Natha then established an ashram in the lower regions of the Himalayas, and he established the cult of the Lingam and the Yoni there.[131]

The Natha Yogis have some songs containing references to John the Baptist. This legend about Jesus in the Hindu sutras is worthy of serious consideration. We find a parallel legend in another work in Sanskrit on the ancient history of Kashmir. There, the author mentions Isana instead of Chetan Natha. This legend will be discussed later.[132]

First Aid

They took Jesus Christ down from the cross and wrapped his body in a clean linen cloth. This linen was pasted with spices. They laid him in a new sepulchre, which existed in the garden, near the site of crucifixion.

The women also accompanied them to the sepulchre. Nicodemus had brought a mixture of myrrh and aloes with him.[133] The other devotees prepared spices and ointments for the Lord.[134] Nicodemus spread strong spices and healing salves on long pieces of byssus, which he had brought. He also spread balsam in both the nail-pierced hands of Jesus Christ.[135] The myrrh and aloe was reduced to powder and inserted between the bandages, which were wound, fold upon fold.[136]

In these medical operations, they were helped by the Essenes. This pious sect was fully instructed in the healing virtues of medicinal plants, roots and stones.[137] At midnight, Nicodemus and other devotees found that Jesus was breathing.[138] As the place was not safe, he was taken out of the sepulchre to some other safer place.

Medical Relief

The high priest anticipated secret plans between Joseph and the Galileans regarding saving the life of Jesus. He also thought that Pilate and Joseph were plotting against the Jews. Accordingly he sent his spies to enquire about the secret friends of Jesus Christ. An Essene, dressed in the white robe, obscured by the morning mist, descended from the mountain, and pulled aside the stone of the sepulchre. The guards and the spies were seized with a great fear and fled away, spreading the report that an angel had driven away the stone. In the meanwhile, twenty-four Essenes, led by Joseph and Nicodemus, arrived at the grotto. They saw the white-robed Essene supporting the head of the revived Jesus on his breast. Then Joseph embraced the Lord with tears in his eyes. When Jesus recognized his friend, he asked, Where am I? They gave him some bread dipped in honey and he felt greatly refreshed. He became conscious of the wounds, but the balsam which Nicodemus had spread upon them had a soothing effect. After the byssus wrappings had been taken off and the muckender was removed from his head, Jesus was removed to a house belonging to an Essene. Before departure they annihilated every trace of the byssus wrapping, the medicines and the drugs used. Jesus was kept in concealment for safety's sake. After his recovery, he was clothed in white robes of a gardener. Nicodemus again tied up his wounds, gave him a medical draught and advised him to rest himself in quiet. But he said:

> I fear not death,
> For I have fulfilled it;
> And the enemies shall acknowledge,
> That God has saved me;
> And wills not that I die eternally.

After that Jesus Christ went forth upon his journey.[139] As it was cold, the Essenes gave him a warm mantle in which he wrapped himself.

Ointment of Jesus

The famous *Marham-i-Issa* or the Ointment of Jesus, which cured his wounds has been mentioned in many medical treatises such as the Canon of Avicenna, *Sharh-i-Qanun, Hawi-Kabir* by Rhazes, Liber Regius by Haly Abbas, Hesagps of Jarjani.[140] This ointment is also known as the Ointment of Twelve, due to the fact that Jesus had twelve disciples. According to Avicenna, this balm has miraculous powers of healing wounds.[141] It can eliminate pus and replace worn-out flesh.[142] It is effective to cure wounds and provides new flesh to fill up cavities. It is helpful in circulating blood and removal of numbness.[143] The Ointment of Jesus contains:

1. White Wax.
2. Gum Gugal also known as Balsamo Dendron Mukul.
3. Plumbi Oxidum.
4. Myrrh.
5. Galbanum.
6. Aristoelchia Longa.
7. Subacetate of Copper.
8. Gum Ammonicum.
9. Rasin Pinuslongifolia.
10. Olibanum.
11. Rasin.
12. Olive Oil.

It is necessary to mention that in all Arabic and Persian works, the ointment has been mentioned under the caption of *Sheliakh, Salieka, Zaliekha,* which may mean the Ointment of the Prophets or the Ointment of Twelve.[144]

Another Version

Many treatises have been written on the question of physical death or otherwise the survival of Jesus Christ. Dr. William Stroud published his research from London in the year 1887. Prior to him the issue was medically examined by Dr. Nagels Bibeluber-setzung, in 1881, and later the issue was taken up by Dr. O. Streffe, who compiled his dissertation under the title: *Physiologische Unmoglichkeit des Todes Christi am Kreuze,* which was published in Bonn in 1912. *The Life of Christ,* reprinted by Stockton-Doty Press, California, gives the following version:

> Master Yessu, although maltreated beyond the term of brutal, wounded with very great loss of blood, enough to cause death to any ordinary being, and though having suffered physically, mentally, and spiritually, the agony and bloody sweat of a Son of God unrecognized by his people, recovered more rapidly than his best friends had expected, and once down from the cross and his wounds given the necessary attention, it became only a question of nature doing the rest. His inner circle of friends had determined to save him at any cost, and

their knowledge and understanding of the higher sciences obtained from him, were now to be brought to a test. Thus, as soon as the body had been taken down from the cross, it was interred in the private sepulchre, and after the stone door had been carefully sealed, the Master's friends entered the secret passageway leading thereto. Here, they set to work at once. When he was taken from the cross, they knew that he was not dead but merely in an unconscious condition, superinduced by the opiate which had been so ingeniously administered; for under the cover of night they had determined to do a desperate act, had not the arrival of the imperial edict made matters much more favorable for them.

Once the body was brought to the sepulchre and away from public gaze, Joseph of Arimathea, Nicodemus, Mathaeli and others set to work to do all within their power to revive their beloved Master. It was nearly midnight when the body of their Lord had been sufficiently revived to warrant his removal to the house of Joseph.[145]

In the Gospels there is no mention of the washing of the wounded body of Jesus, but there is no doubt that it was anointed with herbs and balms and then wrapped. As Jesus was still alive at the time he was wrapped, his sweat produced an imprint on the cloth. At the same time, the ointment used for healing wounds also had a chemical effect on the shroud. As time passed on, his energy returned, his body became warm and this left a permanent image. It not only carried the scourge marks but also depicts the flow of blood, especially from the spear wound. According to Professor Giovanni Batista, the body that was wrapped up in this shroud was a person of the AB positive blood-group.[146] As is known to anthropologists, Jesus belonged, broadly speaking, to the Caucasoid stock and principally to the Mediterranean race. Basically, his blood group should be A, but as he lived east of the Mediterranean, the incidence of B is possible in varying frequency.

The Tomb

We know very little about the tomb in which the body of Jesus was laid by his friends. At this same time, it cannot be denied that he was to be buried according to the Jewish custom. In case of important individuals, the body was laid on a shelf within a rock-cut tomb. After decomposition, the bones would be collected and stored in a wooden or stone chest, to make room for other dead members of the family. It is noteworthy that placing of bodies in a casket is a Buddhist custom of preserving the relics of the *Bodhisattva*. The tomb for Jesus Christ was hewn out of a rock.[146] This tomb was a new one, wherein was never man yet laid.[147] The tomb existed in a garden close to Golgotha.

Though tombs of the same period have been found in Jerusalem, the tombs cut into rocks have not been found. So is the case with the tomb, which was prepared for Jesus Christ by Joseph of Arimathea. It is recorded that Constantine the Great ordered cutting away of the rocks for building a basilica, in about 326 A.D. Up till now, the archaeologists have failed to find any relics or remains of Jesus, which proves that we have to find his grave elsewhere. The Freemason Society in Germany has gotten hold of a slab engraved by the Essenes. In it, they have mentioned that Jesus did not die on the cross but was saved owing to circumstances. Firstly, he remained at the cross for hardly a few hours, and secondly, he was properly nursed by the Essenes. It was they who protected him and then took him away out of the reach of the Jews. At the same time, the existence of the Essenes in India cannot be doubted because we have such a type of Order, known as "Sanyasis," who are mendicants but well-versed in herbs and ailments. This slab which is kept concealed by the above Society is out of the reach of the Church.[148]

Edessa

Ezad ascended the throne of Adiabene in 36 A.D. He was a contemporary of Abgar Ukkama of Edessa.[149] It is necessary to mention that Abgar was an Aryan and his kingdom carried on regular trade with India. In fact Edessa was an important trade center on the route between Babylon and Spasinou Charax.[150] One of Abgar's servants, named Ananias, had seen Jesus performing miracles. After his return to his home country, he gave full information about Jesus to Abgar, who was suffering from arthritis and black leprosy. At first he decided to summon Jesus to his court and get cured of illness. But news reached him that the Jews were murmuring against Jesus and wanted to harm him. This being the case, Abgar Ukkama decided to send a letter to Jesus requesting to be cured of illness. Unfortunately, Jesus had already been crucified when Ananias reached Jerusalem. He met Thomas, who gave him the cloth which had wrapped the body of Jesus, when laid in the tomb. Ananias hid this cloth in his bag and returned to Edessa along with Andreas. He handed over this sacred cloth to Abgar, who was cured of his illness and disease.[151] During the period there was an important Jewish community at Edessa. However, it was due to Abgar Ukkama that Christianity spread in his realm and many of the Jews accepted the doctrines. It is for this reason that the early Christian bishops carried Jewish names.

The Holy Shroud

The cloth which covered the body of Jesus in the tomb is now preserved in the cathedral at Turin, Italy. It is 4 meters and 35 centimeters long and 1 meter and 10 centimeters broad. It carries the image of the face and the body of Jesus, in perfect anatomical proportion, giving the height of the body as 1 meter and 62 centimeters. There are blood stains and blots on the shroud, located exactly on the head, hands and right side of the chest. It was carried to Edessa in 30 A.D. It was discovered again in 525 A.D., hidden in a niche. In 639 A.D. it was preserved in the Cathedral of Hagia Sophia. After that it was taken over by the Muslims, who handed it over to Abraham, the bishop of Samossata in 944 A.D. It was taken to Constantinople and preserved there in the Cathedral of Hagia Sophia. It was seen by Abu Nasr Yahya, an Arab Christian writer in the year 1058. It was also seen by the French crusader, Robert de Clari in Constantinople in 1203 A.D. We hear about its disappearance next year at the time, when Constantinople was sacked by the Crusaders. It found its refuge in France and was exposed for the first time in the presence of the royal family of the House of Savoy.[152] It is now permanently preserved in the Royal Chapel of Turin.

In 1898, a first attempt was made to photograph it, but this attempt failed. However, the photographer, Secondo Pia succeeded in his second attempt. He found a "lifelike" image visible in the nega-

The Holy Shroud at Turn
Photo: Enrie, 1931, Turin

tive. In 1931 A.D. the negative image was revealed yet more clearly in the photographs by Giuseppe Enrie. The shroud was shown to the members of the special scientific commission in June, 1969, and the first scientific research conference started its work on it in March 1977.[153]

Scientific tests conducted so far reveal as follows:

a) The antiquity of the linen is confirmed through its herringbone weave, a kind fashionable in the first century A.D.

b) The image on the shroud is three-dimensional rather than flat and as such is not the work of human hands.

c) The pollen on the linen of the type found in Palestine during the first century A.D.

d) The blots and stains on the linen show the presence of myrrh, the ointment used on the wound marks of Jesus Christ.

e) One nail was struck at the crossed feet, between the second and third toes and no bone was damaged.

f) Both the hands were nailed above the fleshy ride of the palms.

g) The spear thrust was aimed between the fifth and the sixth rib, about six inches from the medial line, in an upward angle from the heart.

h) Positive photos of the facial features show Jesus to be of Jewish origin, with long nose, long hair and beard.[154]

The Holy Shroud was lately put to further scientific tests by a team of twenty-seven scientists from the U.S.A. who had been assigned the difficult task of determining whether the shroud was real or a fake. After minute microanalytical and radiocarbon testing the scientists have come to the conclusion that the shroud is the same cloth in which the body of Jesus Christ was wrapped after crucifixion.[155]

Disappearance

Very early in the morning. Mary Magdalene and Mary the mother of James and Salome came to the site of the sepulchre. They had brought sweet spices with them, so that they might anoint Jesus Christ. There were other devotees with them.[156] They saw the stone of the sepulchre had been rolled away.[157] An angel sat upon it whose countenance was like light and his raiment white as snow.[158] They saw a young man sitting on the right side clothed in a long white garment.[159] As they were much perplexed, two men stood by them, who said unto them:

> Why seek ye
> The living among the dead?
> He is not here,
> But is risen;
> Remember:
> How he spake unto you:
> When he was yet in Galilee,
> Saying:
> The Son of man,
> Must be delivered,
> Unto the hands of sinful men,
> And he crucified
> And the third day,
> Rise again.[160]

The young man, who was clothed in a long white garment, told them not to feel frightened, but to go and tell his disciples that Jesus had gone before them to Galilee and they could see him there.[161] Accordingly, they departed quickly from the sepulchre with fear and great joy. They ran to bring disciples to Galilee and see him.[162] But as they were afraid of the Pharisees, they kept the whole incident secret. They did not inform any one about it.[163] However, Mary Magdalene could not keep the secret and she ran to Simon Peter and other disciples whom Jesus loved. She told them that they had taken away the Lord out of the sepulchre.[164]

Hearing it, Peter ran into the sepulchre and looked around the room. He saw the linen clothes laid on the floor.[165] He also saw the napkin that was about his head, not lying with the clothes but in another corner of the room.[166] He departed wondering in himself at the strange incident which had occurred.[167]

The Resurrection

The Gospel of Peter, which was written in 150 A.D., has provided authentic details about the resurrection of Jesus Christ, which are reproduced here:

> Now in the night whereon the Lord's day dawned, as the soldiers were keeping guard two by two in every watch, there came a great sound in the heavens, and they saw the heavens opened and the two men descend thence, shining with a great light, and drawing near unto the sepulchre. And that stone which had been set on the door, rolled away of itself and went back to the side, and the sepulchre was opened and both the young men entered in. When therefore these soldiers saw that, they waked up the centurion and the elders; and while they were yet telling them the things which they had seen, they saw again three men come out of the sepulchre, two of them sustaining the one, and a cross following after them. And of the two, they saw their heads reached unto heaven, but of him that was led by them, that it over-passed the heavens.[168]

The above passage from the apocryphal Gospel reveals that two men shining with a great light entered the sepulchre. But after some time, instead of two, three men came out, the two sustaining the third. It is not a strange coincidence that at the time of transfiguration, Jesus was seen talking to two men, and here gain, he is being taken out of the sepulchre by two men clothed in white garments?[169] It is clear that they were Joseph and Nicodemus, who met Jesus on the mount, at the time of transfiguration, and it was they who again came to the sepulchre at night and took him away to safety.

The news spread into the city, and the priests heard all the details. They held a council, and gave large money to the soldiers, telling them that they should inform the governor that Jesus Christ had been stolen away by his disciples.[170] In the meanwhile Jesus went into solitude, after having a last look of the land from the summit of a mountain. On the advice of Joseph of Arimathea, he had agreed to live with the Essenes.[171]

Walk to Emmaus

Jesus then went to a village called Emmaus, where two villagers met him. One of them, whose name was Cleopas, asked the Lord if he had not heard that Jesus of Nazareth was condemned to death and crucified by the priests. He said unto them:

> O fools,
> And slow of heart,
> To believe all that;
> The prophets have spoken:
> Ought not Christ
> To have suffered these things,
> And to enter into his glory.[172]

As they drew near the village, Jesus was in a hurry and wanted to go further. But the villagers constrained him and invited him for dinner. He accepted their hospitality.

> And it came to pass
> As he sat at meat with them,
> He took bread,
> And blessed it,
> And brake,
> And gave to them.[173]

The above shows that Jesus, after having his meals, which consisted of meat and bread, proceeded further and went into the country.[174]

Meeting with the Disciples

After the crucifixion, the disciples of Jesus, due to fear, had gathered themselves in a house with doors shut. They had heard evidence about the Lord having appeared at several places. While they were absorbed in discussions, Jesus Christ came to them and said unto them:

> Peace be unto you.[175]

OUR LORD'S APPEARANCES AFTER HIS RESURRECTION

ORDER	TIME	TO WHOM	WHERE	RECORD
1	Sunday, April 9, early in the morning	To Mary Magdalene	Near the sepulchre at Jerusalem	Mark 16: 9; John 20: 11-18
2	Sunday morning	To the women returning from the sepulchre	Near Jerusalem	Matt. 28: 9, 10
3	Sunday	To Simon Peter alone	Near Jerusalem	Luke 24: 34
4	Sunday afternoon	To two disciples going to Emmaus	Between Jerusalem and Emmaus, and at Emmaus	Luke 24: 13-31; Mark 16: 12, 13
5	Sunday evening	To the apostles, except Thomas	Jerusalem	John 20: 19-25; Mark 16: 14
6	Sunday evening, April 16	To the apostles, Thomas being present	Jerusalem	John 20: 26-29
7	Last of April or first of May	To seven disciples, fishing	Sea of Galilee	John 21: 1-13
8	Last of April or first of May	To the eleven disciples on a mountain	Galilee	Matt. 28: 16-20; Mark 16: 15-18
9	Last of April or first of May	To above five hundred brethren at once	Galilee	I Cor. 15: 6
10	May	To James only	Jerusalem, probably	I Cor. 15: 7
11	Thursday, May 18	To all the apostles at his ascension	Mount of Olives, near Bethany	Mark 16: 19-20; Luke 24: 50, 51; Acts 1: 6-12
12	Jesus appeared to Paul about six years later, near Damascus, A.D. 36. Acts 9: 3, 4; I Cor. 15: 8.			

The disciples felt terrified, fearing that it was the spirit of the Lord speaking to them. But he told them:

> Why are ye troubled;
> And why do thoughts arise in your hearts?
> Behold my hands and my feet,
> That it is I myself;
> Handle me,
> And see;
> For a spirit hath not flesh and bones,
> As ye see me have.
> And when he had thus spoken;
> He showed them his hands, and his feet.
> And while they yet believed not, for joy,
> And wondered,
> He said unto them,
> Have ye here any meat,
> And they gave him

A piece of a boiled fish.
And of honeycomb.
And he took it.
And did eat before them.[176]

After having spoken with his disciples and after eating boiled fish and honeycomb, Jesus Christ departed to other lands.

Unbelievers

It is a strange coincidence that those who believe in the holy scriptures, at the same time believe partly or have no faith in certain portions of the Bible. Some are of opinion that the facts given in the Gospels about the later events after crucifixion are only hallucinations, and no credit could be given to these accounts. If whatever is written about the Lord in the Gospels is incredible, then it would be better to wash off our hands and declare openly that the Gospels are inauthentic. There were people even during the lifetime of the Lord who did not believe in having seen Jesus Christ. One such was Thomas, who did not believe that Jesus Christ was alive and had eaten food. At the moment when Thomas was in the company of the apostles, Jesus Christ came and told him:

Reach hither thy finger,
And behold my hands,
And reach hither thy hand
And thrust it into my side,
And be not faithless,
But believing.[177]

Lately, some Christians, whose sincerity cannot be doubted, have questioned the physical resurrection of Jesus Christ. For centuries, the Christians were told that Jesus had died for their sins on the cross. As such, they doubted the physical resurrection from the dead until they subscribed to the survival of Jesus from crucifixion. It must be admitted that Jesus Christ was created for a special role within the divine purpose.

Had Jesus merely taught for one year and then died on the cross, it is not difficult to think that his teachings would have lasted for a fortnight. But God willed that he should be saved so that his mission could be made permanent. His physical resurrection may be termed a miracle, but it must be recognized that many a miracle in world mythologies have been established by scientific inquiries as true. There is no reason to disbelieve that Jesus was not seen alive physically by his disciples and devotees, and that he ate and drank with them.

Sea of Tiberias

Another incident, where Jesus Christ met his seven disciples at the sea of Tiberias, has been recorded in the Gospels. He showed himself to them when the disciples had gone there for fishing. They went forth and entered into a ship. In the morning they saw the Lord standing on the shore. He told them to bring the fish which they had caught, and dine with him.[178] So when they had dined, Jesus said:

> Feed my sheep.[179]
> Go ye into all the world,
> And preach the Gospel,
> To every creature.[180]

Jesus led them out as far as to Bethany and, after lifting up his hands, blessed them. After this, he parted away from his disciples.[181]

If Jesus was dead, there was no need for him to eat flesh with his disciples, because the dead do not dine! If he was dead, there was no need for him to give instructions to his disciples, for he had already instructed them in the way of God! If he was not alive, there was no occasion to raise his hands up, and bless them! Such and other questions when answered logically testify to the physical resurrection of Jesus Christ. On the testimony of the above narratives, supported by the Oriental sources, it will be clear in subsequent pages that Jesus Christ, after having been saved from death by his devoted disciples, proceeded towards the East.

Verdict on Second Coming

It cannot be denied that Jesus had designated himself as the Son of God and had pledged his whole person behind the truth of his proclamation. It is also a fact that the central content of his proclamation was not himself but the Kingdom of God. His word was the word of God, and there is no reason to doubt the sincerity of his words. Jesus Christ has expressed very clearly his mission and his work, and the apostles have tried their best to record his words. What does he say about his second coming?

While imparting special instructions to his disciples regarding missionary work, he told them about the dangers they had to face. He further told them to flee to the next city, in case they are persecuted, and at the same time informed them that he would come himself to see them. Here is the relevant passage on the subject:

> But when they persecute you in this city,
> Flee ye into another;
> For verily I say unto you,
> Ye shall have not gone over the cities of Israel,
> Till the Son of man be come.[182]

The above prediction made by Jesus Christ is an important proof of his second coming. At another place, Jesus predicted the overthrow of Jerusalem and his second coming to test the faithfulness of his disciples. He clearly tells them that he would come again during their life time, along with angels. The event of his coming is not to occur in the future but within the lifetime of his disciples, to whom he spoke. He predicted as follows:

> But I tell you a truth,
> There be some standing here,
> Which shall not taste of death,
> Till they see the kingdom of God.[183]
> Verily I say unto you,
> There be some standing here,
> Which shall not taste of death,
> Till they see the Son of man coming in his kingdom.[184]
> And he said unto them,

Verily I say unto you,
That there be some of them that stand here,
Which shall not taste of death,
Till they have seen the kingdom of God come with power.[185]

The above declarations are a clear verdict on the visible coming of Jesus Christ, during the lifetime of his disciples. That being the case, seeking philosophical explanations of the testament given by him seems unwarranted. When he has made a definite and positive statement about his coming again among his disciples, it is not fair to doubt the sincerity of the evangelists, who meant that Jesus would return physically and not spiritually. Later events in the life of Jesus Christ have proved that the predictions made by Jesus Christ about himself were true and correct.

A woman healed by touching the garment of Jesus (Bida)

Miracles of Jesus Christ

Miracles are considered marvelous events or wonderful acts done by a saint with the help of some supernatural agency. Many remarkable occurrences in the life of Jesus Christ testify to his being a supernatural man.

The wonders done by him may look incredible to some, but to those who have read something about spiritual matters, all these miracles of Jesus Christ have an air of truth about them. His birth, his travels, his ministry, his crucifixion, and his future life are all miraculous. When there arose a great tempest, he calmed the storm.[186] At that time, the people wondered what sort of man he was that even the winds and the sea obeyed him. He could even walk upon the sea, and the people thought that he was a spirit.[187] There was a man with a spirit of an unclean devil, and when Jesus saw him, he ordered the devil to come out. The devil came out and all felt amazed.[188] They also wondered when, in Galilee, he saved the son of a nobleman who was at the point of death.[189] Similarly, when ten lepers of Samaria cried, "Master, have mercy on us," all of them were cleaned of this dreadful disease.[190] It is clear from the above that it was possible for him to save himself from his enemies.

Jesus Christ was bestowed with the power of restoring eyesight. He touched the eyes of two blind men, and their eyesight returned. They had faith that it was only Jesus who could give them their eyesight, and they obtained their wish, according to their faith. It is recorded in the Gospels that Jesus could heal the sick, restore hearing to the deaf, and make the dumb to speak.[191] The Pharisees, who were spiritually blind, did not believe in these miracles. But it was a miracle of God which materialized in saving Jesus on the cross.

Jesus healed the man who had dropsy and also healed a crippled woman on the Sabbath day. When the Pharisees said that no one should work on the Sabbath day, he questioned them saying: "Which of you will not pull out an ass or an ox, fallen in a pit?" They could not answer him.[192] When he was in the wilderness, a great multitude came to see him, and was with him for three days. He felt compassion on them, for they had nothing to eat. His disciples came to him, and informed him that they had only seven loaves, and it was impossible for them to feed four thousand people assembled there. He did break the loaves, and went on giving bread to his disciples, who went on placing these before the multitude. About four thousand of the people ate these seven loaves, and their hunger was satisfied completely.[193] When the Pharisees demanded a sign, he admonished them saying that only a wicked and adulterous nation seeks a sign.[194]

Prayers of Jesus Christ

Did God hear Jesus Christ? This is an important question often asked of us. Our answer is yes—and let us quote from the scriptures. It is recorded that when Abraham prayed, God healed Abimelech.[195] Again, when Moses prayed, the fire was quenched.[196] The Prophets would pray and their prayers were heard. In the same way, Jesus Christ also prayed and his prayers were heard by God. Jesus declared:

> And all things,
> Whatsoever ye shall ask in prayer,
> Believing,
> Ye shall receive.[197]

Jesus would go out to a mountain for prayers, and continue praying during the night. He would tell them that he would pray to the Father, and that He would give them another Comforter, to abide with them forever.[198]

Before Jesus Christ is arrested, he prays for his disciples as follows:

> I pray for them:
> I pray not for the world,
> But for them,
> Which thou hast given me;
> For they are thine.
> I pray not that thou shouldst
> Take them out of the world,
> But that thou shouldst,
> Keep them from the evil.
> Neither pray I for those alone,

But for them also,
Which shall believe in me,
Through their word.[199]

During his prayers at Gethsemane, Jesus prayed:

O my Father,
If it is possible,
Let this cup pass from me:
Nevertheless,
Not as I will,
But as thou wilt.[200]

From the above, it is clear that even though Jesus Christ was resigned to the will of God, he never wished to die. The above would disprove the assumption of some scholars that Jesus Christ wanted to die and bring death upon himself in the expectation that it would result in a *parousia*—or manifestation—of the Jewish Messiah, of himself.[201] On another occasion, he prayed in the garden on the Mount of Olives as follows:

And he was withdrawn from them,
About a stone's cast,
And kneeled down,
And prayed,
Saying:
Father,
If thou be willing,
Remove this cup from me:
Nevertheless,
Not my will,
But thine,
Be done.[202]

The above prayer also makes it clear that Jesus never desired to die but prayed for his survival. When Jesus was at Gethsemane with his disciples, he took with him Peter, James and John for prayers. But after a while he told them to wait, himself going forward, and fell on the ground. Jesus prayed that the hour might pass for him. He said:

> Abba, Father,
> All things are possible unto thee
> Take away this cup from me:
> Nevertheless,
> Not what I will,
> But what thou wilt.[203]

It is understood that, apprehending danger to his life, Jesus went to Gethsemane, the garden on the Mount of Olives, and again at Gethsemane. He prayed thrice, imploring God that the cup of death be removed from him. He had already declared that all our prayers are heard by God, and his prayer was also heard. The cup of death was taken away from him, in a miraculous way.

Jesus had declared that he was the good shepherd, and he knew his sheep. He had predicted:

> And other sheep I have,
> Which are not of this fold:
> Them also I must bring,
> And they shall hear my voice;
> And there shall be one fold,
> And one shepherd.
> Therefore doth my Father love me,
> Because I lay down my life,
> That I might take it again.
> No man taketh it from me,
> But I lay it down of myself.
> I have power to lay it down,
> I have power to take it again.[204]

Here Jesus informs us that there are other tribes and races who are to be brought into his fold. He also tells us that these tribes and races will hear him and believe him. He declares that no man on earth can take his life, for his Father has given him power to lay down his life or take it again. This clearly reveals that nobody on this earth could kill Jesus, and even if they willed, he had full power over his life.

The Cross

The cross as a religious symbol originated in Jerusalem and then spread towards the east and the west. Prior to it, we have found the swastika, which has been termed by some as the "broken cross," in Iran and Central Asia, buried in ancient graves. Its history goes back to 5000 B.C. Proper crosses have been found at Kashan in Iran belonging to the pre-Christian era. Even a cross during the Muslim period in Iran and made by Mirjan bin Abdullah has been found. It is on a decorated wooden door with an Arabic inscription.[205]

It was some time before 1925 that Rev. Gergan, a neo-Christian of Ladakh, told the Moravian missionaries about the existence of the crosses in that region. Accordingly, A. H. Francke of the Mission at Leh published the photograph of one of them in 1925 in the *German Academy* magazine.[206] Crosses like these were located in Afghanistan, Kafirstan and the North West Frontier region of India. It was very significant that the crosses found at Tangtse in Ladakh were accompanied with inscriptions and the name of Jesus Christ. As these inscriptions were written in Aramaic, it was clear that they belonged to the first or the second century of the Christian era. Secondly, the existence of such crosses in the region on such a vast scale and covering such a vast region proved early migration of the Christians towards the east, not only the west. Tangtse is a large village situated in the Shayok valley, 61 miles from Leh by bridle path, at a height of 12,900 feet above sea level. Here, a resident of Samarkand, Charansar, who was probably a Tartar, had immortalized himself and his tribe by engraving these eight-pointed crosses with the name of "Yuzu" on boulders.

Initially the Christian scholars designated these inscriptions as belonging to the Sogdiens but later on changed their mind and attributed them to the Nestorians. The North India Expedition from Yale University to Kashmir in 1932 declared:

> Dr. de Terra and I examined the rock engravings at Drang-tse, a few miles west of the Panggong Tso. Apart from the intrinsic interest of the crosses and the Soghdian inscription described by these authors, the rock has certain other points of significance to the geologist and biologist. The inscriptions are cut in the dark brown patina or 'desert

varnish" and show white color of the granite beneath this patina. It is clear that no desert patination has occurred since the visit of the Nestorian from Samarkand.[207]

This shows that the Christian scholars wanted to sidetrack the main issue as to how Christian crosses with the name of Jesus had reached Ladakh in the North of Kashmir. According to another Christian scholar, these inscriptions were written in Syriac script, which was the ecclesiastical language of the Sogdiens, who were Nestorian Christians from Bactria.[208] However, the attribution of these crosses to the Nestorians was challenged by Tucci, when he declared that many crosses have been dug out in the Chinese territories and there exists an element of doubt in attributing these crosses to the Nestorians.[209] In fact, such crosses in the northwest of India can be identified as sign boards and symbols carried by early Christians to the East.

At Char-Sada, near Taxila, such crosses are shown on slabs with donkeys. These slabs also depict scenes of crucifixion and date back to about the first century. There are historical proofs of the existence of both Jesus and Thomas at Taxila. The discovery of the crosses in Ladakh also indicates the presence of Jesus in that country.

Crosses in Ladakh

CHAPTER FIVE

Jesus Christ in the East

I am not sent but unto the lost sheep of the house of Israel.
Matthew

IN THE LIGHT OF OUR NEW KNOWLEDGE of the Dead Sea Scrolls, it can scarcely be doubted that John the Baptist belonged to the Essenes. Jesus was baptized by him and his followers became attached to Jesus Christ.[1] Members belonging to this Order were termed as pious. They would hold their meetings very secretly away from habitations. Every member of this brotherhood had to take an oath that he would always take the side of justice, even at the cost of his life. They would use white garments and lead pious lives. Their conduct was orderly and neither bribe not torture could make them false to their brotherhood.[2] Joseph of Arimathea, Nicodemus and Mary Magdalene belonged to the same brotherhood. Jesus would often retire to the wilderness and mountains to meet these friends. When his enemies sought to take him, he would escape and take shelter in a secret place.[3] The Essenes had a secret shelter on the top of the Mount of Olives.[4] Jesus belonged to this brotherhood himself.[5] Some members of this very sect had entered the sepulchre to help Jesus out to safety. After having been saved, Jesus was nursed by them. Their writings have been unearthed from the Dead Sea, which reveal that Jesus lived with them after the event of the crucifixion.

Dead Sea Scrolls

A careful study of the Dead Sea Scrolls reveals that the Jews and their leaders left no stone unturned to persecute the True Master. They not only opposed him but scoffed at him and made him a

199

scapegoat by a wrong verdict. Jesus Christ, during his stay with the brotherhood of the Essenes, gives some details about his misfortunes and thanks God for saving him from out of the hands of his enemies. He declares:

> God, I thank Thee,
> For again giving me,
> A new lease of life.
> For saving me from death:
> And,
> Surrounding me,
> With a defensive wall.
> The cruel wanted to take my life,
> But,
> I stood firm on Your commandments.
> They are the supporters of the wicked,
> And,
> Do not understand Thee.
> Your grace is my guardian:
> Thou hast saved me;
> And,
> Thou willed that,
> They could not catch my soul.
> God,
> Thou came to the rescue of this humble servant,
> It is Thee,
> Who saved my life from the clutches of the powerful.

The above are excerpts from the prayers contained in the Dead Sea Scrolls. It is evident that the wicked wanted to persecute the True Master and then kill him. But he was saved by God and rescued from the enemy. Who is this True Master, who sings the praises of God? Who is he who thanks God for saving his life? The Dead Scrolls have established the link between Jesus Christ and the Essenes.

It is an historical fact that the Gospels have been revised and recast by various compilers from time to time. The net result has been that some very important material which informed us about matters not to the liking of the bishops has been deleted. One such example is the last page of the Gospel of Mark, which was salvaged by the famous Bible scholar, C. R. Gregory, who wrote *The Canon and the Text of the New Testament*.

The salvaged verses are as follows:

> And all the things announced,
> To those about Peter briefly:
> They spread about,
> And after that,
> Jesus himself appeared from the east,
> And out to the west he sent out,
> By them the sacred,
> And uncorrupted preaching,
> Of the eternal Salvations.
>   Amen.

The above verses, which were deleted from the Gospel of Mark, clearly inform us that Jesus appeared from the east and directed his disciples to spread his teachings in the west. This also proves his second life, which has altogether been suppressed by the Church.

Testament

Jesus Christ had prayed to God to save him, and he was saved. He had suffered untold miseries but he was always thankful to God.

> I was sold into slavery,
> And the Lord of all made me free:
> I was taken into captivity,
> And his strong hand succored me;
> I was beset with hunger,
> And the Lord himself nourished me:
> I was alone,
> And God comforted me:
> I was sick,
> And the Lord visited me:
> I was in prison,
> And my Lord showed favor to me;
> In bonds,
> And he released me.[6]

Here Jesus Christ tells about his misfortunes, imprisonment, captivity, illness, etc. and how God saved him. This is the testament of Jesus Christ, who himself claims that he was saved by God.

> O God, I thank thee,
> For bringing me
> Out of the well of death;
> Thou brought me on earth;
> So that I could traverse on its vast surface.

Flight of Jesus Christ

Jesus Christ told his disciples that he would not tell them about his destination because he wished to keep it as secret.

He rose and hastily went away through the gathering mist. It was rumored that he had been taken up by the clouds. This was simply a mythological tale.[7]

Jesus, though officially crucified in about 30 A.D., escaped alive towards the East, and in about 36 A.D. was seen on the road to Damascus by Paul, who had been sent by the Romans to bring him back for a second crucifixion.[8]

The Conversion of Paul

Paul had been deputed by the Romans to intercept Jesus Christ. He had journeyed to Damascus, when he heard a voice; "Saul, why persecutest thou me?" He asked who he was. He heard:

> I am Jesus whom thou persecutest;
> It is hard for thee to kick
> against the pricks.
> Arise and go into the city,
> And it shall be told thee
> What thou must do."[9]

Jesus had a disciple at Damascus named Ananias, who was directed by him to go to Paul, and inform him that he was the chosen vessel, and that he must preach in the name of Jesus Christ in Israel.[10]

Accordingly, Paul contacted the other disciples of Jesus Christ and spent a few days with them at Damascus. After that he preached Christ in the synagogues and made many converts.[11] He also went to Jerusalem and then to Tarsus, and continued missionary activities in collaboration with Barnabas and John.[12] The above account has

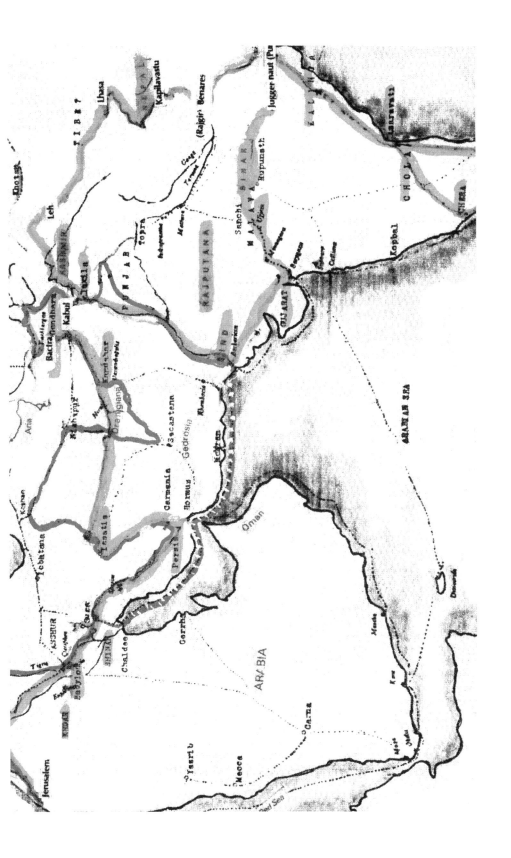

been called a vision by the compilers of "Acts." Visions are real and do exist, but they do not arise in dull brains. After all, Paul was only a tent-maker.[13]

The Apostles still feared that the Romans might pursue Christ, and thus invented the theory of visions, and intermingled fact with imagination. Another confusion arises about Paul, because he was also known as Saul in the beginning.[14] If a vision could be termed unreal, then the basis of all mythology in the world would be removed and we would be left blank. Most of the stories given in mythology have now stood the scientific test. Was the great flood during the day of Noah a vision? Was the space craft of Ezekiel a vision? If all these facts are visions, then the virgin birth of Jesus, his crucifixion, and even his existence on this earth could be termed as a vision and there would arise no need to believe in Jesus Christ or his mission. It is a historical fact that Paul conducted a series of long missionary tours to far-off countries, including Greece and Asia Minor.[15]

Jesus Christ lived in the house of Ananias at that time. But when the Jews sent a commission to Damascus, he left the place and reached Babylon. As he had visited the East in his childhood, he knew the routes and topography of these countries. He had already been saved and now on this strange odyssey, God guided him, so that he could be saved from further persecution.[16] Jesus and his mother had to migrate from Palestine and they departed for a far-off country. Both of them traversed from country to country.[17] Some of his devotees followed him from place to place. During his journey toward the East, Jesus was accompanied by Mary his Mother, Peter the Apostle, and another Mary who can be no other person than Mary Magdalene. It cannot be denied that Mary Magdalene had taken a personal interest in the affairs of Jesus Christ. She had been possessed by demons which were cast out by the Lord.[18] She had stood by the cross during the time of the crucifixion.[19] She watched the burial of Jesus Christ and came early to the sepulchre.[20] She also saw the risen Lord, and the event is described in the Gospel of John as follows:

> But Mary stood without at the sepulchre,
> And as she wept,
> She stooped down,

And looked into the sepulchre,
And seeth two angels in white sitting,
The one at the head,
And the other at the feet,
Where the body of Jesus had lain.[21]
Jesus saith unto her, Mary,
She turned herself, and saith unto him,
Rabboni;
Which is to say,
Master.[22]

According to the Gospel of Philip, Mary Magdalene was the consort of Jesus Christ. As such, it is obvious that of the two who accompanied Jesus Christ on his migration towards the east, one was Mary, the mother of the Lord, while the other one must have been Mary Magdalene, the consort of Jesus Christ.[23]

It is a strange coincidence that the successor of Buddha has been called Rahula. When he is separated from his mother, a lady devotee named Magdaliyana acts as a messenger between him and the mother. The word Rahula may mean *Ruh-Allah*, or the Spirit of God, and Magdaliyana, the lady messenger, may refer to Mary Magdalene, who was so much attached to Jesus Christ.[24] It is also strange that the Tomb of Mary has been located about six miles from Kashgar in Central Asia.

It is probable that the tomb in question is that of Mary Magdalene.[25]

Jesus Christ in Parthia

We are informed by the Gospel of Philip that after having been saved from crucifixion, Jesus Christ was nursed by his friends and disciples and remained in hiding for some time. During this period, he imparted special spiritual knowledge to Peter and James. After having remained with them for a period of about one year and a half, he made up his mind to leave them. He appointed James as his successor and migrated.[26] It has already been mentioned that Thomas had already been deputed to Parthia and India by Jesus. As such, it is but natural that Jesus Christ felt safe to travel in these lands. At that period, the Parthian empire extended right from Antioch and Palmyria to Kabul on one side and from the Caspian Sea to the Arabian Sea. He wanted to avoid the limits of the Romans and, as such, took the first opportunity to reach Damascus. From that place he went to the city of Nisibis, which had a colony of exiled Jews.[27] The city, being the meeting ground of many caravan routes, was full of men of all nations busy in trade and commerce.[28] Jesus Christ tried his best to conceal his identity, and it was at this place that he came to be known as Yuzu-Asaph. He wore clothes and a turban of white fleece and carried a rod in his hand. He set a seal of silence on his lips, and began his journey further.[29] Nisibis lay on the silk route from Syria to Mossul and beyond, towards the east. Jesus had traveled incognito to this place.

Nisibis

It is related by Josephus that the king of Adiabene sent his son Ezad to stay with Abennerigos, the king of Spasinou Charax, at the head of the Persian Gulf. The small principality of Adiabene existed between Tabriz and Mossul, on the banks of the river Tigris. Ezad returned home to ascend the throne of Adiabene on the death of his father. It was Ananias who had converted Ezad and his queens. After some years the king of Parthia accorded him to rule over Nisibis with the result that his kingdom extended right up to the banks of the Mediterranean.[30] We know already that it was Ananias who had reached Jerusalem with a letter from Abgar Ukkama for Jesus. It was too late and Jesus had been crucified. It was Thomas who gave the shroud to him for Abgar. Both Ezad and Abgar were contemporaries of Jesus Christ. If seems that from Damascus Jesus and his party reached Nisibis, which was a safe place for them. Maybe Ananias wished to carry Jesus to Edessa but the proximity of the Roman capitol prevented Jesus from proceeding westward. As such, Jesus moved towards the east and reached Mossul, and from that place to Babylon, which was on the banks of the Euphrates.

We are informed that Jesus preached his doctrines in Nisibis and many accepted him. At the same time the orthodox became his enemies and tried to kill him.[31] Early evidence of Christianity at Nisibis is provided by an inscription on a grave which reads as follows:

I saw the Syrian plain, and all the cities—even Nisibis, having crossed the Euphrates.

Everywhere I found people with whom to speak.[32]

Jesus in Persia

From Babylon, Jesus proceeded to Ur and from that place to Kharax, which was the capital of the kingdom of Mesene. It was the main port to which ships brought the products of India and the far east. From that place, the goods were transported up the river Euphrates to Babylon, then to Arbel in Adiabene and thence to Nisibis and Edessa in the west.[33] It was possible for Jesus to take a sea route to India but he avoided it and instead crossed into the Persian empire.

In Persian works, we hear about Yuzu-Asaph, which means Yuzu, who is the leader of those lepers who have been cured by him. Here is the report given in the Persian dictionary:

> In the days of Hazrat Isa, when lepers were cured by him, they, on being admitted among the healthy people, were known as Asaph. Thus Hazrat Isa, who cured lepers, also came to be known as Yuzu-Asaph, for he not only cured them but gathered them under his merciful protection.[34]

Jesus Christ was known in Persia as Yuzu-Asaph. His sayings and teachings in the region, as recorded in the Iranian traditions, are the same as those of Jesus Christ.[35] This shows that his preachings were popular among the Persians. It is clear that after the advent of Islam, the Christians, the Jews and the Zoroastrians lost importance and were reduced in numbers. But the sayings and parables of Jesus Christ continued in their traditions and lived afterwards as those of Yuz-Asaph. From Nisibis two routes led toward the east; one passed through Nishapur and Herat to Kabul, and the other through Susa, and Hermuz to Sind. Jesus Christ took the former route.

It may be recalled that from the beginning of the second millennium B.C. till about 1200 B.C., the Hittites inhabited Asia Minor. From the middle of the 13th century B.C. the Hurrians formed one of the most powerful states of western Asia, which included Mesopotamia,

Syria, and Assyria. The Hurrians worshipped the Indian gods Varuna, Indra, Mittra, and the Matsiya, besides other deities. The Assyrians consolidated their supremacy in the region at the end of the 9th century B.C. However, the creators of the first flowering of civilization which connected the east with the west were the Sumerians, who had settled in Mesopotamia in about 3000 B.C.[36]

It may be mentioned that trade routes, both by sea and land, between India and other countries in the west have existed since ancient times. It was in about 3100 B.C. that the seafaring Sumerians established their colonies in the Indus Valley region, right from Mohenjo-daro to Kashmir. They exploited the economic and commercial resources of the region. The Sumerian seals excavated at Mohenjo-daro and Harappa have revealed that the Indus Valley region was an abode of Amorites or the seafaring people, who were fire and sun worshippers.[37]

From Kabul, the trade route went to Peshawar, and then to Taxila. Jesus Christ and his companions had to bear many hardships during their travel from Herat to Kabul, and then to Taxila. They had lived on wild fruits and vegetables. Jesus Christ had walked on foot, but some of his companions brought a horse for him. Jesus refused to have the horse, and journeyed on foot. During his travels he had to face many hardships. It is reported that he was arrested, but as he had healed the sick, the governor of the city became his devotee. Many among the people and the soldiers became his disciples. He preached among them and they became happy to hear his words.[38]

Apostolate

We do not have much information as to what happened to the followers, friends and devotees of Jesus Christ after his departure towards the East. One thing is clear: that the hostility of the Jews to the followers of Christianity became increasingly implacable. We know that James, the brother of Jesus Christ, was chosen as their leader by the early Christian community at Jerusalem. But Herod Agrippa took savage measures against him and got him executed. It is also recorded that Peter was also imprisoned by him. Thus, the early Apostolate was shifted to Antioch in Syria. It was here that Paul met Peter and got himself enlisted as the disciple of the Lord.[39] It is to his credit that he carried the message of Jesus Christ to far-off lands. His Apostles carried his mission through the ancient trade routes to various cities of Arabia, Syria, Rome, Alexandria, Italy, Egypt, Persia and Armenia.

Through the efforts of the Apostles, Christianity became very popular among the masses. Seeing this, the enmity of the followers of Judaism toward the new faith became acute. The Apostles had preached among the poor with the result that a good number of the Pagans became Christians. The Jews could not tolerate the popularity of Christianity and thought of doing something to attract the masses. Out of frustration, they raised up the banner of revolt against the Romans, who had subjugated the Holy Land. The Pharisees saw that it was absolutely necessary for them to establish their own theocratic kingdom. But they failed against the might of the Romans, who ravaged and destroyed nearly all Jewish settlements. The Roman soldiers stormed Jerusalem and burnt down the Temple in 70 A.D. Thousands perished in the revolt, but many more thousands were carried off as slaves by the Romans. According to one estimate, nearly eleven thousand prisoners died of starvation.[40] While lamenting over Jerusalem, Jesus Christ had already predicted its destruction:

> O Jerusalem,
> Jerusalem,
> Thou that kills the prophets,
> And stonest them which are sent to thee,
> Behold,
> Your house is left unto you desolate
> For I say unto you,
> Ye shall not see me henceforth.[41]

The Romans wanted to annihilate the Jews from their camps. As such they devastated their settlements by killing all capable of bearing arms. Josephus has described the destruction of the Jews as follows:

One could see the whole lake red with blood and covered with corpses, for not a man escaped.[42]

Thus, it would be seen that the mission of Judaism failed but the kingdom of God remained solid as a rock.

Jesus delivered many sermons in Persia, and he was welcomed by the people, who listened to him devoutly. The high priest got him arrested, and he was asked about which new God he was speaking to the people when Zoroaster only had the privilege of communion with the Supreme Being. He was also told that the laws were given to Zoroaster by God, and he should not sow doubts in the heart of believers. On hearing this, Jesus said unto them:

It is not of a new God that I speak:
But of our Heavenly Father,
Who has existed since all time;
And who will still be after,
The end of all things.
It is of Him,
That I have discoursed to the people,
Who,
Like unto innocent children,
Are not yet capable,
Of comprehending God,
By the simple strength of their intelligence;
Or of Penetrating,
Into His divine,
And spiritual sublimity.[43]

In the Name of the Heavenly Father

Jesus told them that he spoke in the name of the Heavenly Father. He explained that just as a baby discovers in the darkness its mother's breast, in the same way, people who have been led into error by erroneous doctrine do recognize by instinct their Heavenly Father.

Jesus paused a while in many a hamlet, town and city in Persia. He preached and healed among the common people, who followed him in throngs. He also attended a feast in Persepolis. He spoke to the priests in these words:

There is a Silence where the soul may meet its God,
And there the fount of wisdom is,
And all who enter are immersed in light,
And filled with wisdom, love and power.
The Silence is not circumscribed;
Is not a place closed in with wall, or rocky steeps,
Nor guarded by the swords of men!
Men carry with them all the time the secret place,
Where they may meet their God.
It matters not where men abide,
On mountain top, in deepest vale or in the quiet home;
They may at once,
At any time,
Flung wide the door,
And find the Silence,
Find the house of God:
It is within the soul.[44]

During his short sojourn in Persia, Jesus sat in silence in the prayer hall of the Magi priests for seven days. Then he spoke on the origin of evil and good.

He told them not to worship the Sun, for it was but a part of the cosmos which God has created for humanity. It is to God and to God alone that we owe all that we possess in this world. On hearing him, the priests asked how could a people live according to the rules of justice if it had no preceptor? Jesus replied that so long as the people had no priests, the natural law governed them, and they preserved the candor of their souls. He further explained that, when their souls were with God, they could commune with the Father without the medium of any idol or animal or the Sun or the fire. He said:

You contend,
That one must worship the sun,
The spirit of good and of evil:
Well:
I say unto you;
Your doctrine is a false one:
The sun acting not spontaneously,
But according to the will of,
The invisible Creator,
Who gave it birth.

The Eternal Spirit is the soul of all,
That is animate.
You commit a great sin in dividing it,
Into a spirit of evil,
And a spirit of good:
For there is no God outside the good.
Who,
Like unto the father of a family,
Does but good to His children,
Forgiving all their faults:
If they repent.
Wherefore I say unto you,
Beware of the day of judgment,
For God will inflict a terrible chastisement.
Upon all those,
Who shall have led His Children astray,
From the right path.[45]

We have no information about the route taken by Jesus and his companions on their onward march towards the East. Maybe they visited Hamadan and Nishapur, from which city there are two roads, one leading to Afghanistan via Herat and thence to Kandhar and the other leading to Bokhara and Samarkand. The tomb of Mary Magdalene has been located near Kashgar in Central Asia. It is probable that Jesus took her to Bokhara, then to Samarkand and thence to Kashgar. After her demise, Jesus came back to Balkh and thence took the route along the bank of the river Indus and reached Sind. We will deal with this odyssey in subsequent pages.

Jesus in Sind

It is of value, at this point in the narrative, to examine the various sources we have that give us evidence concerning the "missing years of Jesus"—from the age of thirteen through twenty-nine, when he returned to Israel. In a previous chapter we made a brief reference to his stay in India during that time. It is our belief that it was as a result of the profound learnings made by Jesus during this earlier stay in the East that he now knew that his life, having been completed in the West, concerned his mission there.

Let us examine these sources. Piecing together many documents including *The Life of St. Issa, The Aquarian Gospel of Jesus the Christ* and *The Unknown Life of Jesus Christ* (among others) tells us that at the age of thirteen, Jesus left his parental house in secret and departed with the merchants toward Sind.[46] His main object in leaving his country was to perfect himself in the Divine Word and to study the law of great Buddhas.[47]

In the course of his fourteenth year he reached Sind and established himself among the Aryans. After crossing the five rivers of the Punjab, he reached Rajputana and from that region, he proceeded towards Gujarat. Here he came into contact with the followers of Jainism. His fame had spread throughout and the Jains requested him to dwell among them. But he proceeded further and reached Orissa and was welcomed by the priests. They taught him the occult sciences.

He then went to the holy cities of Rajagiri and Benaras and everyone loved him. He had spent six years in his travels. As he freely mixed with the low caste *Vaishyas* and *Shudras*, the upper caste *Brahmanas* and *Khistriyas* disliked his attitude. They told him:

> Death only can set them free,
> From their servitude:
> Leave them then,
> And come;
> And worship with us,
> The gods,
> Who will become incensed,
> Against thee;
> If thou dost disobey them.[48]

But he did not listen to their discourses and disliked their attitude. After that event he started preaching against the *Brahmanas* and the *Khistriyas*. When Jesus saw the *Shudras* and the *Vaishyas* drawing near him, he said:

> The Holy One has said:
> That all his children shall be free,
> And every soul is a child of God.

The Shudras shall be as free as priests,
The farmer shall walk hand in hand with the king;
For all the world will own the brotherhood of man.
O men,
Arise.
Be conscious of your powers,
For he who wills need not remain a slave.
Just live as you would have your brother live,
Unfold each day as does the flower;
For earth is yours,
And God will bring you to your own.[49]

Sermons

Jesus inveighed against the act of a man arrogating to himself the power to deprive his fellow beings of their rights of humanity. He had spent nearly six years in India and could speak in the local language. He lived with the poor masses, to whom he gave many sermons. He preached:

God, the Father,
Makes no difference between His children,
All to Him are equally dear.
Fear thy God,
Bend the knee before Him alone,
Bring thy offerings to Him alone.[50]

He denied the gods invented by the people and told them that God has willed and created the universe. He alone has existed since all eternity, and His existence will have no end. He has no equal either in the heavens or on earth and has not shared His power with any living being. He alone is omnipotent!

He willed it,
And the world appeared;
In a divine thought:
He gathered together;
The waters,
Separating from them,
The dry portion of the globe.
He is the principle,

Of the mysterious existence of man,
In whom,
He has breathed,
A part of His Being.[51]

He warned them as follows:

The anger of God,
Will soon be let loose against man,
For he has forgotten his Creator;
For he has filled His temples,
With abominations;
For he worships;
A crowd of creatures,
Which God hath made subordinate to him.
For to do honor to stones and metals,
He sacrifices human beings,
In whom dwells,
A part of the spirit of the Most High.
Those,
Who deprive their brethren,
Of divine happiness;
Shall be deprived of it themselves.[52]

Jesus taught equality of human beings and made a prophesy that the *Brahmanas* and the *Khistriyas* shall become the *Shudras*; and with the *Shudras,* God shall dwell everlastingly. He told them that on the day of the last judgment, the *Shudras* and the *Vaishyas* will be forgiven because of their ignorance, while the *Brahmanas* and the *Khistriyas* shall be punished for their arrogance.

The above sermons of Jesus contain much philosophical content. He talks of God as the Father of all human beings and exhorts all to bow before him alone. He is the eternal soul and the impetus behind all creation; His will separated water from earth, created the continents. To Him, there is no difference between human beings, for all are His children. As such, all have to bow before Him, and none else.

His words and works caused unrest through all the land. The poor followed him in throngs but the priests resolved to drive him out of India. All the *Brahmana* priests met in a council and employed a murderer with the mission to kill Jesus.[53]

In Communion with Buddha

Having been informed about the plot and advised by friends to depart, Jesus left the place by night. With haste, he journeyed to the north, and reached Kapilavastu, the birthplace of Sakyamuni Buddha. The Buddhists opened wide the doors of a monastery for him, and he started living among the monks. He witnessed their religious rites and participated in their prayers. A time came when he fully understood the words of the Master and began to teach on the same lines. The head lama declared in a congregation:

> We stand today upon a crest of time,
> Six times ago a master soul was born,

Buddha, Kashmir, 8th century

Who gave a glory light to man,
And now a master sage stands here.
This Hebrew prophet is the rising star of wisdom,
He brings to us a knowledge of God;
And all the world will hear his words,
Will heed his words,
And glorify his name.[54]

Departure

He lived among the Buddhists for six years. He learned and taught in the monastery where he abode.

> Whom the Buddha had elected to spread his holy word, had become a perfect expositor of the sacred writings.[55]

Then he left Nepal and the Himalayan mountains and went towards the West, preaching to the diverse peoples the supreme perfection of man in these words:

> He who shall have regained his original purity;
> Will die having obtained,
> Remission for his sins;
> And he will have the right,
> To contemplate the majesty of God.
> The Eternal Law-giver is one;
> There is no other God but Him;
> He has not shared the world with anyone,
> Neither has He informed anyone of,
> His intentions.

One day, in silent meditation, Jesus sat beside a spring among the poor people. He saw the hard-drawn lines of toil on every brow, and his heart was stirred with pity for these poor toilers, and he said:

> Cease to seek for heaven in the sky;
> Just open up the windows of your hearts,
> And like a flood of light,
> Heaven will come,
> And bring a boundless joy;
> Then toil will be no cruel task.[56]

Jesus continued his sermon as follows:

> Even as a father would act.
> Towards his children,
> So will God judge men,
> After their deaths:
> According to the Laws of his mercy.
> Never would he so humiliate his child,
> As to transmigrate his soul,
> As in a purgatory,
> Into the body of an animal.[57]

Here, Jesus speaks of God as Father and human beings as his children. God the father, being merciful, will judge every one according to the laws of mercy and never would humiliate his children. According to the above text, he further explains as follows:

> All things have been sacrificed to man,
> Who is directly,
> And intimately,
> Associated with Me:
> His Father:
> Therefore,
> He who shall have stolen from
> Me:
> My child;
> Will be severely judged,
> And chastised by the divine law.

Here Jesus speaks of God as the father of humanity, which is intimately and directly connected with him. According to him, all men are his children and he is the father to them.

> Man is naught before the eternal Judge,
> As the animal is naught before man.
> Wherefore,
> I say unto thee:
> Leave your idols;
> And perform not rites,
> Which separate you from your Father:
> Associate ye not with the priests,

From whom the heavens,
Have turned away.[58]

The Tibetan Gospel

The above narrative, translated by Nicolas Notovitch from several scrolls found in the Hemis monastery in Ladakh, provides invaluable information about the missing years of Jesus.

Hippolytus, the Bishop of Rome in about 220 A.D., mentions a Judaeo-Christian scripture of the land of the Seres in Parthia. According to an old tradition, this holy book of revelations had fallen from heaven, and dealt with the "Hidden power." Eli the Prophet, who was the incarnation of God, received it. During the period of Hippolytus, the name Seres denoted a nation which produced silk and lived above India. Thus, the holy book of revelation was the Tibetan Gospel.[59] It is interesting to note that Nicolas Notovitch translated the scrolls about the life of Jesus from the Hemis monastery in Ladakh. It is also important that the western Christians of the third century knew of the Eastern books on Christianity. The Hemis scrolls, therefore, are not as unusual as these seemed to be at first sight.[60]

This would reveal that Jesus was very much respected by the common people, who adored him and wished that he could stay with them. The above scrolls also establish the fact that Jesus learned many occult sciences in India.

According to the Hemis scrolls, Jesus had been elected to remind a deprived humanity of the true God. Since his departure from Jerusalem, the pagans had inflicted still more atrocious sufferings on the Israelites. Many among them had already begun to abandon the laws of their God and those of Moses in the hope of appeasing their savage conquerors.[61]

Nicolas Notovitch published his translation of the Hemis scrolls in 1890, calling his work, *The Life of Saint Issa*. Subsequently in 1894 the book was published in French entitled, *La Vie Inconnue de Jesus* and in English as *The Unknown Life of Christ*. At the time of publication of his work, Notovitch knew that the Church would repudiate his find as a fabrication. He therefore suggested organization of a scien-

Ladakh, the land of celebrations

tific expedition to Ladakh for verification of his discovery. From the outset, the book became a source of great controversy. The Church denied the very existence of Nicolas Notovitch and even of the Hemis monastery. But when it came to light that Nicolas Notovitch had visited Kashmir and Ladakh and met many important officials of the Indian and state governments, the Church took another course. At the insistence of the Church, the then British government in India directed the famous Orientalist, Max Muller, and a professor of Agra, Archibald Douglas, to conduct on-the-spot inquiries. Both of them published their findings in newspapers and concluded that Nicolas Notovitch was a fraud.[62] In 1894, the Church deputed a neo-convert, Ahmad Shah, to Ladakh in the disguise of a *hakim*, but with the main aim to find any means "to refute the findings of Nicolas Notovitch."[63] He remained in Ladakh for four years and wrote a book with the title of *Four Years in Tibet*. It is probable that out of the great fear of the then British Government in India, the Buddhist lama concealed the scrolls or handed over some fragments to Ahmad Shah.

In 1922, Swami Abhedananda, the world famous Vedantist, visited Ladakh and learned from the lamas of the Hemis monastery that the account about the coming of Jesus Christ to India was indeed correct.[64] With the help of the lama, he obtained a translation of a few pages from the Tibetan manuscript. We will conclude this issue with the remark that the Buddhists of Ladakh and Tibet have scrolls about the life of Jesus hidden among the innumerable manuscripts housed in dark cells. According to the Buddhists, Jesus had become a perfect expositor of the sacred writings, for he had been elected by Buddha to spread his holy word.[65]

Buddhism and Christianity

Buddhism and Christianity have many similarities. The following information recorded in 1812 by a traveller to Ladakh is interesting:

> Every Tibetan makes one of his sons a Lama, or one who has forsaken the world. Both male and female Lamas remain unmarried, and are the spiritual guides of the people. They do not worship the idols kept in their temples, which they declare are merely representations

Mask dance at Hemis, Ladakh

of departed saints and Lamas, to contemplate which is considered an act of piety. When a Lama or great man dies, his body is burned, and a sculptured representation of him is placed on his tomb. Some of these figures are said to represent a certain prophet who is still alive in the waters and forests, the former being under his complete control. Others again consider the figure to represent a prophet who is living in the heavens, which would appear to point to Jesus Christ. The Tibetans consider their scripture to be inspired; this book contains many moral precepts and exhortations to worship God, to fulfill a promise, to speak the truth, to abandon what is evil, and such like. It also commands that if any man take away thy sheet give him thy cloak also. Again, 'if any man strike thee on one cheek tell him so strike the other also'. With the exception of the custom of burning the dead, many of their observances are similar to those of Christians.

The traveler noticed other similarities which are noteworthy and are reproduced below:

They are forbidden to eat the flesh of the horse or camel, and they are allowed but one wife. Their great feast again is held at the time when the sun enters Capricorn, corresponding with Christmas. From this time their year commences, but I was unable to ascertain the exact date. Another similar custom is that a man, when taking an oath, swears by Kunchok-Sum. Kunchok meaning God, and Sum, three, that is by the three Gods of the Trinity. In the infliction on themselves of heavy penances also, the Lamas resemble Christian priests. I was informed by an aged man that he had ascertained beyond all doubt that some portions of the Bible had been revealed to the Tibetans, but that, in consequence of their not being in possession of the whole book, the practices of burning the dead, and the doctrine of transmigration of souls have been admitted as a portion of their practice, and faith. The Tibetans assert that their original scripture was in a language now become unintelligible to them, and has been translated into their own tongue.[66]

It may be pointed out that striking similarities between the moral teachings of Buddha and Jesus Christ lead us to think that Mahayana Buddhism borrowed much from Christianity. When we look at the events and the timing of the Fourth Buddhist Council, this possibility becomes even more plausible, since the Council took place at a time when sources place him and his followers in that part of the world.

The Fourth Buddhist Council

Several legends have depicted the great Kushana king, Kanishka as the patron of Buddhism. He is said to have convened the 4th Buddhist Council in Kashmir in about 78 A.D. Besides a large audience, this Council was attended to by 500 *Arhats*, 500 *Bodhisattvas* and 500 *Pandittas*. This Council paved the way for the acceptance of Mahayana, the progressive school of thought in Buddhism.[67] It is recorded in the Buddhist canon that after the Buddha, another redeemer or the next *Bodhisattva* will come, and he will be called *Metteyya*. He will be the leader of a band of disciples.[68] It is for this reason that the Buddhist Lamas reached Palestine, in search of their Bodhisattva, at the time of the birth of Jesus. It is also recorded in the prophesy concerning *Metteyya* that he will come at the time when the religion of the Buddha will be forgotten and the new Bodhisattva will show them the way. In this context, it remains to be seen as to what part Jesus played—if he actually did—in the 4th Buddhist Council held in Kashmir.

It may be mentioned that the word *Metteyya* is no other than the word Messiah, because the sound of "t" changes into "s" in Arabic or Persian.[69] It is interesting to note that Jesus is mentioned as *Mi-shi-ho* in the Chinese Buddhist canon of the 8th century A.D.[70] Examination of Buddhist iconography shows that all Bodhisattvas stand or sit on a lotus throne. Some show their hands and palms with round marks. Those statues of the Mahayana period, with marks on palms and feet, symbolically depict the wounds of crucifixion. This fact is immortal evidence for the identity of Jesus as the teacher of the Mahayana monks.[71]

We are struck by the extraordinary similarity between the doctrines and rituals of Buddhism and the Catholic Church. The dress of the monks in both the religions was remarkably the same, as can be verified from early paintings. "The ranks of the various orders in the Monasteries bear a resemblance to the monastic orders in the Roman Church. The Buddhists make suffrages, alms, prayers and sacrifices like the Catholics, and the Buddhists take vows of celibacy, poverty, chastity and obedience like the Catholic monks. The Buddhists use holy water and singing services. The Buddhist liturgy also resembles the Eastern Christian liturgies.[72]

It may be pointed out that due to the striking similarity between the two religions, most thinkers believe that Christianity is the Buddhism of the West. Both Jesus as well as Buddha are called Saviours in their respective scriptures and it is a strange coincidence that both make the same claim when they say: I am the Light and the Way.[73] Titles which have been ascribed to Jesus in the Gospels have been similarly ascribed to the Buddha in the Buddhist scriptures. Both have called themselves Light, Master, Blessed, Prince and the Refuge. Both fasted at the time of temptation and the fast lasted for forty days.

The Buddha describes alms-giving as "good seed sown on good soil that yields an abundance of fruits." Jesus says the same thing when he says that alms-giving means providing ourselves "with a treasure in the heaven."[74] In the *Lalita Vistara*, a famous Buddhist scripture, the Buddha declares that "the shepherd who is full of wisdom" will guide those who have fallen over the great precipice." In the same manner, Jesus Christ says:

> I am the good shepherd:
> The good shepherd giveth his life for the sheep.[75]

There is a striking resemblance between the teachings of both the masters. It seems that Buddhism had prepared the way for Christianity. It is a historical fact that Ashoka collected about eighty thousand Buddhist monks who were sent by him for missionary work to China, Persia, Babylonia, Syria, Palestine and Egypt. It was due to the influence of their teachings that many mystical sects like the Therapeutae, Essenes and Zoroastrians became popular among the followers of Judaism. Jesus had received his early education under the guidance of the Essene masters and it is for this reason that we find traces among them of Buddhist virtues like nonviolence, brotherhood, kindness, love and piety.

As times passes on, documents are forthcoming which show that Jesus visited Tibet and Ladakh. According to one source, Jesus went to Tibet and stayed for some time in the chief monastery. He did not preach there but absorbed himself in meditation. After some time, he reached Ladakh and was received well by the Buddhist monks.

Jesus Approaching Ladakh.
Oil painting by J. Michael Spooner, published in the *Lost Years of Jesus*
by Elizabeth Clare Prophet.
Courtesy: Summit University Press, Livingstone.

There he healed a dying child, and his fame spread far and wide. He said in a sermon:

> My Father God is king of all mankind.
> And he has sent me forth,
> With all the bounties of his matchless love,
> And boundless wealth:
> I go my way,
> But we will meet again;
> For in my Fatherland is room for all,
> I will prepare a place for you.

Jesus raised his hands in silent benediction, and then went his way.[76]

They Seek Miracles

Jesus Christ preached against idol worship saying:

> Wherefore I say unto you,
> Leave your idols,
> And perform not rites.
> Which separate you from your Father.[77]

For the reproaches he made against them, the priests asked him to do a miracle. But he answered:

> The miracles of our God have been worked.
> Since the first day;
> When the universe was created;
> They take place every day,
> And at every moment;
> Whosoever seeth them not,
> Is deprived,
> Of one of the fairest gifts of life.
> But woe unto you.
> Ye enemies of men!
> If it be not a favor that you await.
> But rather the wrath of the Father;
> Woe unto you.
> If ye expect miracles,
> To bear witness to His power.[78]

Seeing the powerlessness of their priests, the pagan people developed a great faith in the saying of Jesus. They broke their idols to pieces, and the priests fled away to safety. Jesus told the people not to strive to see God with their own eyes, but to endeavor to feel him in their hearts. He further preached:

> Abstain from consuming human sacrifices;
> Immolate no creature to whom life has been given;
> Do not steal the goods of your neighbor;
> Deceive no one so as not to be yourselves deceived.

Jesus Christ then passed by the way of Kashmir, where he joined a caravan of merchants. When they heard him speak like a prophet, and when they came to know that he wanted to travel to Persia, they gave him a Bactrian beast. Having reached the Punjab, Jesus performed many miracles and healed many among the sick.[79]

Thomas the Apostle of India

Thomas, who was also called Didymus, holds the seventh position among the chief disciples of Jesus Christ. He considered Jesus as his God.[80] His real name was Judas and as such his Gospel is known as the Acts of Judas Thomas. He is considered to be the twin brother of Jesus. When the disciples of the Lord divided the whole world for missionary work, India fell to his lot. He is known as the apostle of Parthia and India.[81] In the beginning, he was reluctant to go on a long journey, for he wanted to die for Jesus Christ.[82]

At that time, an Indian merchant named Habban arrived in the south of Palestine. In obedience to the commands of the Master, Thomas sailed with Habban towards the east.[83]

At the time of nominating his disciples, Jesus had asked him to work within the Parthian empire, which included the northwestern areas of India also. The Parthian empire extended from the Euphrates to the Indus and from the Arabian Sea to the Caspian Sea. Thomas was known as the evangelist of Parthia and India.[84] He preached to the Parthians, Medes, Persians, Bactrians, Indians and Hyrecaneans.[85]

Among the Graeco-Bactrian rulers of Kashmir whose coins have been found in that region, mention may be made of Euthydemus (220 B.C.), Eucratides (180 B.C.), Hippostratus (140 B.C.), Menander the Great (110 B.C.), Antimacjus II (100 B.C.), Azilises (20 B.C.), Spalagadames, Vonoes, Spalyrises (10 A.D.), Gondaphares (50 A.D.), and Abdagases (100 A.D.). It was during the rule of Gondaphares that Thomas crossed the borders of India. Then he reached Attock, where he was introduced to the ruler, Gondaphares, by Abdagases.[86] Gondaphares, after combining the territories held by the Parthians and the Sakes, had established his kingdom in the northwest of India, and reigned from 21 A.D. to 50 A.D.[87] It was in about 48 A.D. that Thomas supervised the building of the palace for the king.

In the meanwhile, Jesus, along with his mother and a few disciples, reached Taxila. He was invited by the king to attend the marriage ceremony of Abdagases. Circumstances leading to the meeting of Jesus with Thomas will be dealt with subsequently.

Taxila

The valley of Taxila, near Rawalpindi in Pakistan, occupies an important place on the trade routes which used to connect India with central and western Asia. In the beginning of the fifth century B.C. it formed an important region, included in the Achaemenid Empire of Persia. It was in 326 B.C. that Alexander the Great halted here for some weeks as a guest of Ambhi, the king of Taxila. The Bactrians occupied the region in about 231 B.C. with the result that many Buddhists migrated from this place to Khotan.[88] Taxila was swept away by the Scythians and the Parthians in about the first century B.C. After the death of Azes II, the kingdoms of Taxila and Arachosia were united under the rule of Gondaphares, who figures in early Christian writings of the same period as the king to whose court Thomas the Apostle was sent.[89]

In the Kingdom of Gondaphares

Our task in locating the places visited by Jesus becomes very difficult for the reason that during this period northwestern India witnessed many political upheavals. Information obtained from various sources reveal that the region came under the control of many kings, fighting each other for supremacy. We find the Scythian overlords trying to oust the Parthian, with the result that Gondaphares seems to have controlled the northern regions, with his capital at Taxila. We have some references to him and his brother Gad, and it is now established that Gondaphares ruled in Taxila during 25-60 A.D. Coins of the period, and some inscriptions found at Takht Bhai, are conclusive proof of the fact that Gondaphares established a kingdom during the period.[90] Coins of Gondaphares have been found in Kashmir also. Antiquities relating to him, his brother Gad, and Abdagases have been excavated at Char Sadah.[91] Among the antiquities found there, the statues of Thomas and Peter have been identified. Archeological findings at Char Sadah also include a large number of slabs exhibiting crucifixion. All this establishes the fact that Char Sadah had become an important center of Christianity in the mid-first century A.D.

Gondaphares as a Christian king, first-century stone slab

Among the famous relics found at Taxila is an inscription in Aramaic mentioning construction of a palace of cedar and ivory by a foreign carpenter who was a pious devotee of the Son of God.[92] The inscription reads as follows:

> Dear foreign carpenter,
> Pious devotee of the Son of God,
> Built this palace of cedar and ivory,
> For the king.

In the inscription *priya* means dear, *rideshiya* means a foreigner, *nagruda* means a carpenter, and *Rudradeva* means the Son of God.[93]

It is mentioned in several historical works that Gondaphares desired of Thomas to build a palace for him. The apostle promised to complete the work within six months but expended all the money given to him in alms-giving. When the king asked him to account for it, he explained that he was building a place for the king in heaven, not with hands but which was everlasting.

> He preached with such zeal and grace that the king, his brother Gad and multitudes of the people embraced the faith. Many signs and wonders were wrought by the holy apostle.[94]

We have succeeded in obtaining information about the presence of Jesus Christ at Taxila at the marriage ceremony in the royal family of Gondaphares. As the incident is of vital importance, let us quote fully:

> And the king requested the groomsman to go out of the bridal chamber.
> And when all the people had gone out, and the door of the bridal chamber was closed, the bridegroom raised up the curtain, that he might bring the bride to himself.
> And he saw our Lord, in the likeness of Judas, who was standing and talking with the bride.
> And the bridegroom said to him: Lo, thou didst go out at first; how art thou still here?
> Our Lord saith to him: I am not Judas, but I am the brother of Judas.
> And our Lord sat down on the bed, and let the young people sit down on the chairs,
> And began to speak to them.[95]

Jesus and his son Ahoia-Kim in Taxila, 60 A.D.

The above conclusively proves the presence of Jesus Christ at Taxila. The incident is also given in the Acta Thomas, which is reproduced here:

> Thomas after the ceremonies left the palace. The bridegroom lifted the curtain which separated him from the bride. He saw Thomas, as he supposed, conversing with her. Then he asked in surprise:
> How canst thou be found here? Did I not see thee go out before all?
> And the Lord answered:
> I am not Judas Thomas, but his brother.[96]

As the marriage ceremony was performed in 49 A.D., it is an established fact that Jesus Christ had reached Taxila at that period.

Statue of Jesus

While describing the statues found in cell 29, Marshall, who excavated these antiquities at Taxila, says that the dress and bearded head of a peculiarly distinctive style proves him to be a foreigner. All the figures in the group are shown barefooted except the central figure, which appears to have sandals. This particular bearded figure has the peaked cap of a Syrian traveller, tunic to the knees, as was worn in Syria, and strangely enough, boots without laces or latchets. This figure has definite and distinctive Jewish features.[97]

It is due to their dress and physical features that these statues have been called the statues of foreigners.[98] These were found at Julian, Taxila, where an Assyrian type of monastery was built by Julian, who accompanied Thomas during his travels to India. Near this monastery, there existed the palace of the king Gondaphares. From the palace, an Aramaic inscription has been excavated giving some little information about the pious carpenter, a disciple of the Son of God who constructed it from cedar and ivory.

All these hints lead us to the conclusion that the figure with a peaked cap is none other than Jesus, the Son of God. Just as some of the statues excavated at Taxila have been designated as those of foreigners, on the same consideration the figures on the stone slabs, found at Khurhom, in the Lolab valley of Kashmir, have been described as those of foreigners.

Mary the Mother

Mary, the mother of Jesus, commands much respect among the Christians. One reason is that she agreed to conceive Jesus and thus helped God to manifest Himself in flesh in this world. As Jesus was considered an incarnation of God, Thomas addressed him as "My Lord and my God."[99] Leaving aside mythology, we can assign another reason to the greatness of Mary. She not only nourished Jesus like other mothers but also took great pains to get him educated by the Essenes in Egypt. At the feast of the Passover at Jerusalem, when Jesus is lost to his parents, she feels greatly worried and searches for him from place to place. When at last she finds him, she says, "Son, why hast thou thus dealt with us?"

The Gospels do not provide us with full information about Mary's role during the ministry of Jesus. Like every mother, she feels perturbed over his ministry.[100] She is present at the wedding at Cana and tells Jesus that there is no wine for the guests.[101] Then we find her at the time of crucifixion, when Jesus addresses her as the mother of humanity.

> When Jesus therefore saw his mother,
> And the disciple standing by,
> Whom he loved,
> He saith unto his mother,
> Woman,
> Behold thy son!
> Then saith he to the disciple,
> Behold thy mother.[102]

The above would show that Mary was given the title of the mother of all mankind by Jesus who addressed her as woman but told his disciple that she was the mother. We are also informed that Mary was present in the meeting at Jerusalem when Matthias was included in the group of Apostles.[103] After the resurrection, she accompanied Jesus Christ on a long journey towards the East. According to the Gospel of Philip, both she and Mary Magdalene accompanied him. In about 49 A.D. they seem to have reached Taxila. Due to a political upheaval, when the Kushans attacked the region for

establishment of their supremacy, Jesus had to flee towards the ad-
joining hills. Mary, the mother of Jesus Christ, died on the way, and
was buried at a place called Mari then, and now called Murree.[104]
Research conducted about the resting place of Mary the mother
indicates that she is buried on the hill of Murree.[105] The place was
known as Mari till 1875, when the spelling was changed to Murree.
The tomb is described as *Mai-Mari-de-Asthan,* or, the resting place
of Mother Mary.[106] Mumtaz Ahmad Farouqi, who has conducted
exhaustive research on the Tomb of Mary, has propounded that:

> Mary belonged to the priestly class of the Israelites, and it was befit-
> ting that she should be buried on the top of a hill. According to the local
> tradition, the Tomb is the resting place of Mother Mary.

The shrine has been worshipped by the Hindus in the past, and
the Muslims make their offerings and light up earthen lamps filled
up with oil, on Thursdays. In 1898, Richardson, the Garrison Engi-
neer, wished to demolish the tomb at the time of the construction
of the defense tower. Shortly afterwards he died in an accident, and
the locals connect the incident with his evil intentions towards the
tomb. The grave, which is still facing east, has now been repaired.
In 1931 A.D. the Commandant made a complaint to the Municipal
Committee that a red flag with a white circle in the center had been
planted by someone at the site. Further investigations conducted
by the revenue authorities established that the site was an ancient
historical monument, to which the local populace, both Hindus and
Muslims, have offered homage since ancient times.[107]

It is a fact that popular local tradition provides valuable assistance in research and can be accepted as supplementing the historical records. In the present case, when ancient documents are not
available, we have no option but to accept the local tradition, which
emphasizes that the site is known as the resting place of Mother
Mary. In the interest of research it is demanded that the grave be
opened and the remains put to scientific tests, so that the issue
may be resolved. Till then, we will have no option but to believe
that Mary Magdalene is buried at Kashgar and Mary the Mother is
buried at Murree.

The Tomb of Mary
Muree, Pakistan

The Valley of Kashmir

The valley of Kashmir has been described as paradise on earth by many famous writers. It is bounded by the Himalayas and its rocks range in age to the earliest Paleozoic period. The discovery of a massive flake, a crude hand axe and stone tools in the valley have proved the existence of well stratified deposits dating back to glacial periods. It can be said that the valley of Kashmir may have been the repository of earliest human cultures. Traces of middle Paleolithic and Neolithic cultures have been found in Kashmir. The

*Ice-capped mountains
at the Thajiwas glacier*

later culture can be placed around 2500 B.C. The Neolithic culture of Kashmir has close affinity with the similar cultures discovered in Italy and Central Asia. The etymology of Kashmir is attributed to the name of the valley given by its inhabitants as *Kasheer*. The people call themselves as *Kushur*. It is also claimed that many tribes settled in the valley during prehistoric times and prominent among these was the Kassites or Kush tribe, who founded habitations with the name of Kush, such as Kashan in Iran, Kashgar in Central Asia and Hindo-Kush in Afghanistan. This tribe belonged to the sons of Cush, who were ordered to migrate to the land of fat pastures.[108] The Kushans founded their empire in the first century A.D. and held the fourth Buddhist Council in Kashmir. Prior to the advent of Christianity, the Buddhists had established their *Viharas*, right up from Kashmir to Iran, Syria and the Dead Sea.

The Silk Route

In the ancient world, the countries in southwest Asia formed one compact unit. During the sixth century B.C., Iran, Afghanistan, Pakistan, and some regions of northern India formed part of the Achaemenian dominion of Cyrus and Darius.[109] The people living in this vast tract of land had close links by way of trade, commerce and culure.

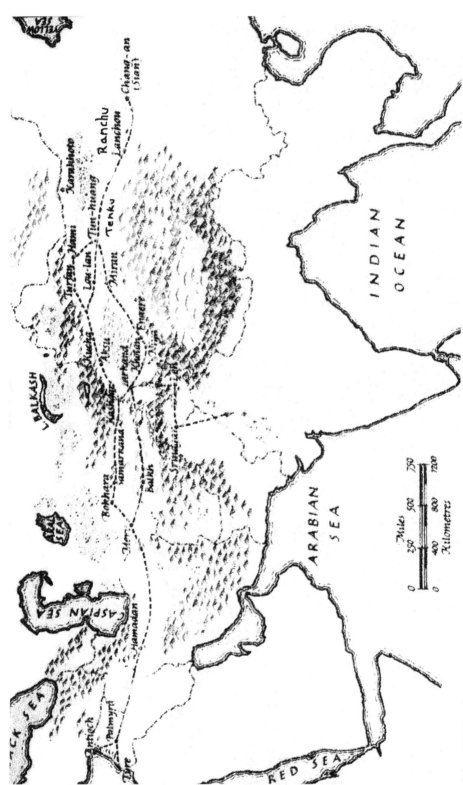

The Silk Road (from *The Lost Years of Jesus* by Elizabeth Clare Prophet)

Prior to the advent of Jesus Christ, Egypt, Iran, Afghanistan and Kashmir were connected by the Silk Route. During the lifetime of Jesus the highway had the following stages:

Jerusalem (Hierosolyma) — Bostra — Damascus — Palmyra — Edessa — Nisseus (Nisibis) — Herat — Bamiyan — Kabul — Khybar — Taxila — Murree — Chitral — Gilgit — Bandipur — Kashmir. From Herat another route lay to Balkh — Badakshan — Ladakh — Kashmir.

It may be mentioned that the valley of Kashmir, though secluded and surrounded by mountains, is located in the region where west, east, south and Central Asia meet. It was an important link in the communication system at the hub of Asia, centripetally uniting all its realms.[110]

From ancient times, the valley of Kashmir had established commercial relations with Afghanistan, Iran and Central Asian countries. Its capital lay on the Silk Route, which connected east with west. Many centuries before the advent of Jesus Christ, the armies of the Greeks penetrated into north India and the Indus basin through land routes of the past. So it is no wonder that any traveler could reach Kashmir from Palestine. These tracks and routes were in existence through all time and were used by emigrants, traders and pilgrims.

Herodotus knew the people of Kaspira or Kashmir, long before the first century A.D.[111] Seven centuries before Christ, the Jews had been transported to the northwest of India and Central Asia, who had established small centers of civilization and trade in these regions, including Kashmir.

Dispersion of Jews

Dispersion of the Jews started with the fall of Samaria in 721 B.C. After that they went on migrating towards the east and settled in far off lands. They settled in Bamyian, Bokhara, Samarkand, Khorasan, Kashmir and Kashgar. Some of their remnants even reached Western China.[112]

It is a historical fact that the Aryans and the Semites intermingled during their dispersion in about 2000 B.C. Some of the Semitic tribes reached the western borders of the Indus valley. But it was during the period of the Assyrian Empire that intimate commercial contacts were established with Iran and Gandhara, which included Kashmir, also. At the time, Media extended its sway right up to the borders of Chitral, and intercommunications between India and the middle east had become well developed. During the reign of Cyrus the Great, the whole region from Thebes in Egypt to Taxila in the Punjab came under the domination of the Persians. With the extension of the Persian Empire by Darius, right up to the northwestern regions of India, the valley of Kashmir, including Hunza, Nagar and Chitral came under direct control of the Persians. Invasion by Alexander the Great, and his stop at Jehlum, proves that he was fully acquainted with the age-old routes from Mesopotamia to the Punjab. His successors established small kingdoms in the northwestern regions of India, and the Greeks ruled over Kashmir. The Greeks continued in Kashmir right up to l A D., when the power was snatched by the Kushans.

It may be pointed out that the Mediterranean people started moving and spreading towards the East, North and West in the beginning of the Neolithic age. One branch migrated towards the northwestern part of the Indian subcontinent. This gigantic race movement started around 5000 B.C.

This physical type forms the basis of the inhabitants in the region. Skeletons found at Mohenjodaro and Harappa in Pakistan include representatives of the aboriginal stock as well as long-headed Mediterraneans who migrated from Mesopotamia.[113] This type is common in Iran, Afghanistan and certain other regions in the northwest of India.[114] Broadly speaking, Kashmiris come under the broad heading of Caucasoids. Ethnologically, they fit in under the Mediterraneans of Armenoid and Nordic type.

The Kashmiri Jews

Most of the Afghan tribes are the descendants of the Jewish tribes. They lived as Jews till they were converted by the Muslims during the days of Khalid.[115] Ethnologically, the overwhelming numbers of inhabitants of Afghanistan are the descendants of the lost tribes of Israel.[116]

As the centuries passed, these ancient tribes of Israel were succeeded in power by Islam and the rule of ten leaders was broken.
Directly and indirectly, the broad mass of population was coerced
to Islamic faith. Despite these changes a segment of population between Iran and Kashmir is still called *Bani Israel,* meaning the sons
of Israel. Even today in the eastern areas from Afghanistan to Kashmir, in more then 350 instances, places and castes bear names which
originate in, or derive from the Old Testament of the Hebrews.[117]

During the ancient period, the valley of Kashmir was occupied by various tribes. Among the prominent tribes mention has
been made of the Nagas, the Pishachas, the Sakas, the Gandharas,
the Khasas and the Tunganas.[118] Most of these tribes were not the
original inhabitants of the valley but came from the north and the
west. It is possible that some of the Jewish tribes might have settled
in the valley also. This is more probable, as Al-Beruni is definite in
stating:

> The Kashmiris are particularly anxious about the natural defences
> of their country. They keep strong vigil and hold on the passes and
> routes leading into it. In former times, they used to allow one or two
> foreigners to enter their country, particularly the Jews.[119]

According to Jesuit Catrou, the author of *The History of the Mughal
Empire,* published in 1708, the Kashmiris are the descendents of the
Jewish tribes which came out of Israel. They built an edifice on a
high mountain near Srinagar, which is still known as the Throne of
Solomon.[120] Another author also writes that the people of Kashmir
are the children of Israel.[121] Bernier wrote in 1644 as follows:

> There are many marks of Judaism to be found in this country. On
> entering the kingdom, the inhabitants in the frontier villages struck me
> as resembling Jews.[122]

The Kashmiris are of a tall, robust frame of body, with manly
features; the women, full formed and handsome with aquiline
noses and features resembling the Jews.[123] Their physical and ethnic
character has always struck observant visitors to the valley and they
have universally connected them with the Jews.[124] Kash or Cush,
the overlord of one Jewish tribe, seems to be the main tribe which

migrated to Kashmir. During their travel when they reached Nisha-pur in Iran, they founded the village of Kashmar; when in Bokhara, they founded a village named Kash; in Samarkand, they founded the villages Kashband, Kashania, and after having founded Kashgar, they came to Kashmir, and named it Kashir, or the country of the Kash tribe.[125]

Jesus Christ had spoken of the Jews as the children of God that had scattered abroad, and he wanted to seek and save the lost sheep of Israel. Therefore there is no wonder that he proceeded towards the east, and reached Kashmir.

Shali-Vahana

Alexander the Great set out toward the East in about 327 B.C. At that time, the valley of Kashmir formed part of Gandhara, with Taxila as its capital. After his return, the Greek soldiers and gener-als scattered themselves in the northwestern regions of India and established small kingdoms in Chitral, Afghanistan, Hazara and Kashmir. Here and there we find evidence, archaeological and nu-mismatic, which prove the fact of the Greek rule in various regions of northwest India. Similarly, we find eleven Greek rulers who held sway over Kashmir.[126]

Kadphises I made himself the master of northern India in about 60 A.D. and his viceroy Kaniska subjugated the valley of Kashmir, some time later in 73 A.D.[127] It was during this period that Shali-Va-hana of Kashmir appeared on the scene as a champion of the Brah-manas, against the Indo-Scythians.[128]

He succeeded in defeating the foreigners and in order to com-memorate his victory, introduced a new era after his name. Known as the Shali-Vahana Era, it was introduced on the first Baisakh 3179 Kalyugi Era, corresponding to the 14th March, 78 A.D.[129]

Jesus Christ and the Kashmiri King

The most important information about the arrival of Jesus Christ in the valley of Kashmir and his meeting with the king of Kashmir has been recorded for posterity by Sutta in his famous Sanskrit work entitled, *Bhavisya-maha-purana*, written in 3191 Laukik era,

विडि कुमार्गगमंसंभगम ॥ २३ ॥ म्लेच्छधर्मस्य वक्तारं मत्यवतपगयणम ॥ इति श्रुत्वा नृपः प्राह धर्मः को भवनां मतः ॥ २४ ॥ श्रुत्वा
यान महागज प्राप्तं मत्स्यग मंश्रये ॥ निर्मर्यादे म्लेच्छदेशे मर्माहोद्धं समागतः ॥ २५ ॥ इशामसी च दस्यूनां प्रादुसुनां भयंकरी ॥ तामहं
म्लेच्छगन प्राप्य मर्मीढन्वमुपागतः ॥ २६ ॥ म्लेच्छेषु स्थापितो धर्मं मया तच्छृण्य भूपते ॥ मानसं निर्मलं कृत्वा मलं दंहे शुभाशुभम ॥२७॥
नगम जपमाप्नाय जपेन निर्मलं पम ॥ न्यायेन सत्यवचसा मनसेक्यन मानवः ॥ २८ ॥ ध्यानेन प्रजयेर्द्शां मूर्यमंडलमंश्थितम ॥
अचलोऽय प्रभुः साक्षात्तथा मूर्याचलः मदा ॥ २९ ॥ तत्त्वानां चलभूतानां कर्षणः स समंततः ॥ इति कृन्वन भूपाल मसीहा विलयं
गना ॥ ३० ॥ इशमूर्तिर्हृदि प्राप्ता नित्यशुद्धा शिवंकरी ॥ इशामसीह इति च मम नाम प्रतिष्ठितम् ॥ ३१ ॥ इति श्रुत्वा स भूपालो
नत्वा तं म्लेच्छपूजकम् ॥ स्थापयामास तं तत्र म्लेच्छस्थाने हि दारुणे ॥ ३२ ॥ स्वराज्यं प्राप्तवान्गजा इयमंधमचीकरन् ॥ गज्यं
कृत्वा स पट्ष्वर्दं स्वर्गलोकमुपाययौ ॥ ३३ ॥ स्वर्गते तृपती तस्मिन्नथा चामीत्तपा शृण ॥ ३४ ॥ इति श्रीभविष्ये महापुगणे प्रति
नगेपर्वणि चतुर्युगखण्डापरपर्याये कलियुगेयितिहासमुच्चये शालिवाहनकाले द्वितीयोऽध्यायः ॥ २ ॥ ७ ॥ ॥ श्रीमृत उवाच ॥ ॥ शालिवा
हनवंशे च राजानो दश चाभवन् ॥ गज्यं पंचशताब्दं च कृत्वा लोकान्तरं ययुः ॥ १ ॥ मर्यादां कमतो लीना जाता भूमंडले तदा ॥ भूपति
दशमो या च भोजगज इति स्मृतः ॥ इष्ट्वा प्रक्षीणमर्र्यादां बली दिग्विजयं ययौ ॥ २ ॥ सेनया दशसाहस्र्या कालिदानं मंथुतः ॥ गन्धर्व्यं
बालगेः मार्ग सिंधुपागमुपाययौ ॥ ३ ॥ जित्वा गान्धारजान्म्लेच्छान्काश्मीरान्राज्यान्वांश्छठान् ॥ तेषां प्राप्य महाकोशं दंडयोग्मयानकार्यन ॥४॥
पन्निम्नग्नन्नं म्लेच्छ आचार्येण समन्वितः ॥ महामद इति ख्यातः शिष्यशास्त्रसमन्वितः ॥ ५ ॥ तृपमेव महादेव मरुस्थलनिवासिनम् ॥
गंगाजलेन संस्नाप्य पंचगव्यसमन्वितैः ॥ चंदनादिभिरभ्यर्च्य तुष्टाव मनसा हरम् ॥ ६ ॥ ॥ भोजराज उवाच ॥ ॥ नमस्ते गिरिजानाथ
मरुस्थलनिवासिने ॥ त्रिपुगसुरनाशाय बहुमायाप्रवर्षिने ॥ ७ ॥ म्लेच्छैर्गुप्ताय शुद्धाय मचिदानन्दरूपिणे ॥ त्वं मां हि किंकरं विद्धि शग्णाय्ं
मुपागतम ॥ ८ ॥ ॥ मृत उवाच ॥ ॥ इति श्रुत्वा स्तवं देवः शब्दमाह नृपाय तम् ॥ गंतव्यं भोजगाजेन महाकालेश्वरस्थले ॥ ९ ॥
म्लेच्छैर्समुदूषिता भूमिर्वाहीका नाम विश्रुता ॥ आर्यधर्मो हि नैवात्र वाहीके देशदारुणे ॥ १० ॥ यभूत्राग्र महामायी योऽस्मी दग्धे मया पुग ॥
त्रिपुगे बलिदैत्येन प्रेषितः पुनरागतः ॥ ११ ॥ अयं.नेः स बरो मत्तः प्राप्तवान्देत्यवर्द्धनः ॥ महामद इति ख्यातः पैशाचकृतितत्परः ॥ १२ ॥

Bhavishay-Maha Purana

corresponding to 115 A.D. Shali-Vahana ruled over the valley of Kashmir and other mountainous regions of the Himalayas during 39-50 A.D. At the time of his succession, the valley and the other parts of his kingdom witnessed attacks by the neighboring tribes from China, Parthia, Bactria, and Sinkiang. These hordes were defeated by him but they left after looting his kingdom. Thus, he succeeded in demarcating the boundaries between the Aryans and the non-Aryans. Sutta further records that the king, during his travels in the Himalayas, met a saintly person near Wien who was fair in color and wore white robes. When the king inquired about his name, the saint replied:

"I am known as the Son of God and born of a virgin." The saint also told him that he had suffered at the hands of the wicked, for he preached human beings to serve the Lord. He further informed the king that his name has been established as Isa-Masiha.

The above information clearly reveals the meeting of Jesus with Shali-Vahana, the king of Kashmir. None except Jesus Christ is known as the Son of God and none except him is known to have been born of a virgin. Secondly, Jesus Christ is known as Isa-Masih in the East, even at present. He is also remembered as *Yusu-Masih*. The above information being very archaic and important is translated as follows:

> In the meanwhile, Shali-Vahana, the grandson of Vikrama-Ditya laid hold on the kingdom of his father. He defeated the invincible Shakas (Scythians) and fought off the hordes from Cheen (China), Tatari (Tartar), Balhika (Bactria), Kam-rupa (Parthia), Roma (Rome) and Khura (Khura-san). He took possession of their treasures, and those who deserved punishment were punished. He defined the boundaries between the Aryan and the Mleechas (Amalekites), declaring this side of the Sindhu (Indus) as the country of the Aryans. This righteous king demarcated the habitat of the Mleechas (Amalekites) beyond the Sindhu (Indus). One day the king of the Shakas (Scythians) came to Himatunga (Himalaya). This King who was very powerful, saw in the mountains of Wien a distinguished person wearing white robes. 'Who are you?' asked the king, and the person replied in a pleasant manner:

> Know me as *Ishvara-putaram* (the Son of God),
> *Kanya-garbam* (Born of the womb of a virgin),
> Being given to the truth,
> And penances:
> I preached the religion to the Mleechas (Amalekites)

> After hearing this, the king asked: "Which religion do you preach?" He answered:

> When the truth had vanished,
> And all bounds of propriety were crossed;
> In the land of the Mleechas (Amalekites):
> I appeared as *Isha-Masih* (Jesu Messiah).
> I received the Messiah-hood, (Christhood)
> In the land of Mleechas

I saith unto them;
Remove all mental and bodily impurities,
Recite the revealed prayer truthfully,
Pray in the right manner,
Repeat within your heart the name of our Lord God,
Meditate upon Him whose abode is in the sun!
When I appeared in the Mleecha country:
The wicked and the guilty underwent pain through my works;
But they made me to suffer at their hands.
I say unto thee:
In truth all power rests with the Lord,
The sun is in the center;
While the cosmos is the contraction of the moving elements;
And the elements, the sun and God are forever.
Perfect, pure and blissful frame of God
Has entered into my heart:
Thus my name has been established,
And promulgated as Isha-Masih!

After having heard this from the lips of the distinguished person, the king returned, making obeisance to him.[130]

The above is the correct translation of the verses from the ancient Sanskrit work entitled *Bhavishya-Maha-Purana*, which was written in 115 A.D. In it we are told that Shali-Vahana, the king of Kashmir, met Jesus Christ at Wien, which place still exists near Srinagar, Kashmir. Jesus is always mentioned in the east as *Yusu-Masih* or *Isa-Masih*, and all those who do not profess Hinduism are termed as Mleechas. The authenticity of this ancient manuscript has been dealt with in the chapter on Sources. However, it may be noted that the manuscript provides most authentic information. Here, Jesus Christ is said to have referred to his sufferings at the hands of the Amalekites, who are termed as Mleechas by the author of the above Sanskrit work. It is also noteworthy that Jesus Christ clearly reveals that he is known as the Son of God, born of a virgin and that he was sent as Messiah to the country of the Amalekites. He also affirms that he taught love, truth and purity but suffered at the hands of the wicked. His statement that the Lord is in the center of the sun and the elements and that God and the sun shall exist forever hints at the ordered system of the cosmos.

After having defeated the Scythians and the other invaders, Shali-Vahana introduced a new era, in the Kalyugi year 3139, which corresponds to 78 A.D. He had to leave for further conquests and it is probable that the above meeting between him and Jesus Christ might have taken place in the same year, or prior to 78 A.D.

Spirit of God

Jesus Christ was the Spirit of God, who assumed the name of Yuzu-Asaph in Kashmir.[131] This tradition has been inherited by the Muslims from the Hindus of ancient times, who also believed that Jesus came to Kashmir and settled here. Here Jesus disclosed his identity to the king of Kashmir in the following words.

"I am known as the Son of God and born of a virgin. As I have preached love, truth and purity of heart, I am called Messiah."[132]

His Ministry in Kashmir

It was during the reign of Gopananda I (79-109 A.D.) that Jesus Christ proclaimed his ministry in Kashmir and spent his later life in the valley. During the period, Sulaiman came for the repairs of a temple dedicated to Solomon. He had the following verses inscribed on the stone pillars of *Takht-i-Sulaiman*.

Yuzu-Asaph, the Yusu of the tribes of Israel proclaimed his prophet-hood, in the year 54.

The translation from the Persian history of Kashmir of the relevant pages is given below:

The new king assumed the name of Gopananda and started his rule in the valley of Kashmir. During his reign, many temples were built and repaired. He invited Sulaiman from Persia for repairs of the cracked dome existing on the top of Mount Solomon. The Hindus raised objections saying that as he was not a Hindu but followed the other religion, he could not repair the sacred temple. During this very period, Yuzu-Asaph arrived from Bait-ul Muqaddas (the Holy Land) and proclaimed his prophethood in the Wadi-a-Aqdas (Holy Valley). He absorbed himself in prayers, day and night, and was very pious and saintly. He called upon the people to follow the words of God and

Takht-i-Sulaiman (Throne of Solomon)

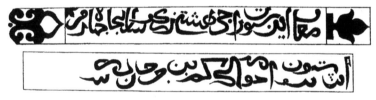

Inscription

In the temple on Shankriyacharya hill in Srinagar, Kashmir, there were four inscriptions on the flank walls encasing the stone stairs. The inscriptions were in Persian in Sulus script. Out of these four, two inscriptions are totally mutilated while the other two were photographed by Maj. H.H. Cole and published in his work entitled, Illustrations of Ancient Buildings in Kashmir, published by W.H. Allen & Co., London, in 1869. Translated into English, these inscriptions read as under:

Mason of this pillar Raji Bhishtay son of Kim, year 54
This pillar honoring Jehoiakim son of Marjan...
It requires to be noted that Yuzu-Asaph married Marjan in Pahalgam, Kashmir.

many became his disciples. The king requested him to bring the people on the right path.

Having completed the repairs of the dome in the year 54, Sulaiman had inscriptions engraved on the stones of the stairs as follows:

> During this period, Yuzu-Asaph proclaimed his prophethood. He was Yusu, the prophet of the children of Israel.
>
> I have seen in a book of the Hindus that this Prophet was really Isa, the Spirit of God, on whom be peace and salutations. He assumed the name of Yuzu-Asaph and spent his life in the valley. After his demise, he was laid to rest in the tomb at Anzmar. It is also said that the rays of prophethood used to emanate from the tomb of this Prophet.[133]

According to the author, Jesus Christ proclaimed his ministry in Kashmir in the year 54, and the event is engraved on the stones of the stairs to the dome of Solomon. It may be mentioned that this ancient edifice was repaired several times after its repairs by Sulaiman. It was also repaired during the reign of Sultan Zain-ul-abidin, in the year 874 A.D. when four pillars were added to its dome. It was under his directions that the earlier inscriptions were translated into Persian and engraved on four pillars. These revised inscriptions were recorded by a Kashmiri historian as follows:

> Mason of this pillar Raji Bihisti Zargar; year 54. This pillar honoring Jehoia-Kim son of Mairjan. Yuz-Asaph proclaimed his prophethood; year 54. He is Yusu, the Prophet of the Children of Israel.[134]

These inscriptions were intact up to the end of the nineteenth century but have been mutilated now. The photograph of only two lines is available at present.[135] It is interesting to note that the year in the inscriptions is given as 54. As the inscriptions were translated into Persian from the original, we have to find out the exact equivalent of the year 54. The Kashmiris used the Laukika Era during ancient times, which began in 3076 B.C.

Accordingly, the year 3154 of the Laukika Era would correspond to 78 A.D. The year mentioned in the inscriptions was engraved as 54, which in reality is 3154, which can rightly be calculated as 78 A.D. It is thus evident that Jesus Christ proclaimed his ministry in Kashmir in the year 78 A.D.

Preaching

Some information though scanty but significant is available about Jesus Christ in Kashmir. It is reported that people came together unto him, the rich and the poor, for blessings and guidance. Jesus said unto them:

> Listen:
> I say unto thee,
> The words of wisdom,
> And truth;
> Ye may be able to make distinction,
> Between right and wrong.
> Indeed this is the religion of those,
> Unto whom the words of God come.
> Whosoever shall discard righteousness
> Shall not enter heaven.[136]

Jesus had once said that those who are persecuted for righteousness shall enter the kingdom of heaven.[137] He repeats the same sermon in Kashmir. He had also said that those who hear the word of God, and keep it, are blessed.[138] Here, Jesus asks people to make distinction between right and wrong, and thus keep the word of God.

> Listen,
> I say unto thee;
> Seek ye the kingdom of heaven,
> Rather than that of the world;
> Woe unto the seekers of the world,
> For they shall perish.[139]

Here Jesus Christ asks them to seek the kingdom of God.[140] At another place, he gave the following sermon:

> Verily,
> I say unto thee;

> Death keeps no time;
> For the hour has come,
> And the birds have no power,
> Over their enemies;
> Save ye with faith.[141]

It has been written in the ancient scriptures that those who do not seek God, they shall be put to death.[142] No one has power on the day of death, nor power to retain Spirit over the Spirit.[143]

> I say unto thee;
> So long as there is light ye travel,
> Keep your good deeds secret,
> Lest these be for show only.
> Blessed are they;
> For they know,
> That they shall be treated in the same way.[144]

The following statement is attributed to Jesus:

> My food is fasting, my natural condition is fear, my dress a sack made from wool. My hearth is the sun in winter, my light in the night is the moon, my conveyance is my feet, my food the berries of the forest. When I go to sleep, I have nothing with me; when I rise I am empty handed. None is richer than me on the earth.
> I advise you to concentrate your thoughts upon God, and lead a detached life. If you have a towering aspiration to meet God, concentrate upon Him.
> Remember; if one employs all energy to attain an aim with clear thoughts, even a thorn may be turned into a rose garland.[145]

According to Jesus, we will receive due reward of our works. He advised people to keep away from worldly desires and do good. He says,

> I say unto thee;
> Shun worldly desires,
> And give up anger,
> And backbiting,
> And keep your hearts pure.[146]

Parable

A parable is a narration of some event, adapted to teach a moral lesson. Jesus taught in parables in a most characteristic and striking way.[147] In the New Testament, we find many parables which deal with loftiest spiritual truth. Here is one such parable which he gave to the common people:

> Behold:
> When a sower goes to sow,
> And sows:
> Some seeds fall by the wayside,
> And are devoured by the birds.
> Some seeds fall upon the stray land,
> And reach the stony foundation,
> and wither away
> And some fall among thorns,
> And grow not.
> And the seeds which fall on good land,
> Grows,
> And brings forth fruit.

Here Jesus repeats the parable of the sower given in the New Testament.[148] But the parable which he taught in Kashmir goes on further as follows:

> By the sower is meant the wise;
> By the seeds is meant his words of wisdom;
> The seeds picked up by the birds,
> Means those who do not understand.
> By the seeds on the stony ground,
> Is meant words of wisdom not heeded.
> By the seeds thrown on stony ground is meant,
> Those who understand but do not comply
> By the seeds which fall on good ground,
> Means those who understand
> Obey,
> And follow.[149]

Crucifixion

Isana lived at Ishbar on the banks of Dal Lake in Srinagar, Kashmir. He was a saint of great repute and his preachings were heard by all, and he had many devotees. One of his chief disciples, Samadhi-mati, was ordered by the king of Kashmir to be imprisoned for ten years. But after some time, he was put on the cross. Isana came and saw three sentences written on the forehead of Samadhi-mati:

> This man will lead a life of poverty:
> After ten years imprisonment;
> He will be put on the stake;
> After resurrection, shall be the king.[150]

When Samadhi-mati was put on the stake, the crowds witnessed his crucifixion. During the night, fairies came and danced around his corpse. Isana felt sad and sat near the site. On the third day, Samadhi-mati came to life. The multitude saw him in amazement and offered him the throne of Kashmir. He refused to accept this offer, but when the people insisted, he agreed to be their king. This extraordinary event as described in the ancient Sanskrit historical work is reproduced here:

> This king had an advisor called Samadhi-mati;
> The greatest of sages,
> Who was distinguished by his wonderful life,
> And devotion to Shiva.
> The wicked raised the king's hatred
> Against that trusted advisor,
> By telling him,
> Beware of this person of wonders.
> Full of wrath,
> The king banished him,
> And reduced him,
> To life-long poverty.
> There spread a mysterious report,
> From house to house,
> Which declared,
> To Samadhi-mati will belong the kingdom.[151]
> Troubled by apprehensions
> The king threw Samadhi-mati in prison,

There he pined
With his legs tormented by cruel fetters.

The above quoted verses reveal that Samadhi-mati was one of the greatest of sages, who was distinguished by his wonderful life and devotion to God. The wicked raised the King's hatred against him. There spread a mysterious report among the people: "To Samadhi-mati will belong the kingdom." Accordingly, the king got troubled by apprehensions and ordered chaining of the saint, whose legs were tormented by cruel fetters.

Then the king ordered
Samadhi-mati be put on the stake;
At night,
By savage executioners.[152]
When the news reached Isana,
The heart of this self-controlled person,
Broke away from control.
He proceeded to the place of execution;
To perform funeral rites
For this suffering man.
He found him,
Reduced to a skeleton;
At which
The wolves tore away,
His flesh,
Held fast by the bones,
Fixed under the foot, of the stake!

The above verses show that the king ordered that the apostle be crucified. Accordingly, he was put on the stake at night by the savage executioners. When Isana heard the news, his heart broke away and he proceeded to the site of execution. There he found the skeleton and his flesh held fast by bones fixed under the feet of the stake.

Keeping off the howling wolves;
He carried away the skeleton;
On his forehead;
The verse inscribed
He will have a life of poverty;
Ten years imprisonment;

Death on the stake;
And still thereafter a throne.[153]
Thus he stayed,
To see
The fulfillment of the prediction,
And watched the skeleton
Then in the middle of the night
While he was awake;
Isana smelt
A heavenly perfume of incense.

The above reveals that Isana carried away the skeleton of the saint. But on his forehead, he saw inscribed that he would have life after death. Thus Isana watched the fulfillment of the prediction. At night, the witches came with incense and heavenly ointments and the skeleton was fitted up with all its limbs.

He saw the witches,
enveloped by a halo of light,
the skeleton in the midst
being fitted up with all its limbs.
He was covered by them;
with heavenly ointments
the spirit of Samadhi-mati
was put into his body.[154]
When the witches departed;
their voice was heard;
He who,
When chosen by us,
was joined with a heavenly body;
will be known on earth;
on account of his noble character,
as *Arya-Raja* or the prince of the Aryans.[155]

The extraordinary event of crucifixion, the only instance recorded in the ancient history of Kashmir, merits serious attention, due to the fact that the crucifixion of Jesus Christ was repeated in Kashmir. It is also a strange coincidence that the dates of Samadhi-mati and Jesus Christ are also almost identical. Further, both the personalities have strong resemblances, with the result that this event has become a mystery.[156]

It is also a strange coincidence that Jesus is called Isa in the East. It is possible that Isana of Kashmir, who is spoken of as a great saint, may be no other personality than Jesus Christ.

It is also possible that his disciple may have been crucified in Kashmir, and may have obtained resurrection at the hands of Isa. The other alternative would be to presume that Isana and Samadhi-mati Arya-raja may be the same person, and Kalhana the historian may be confused while recording the crucifixion of this historical personality. This saint lived at Ishbar, meaning the place of Isa, which is still held in reverence by a section of the people of Kashmir. This fact has been mentioned in various historical works of Kashmir.[157]

Similarities

We now record versions of the three crucifixions, which may be summarized in order to show similarities between them.

> My God, why hast thou forsaken me
> Many bulls have compassed me:
> For dogs have compassed me:
> The assembly of the wicked have enclosed me:
> They pierced my hands and my feet
> But be not thou far from me, O Lord
> O my strength, haste thee to help me:
> I will declare thy name unto my brethren:
> For the kingdom is the Lord's.[158]

This incident pertains to the pre-Christ period and is narrated in the Old Testament. The second incident is reproduced from the New Testament.

> Father, if thou be willing, remove this cup from me.
> They led him away to crucify him:
> They parted his garments:
> And they returned and prepared spices and ointments
> Nicodemus came by night,
> And brought a mixture of myrrh and aloes
> Then took they the body of Jesus
> And wound it in linen clothes with the spices:

> At evening came Jesus and stood in the midst
> And they worshipped him.
> Go ye into all the world and preach.[159]

Now there is the third report of crucifixion, of the post-Jesus period;

> There spread a mysterious report,
> To Samadhi-mati will belong the Kingdom;
> Savage executioners put him on the stake at night.
> Isana found him reduced to a skeleton.
> The wolves tore away his flesh from the bones:
> He smelt a heavenly perfume of incense:
> The *Yogins* covered his body with heavenly ointments:
> The spirit of Samadhi-mati was put into his body;
> The *Yogins* cried,
> He, who was joined with a heavenly body:
> Is chosen as the prince of the Aryans.[160]

It appears that all three personalities who were crucified suffered a similar fate but resurrected after being put on the cross. In the case of the last two personalities, heavenly ointments were used; in the case of Jesus, by his disciples, and in the case of Samadhi-mati, by the *Yogins*. It may be that all the above three personalities are one and the same, or they are different Christs. In the Buddhist mythology, we have the Buddha and then those becoming Buddhas, who are termed Bodhisattvas. All of them belong to the order of Buddha.

In the above mentioned case, it is possible that various personalities belonging to the Order of Jesus Christ may have come to this world at different times.

Jesus and the Jews

Jesus had claimed that he was the expected Messiah but the Jews had rejected him. While the Jews considered themselves as the chosen nation and their God as the God of Israel only, Jesus believed and preached universal brotherhood. He was dissident and as such they crucified him.

Moreover, Jesus had developed strong links with the Essenes, who lived as ascetics around the Valley of Khirbet Qumran. Though other-wordly this monastic order was Jewish in character. They were, in reality, a break-away group, who recognized as their head a "Teacher of Righteousness" instead of Moses. To the Jews, Jesus of Nazareth was not the Messiah for whom they had looked during all these centuries; rather he was their enemy, who had modified the Law.

However, the Messianic movement started by the Messiah or the Christ continued to gain ground, not only at Jerusalem but in the areas dominated by the Romans. Claudius, who was on the Roman throne from 41 A.D. to 54. A.D., had to "drive the Jews out of Rome who were rioting because of Chrestus.[161] This means that a Christian community did exist in Rome just after the departure of the Master. The apostles and their followers spread the word beyond the Jewish communities to the Pagans.

Peter in India

Jesus Christ had predicted that he would be denied thrice by Peter. After he had given the new commandment, Peter asked him where he would go, so that he could follow him. To this question Jesus Christ replied

> Whither I go,
> Thou canst not follow me now;
> But thou shalt follow me afterwards.[162]

The above prophecy clearly reveals that Jesus Christ had predicted that Peter would follow him later on. Thus, we shall have to find out what happened to Peter after the crucifixion.

It is a fact that Peter denied having known Jesus Christ, and as he went out for safety, the cock crowed. When a maid saw him and said that he was one of the disciples, he again denied it. When he was pressed to reveal the truth, he swore that he had never known Jesus Christ. Thus, he denied thrice having known Jesus Christ. He had told a lie and when he thought about what he had done, he felt remorse and wept.[163] Jesus had also predicted that he would build his church on the rock, and the gates of hell should not prevail against it. Addressing Peter, he had declared:

And I will give unto thee
The keys of the kingdom of heaven;
And whatsoever thou shalt bind on earth,
Shall be bound in heaven;
And whatsoever thou shalt loose on earth.
Shall be loosed in heaven.[164]

It is significant that out of all his disciples, Jesus not only informed Peter that he should have to follow him at a later period
but also gave him "the keys of the kingdom of heaven." This would
mean that Jesus Christ made him his successor. It is but natural that
after the flight of Jesus Christ, his successor should follow him to
distant lands.

Soon after the crucifixion, Jesus' disciples met together and Peter
addressed them.[165] After that he started missionary work and added
about three thousand converts to Christianity.[166] Both Peter and
John preached in Jerusalem for some time with the result that the
number of Christians rose to about five thousand.[167] Both of them
were arrested and brought before the Jewish council. The priests
admonished them and warned them not to speak in the name of
the Lord. In the meanwhile, many, including Barnabas, supported
them morally and financially. Among others who supported them
was Ananias, who sold his possessions and presented a part of the
price to Peter.[168]

The apostles of Jesus Christ were persecuted by the Sadducees
and put in the common prison. But the angels by night opened the
doors and set them free. They again started preaching in the name of
Jesus Christ and were again brought before the council. They were
again told to stop their activities, but Peter and the other apostles
said that they ought to obey God rather than men. The priests
wanted to slay them but they were saved through the intervention
of Gamaliel.[169]

After some time, Stephen was arrested and stoned to death.
Peter went to Lydda and healed Aeneas, who had been ill for eight
years.[170] Then he went to Joppa and restored Dorcas to life after
death. Staying for some time there, he proceeded to Caesarea and
converted Cornelius along with other people. It was shortly afterwards that James was killed and Peter was imprisoned under orders
of Herod.[171]

One night, an angel rescued him from the prison. Herod, in anger, got the jail keepers killed for carelessness. Peter departed for Caesarea and lived there for some time. After that we hear of him at Antioch, when Paul rebukes Peter for not eating with the Gentiles.[172]

Paul preached the doctrines among the Romans, the Corinthians, the Galatians, the Ephesians, the Philippians, the Colossians and the Thessalonians. Peter attached much importance to the East and addressed himself to the strangers scattered throughout Pontus, Galatia, Bithynia, Cappadocia and Asia.[173] Addressing the nations in the East he said:

> But ye are a chosen generation
> A royal priesthood,
> A holy nation,
> A peculiar people.
> That ye should show forth the praises
> Of him who hath called you out
> Of darkness into his marvelous light
> Which in time past were not a people,
> But are now the people of God
> Which had not obtained mercy.[174]

While addressing the Asians, Peter praises them as the holy and chosen people. He also tells them that they were not on the right path earlier and they have now come to the right path and obtained the mercy of God. It is significant that he tells them that it all has happened now when Jesus "hath called you out of darkness."

He addresses the Asians from Babylon, which shows that his final goal is not in Europe but in Asia. In his second letter, he does not indicate the name of the place wherefrom he wrote, but his first letter clearly reveals that he wrote from Babylon, in presence of Silvanus and Mark.[175] After this, nothing is known about the whereabouts of Peter, but it is evident that he should have followed Jesus Christ as predicted earlier.[176] Later findings have revealed that, like Thomas, Peter also visited India and reached Taxila.[177] In his research paper, Shaikh Abdul Qadir has drawn attention of scholars to a bronze statue found by the Archeological Survey of India at Char-saddha, a photo whereof has been published without identification.[178]

This bronze statue is an early specimen of Christian antiquities in India. It represents Peter, sitting on a chair, wearing royal attire. His beard and hair are thick and curly. He holds a key in one hand, while the other hand is up in the blessing mood. The statue is a masterpiece of Gandhara Art. According to the Western orientalists, this statue represents Peter, who arrived in Gandhara after the crucifixion.[179]

It may also be pointed out that the skeletal features, thick and heavy hair on head and face, and facial index prove that statue is of a person of the Mediterranean group, belonging to the Mesolithic Natufians of Palestine.

Demise

Like his advent, the demise of Jesus Christ is shrouded in mystery. While the Gospels make him leave this world at the age of 30, the Oriental writers have assigned to him a long life of from 115 to 120 years.

At the approach of death, he sent for his disciple Babad, and expressed his last will to him, about carrying on his mission. He directed him to prepare a tomb for him at the very place he would breathe his last. He then stretched his legs toward the West and kept his head towards the East, and passed away. May God bless him.[180]

According to another account, Jesus Christ left his mortal remains at the ripe age of 120 years.[181] His burial ceremony was performed by Babad in the Jewish style.[182]

Who was this Babad, who was summoned by Jesus Christ, before his demise? Thomas was a twin brother of Jesus Christ, and his real name was Judas. His *Acts Thomae* in Syriac are known as the Acts of Judas Thomae or the Acts of Judas the Twin. Judas is spoken as the brother of Jesus in the Gospels.[183]

Thomas in Aramaic, Didymus in Greek, Thomas in Syriac, Theom in Nestorian, and Tauam in Arabic, means the twin. It may be pointed out that Babad also means the twins who suck milk from the same mother.[184]

This speaks for reason as to why the "another" of the Kamal-Ud-Din speaks of Thomas as Babad.

Jesus Christ passed away in the year 109 A.D. It was a great mourning day for the Kashmiris of that period. According to Jewish custom, the body of the dead had to remain on the shelf, and after decomposition, the bones would be stored in a wooden or stone chest. No information is available on the issue, except that the sacred body of Jesus was laid in the sepulchre, according to the Jewish style.[185] In order to settle the controversy, once for all, it is necessary to open the ground floor of the present tomb, and find out the sacred relic, which might be in a wooden, stone or earthen casket.[186]

A big tomb was raised on his grave and it became a place of pilgrimage for all, whether rich or poor. People came with offerings at the tomb and led prayers there.[187] Thomas, who had always devoted his life to the services of Jesus Christ, felt very much bereaved and left for Malabar to preach among the lost tribes there.[188] Thomas preached among the people of south India and established seven churches there. He suffered martyrdom at Maelapur in Madras and is buried there.

His disciples call themselves the Christians of St. Thomas and they solemnize only two rituals, of Baptism and the Lord's Supper.

The Tomb of Yuzu-Asaph

The Tomb of Yuzu-Asaph is situated in Anzimar, Khanyar, Srinagar, the summer capital of Kashmir. Srinagar, which means the city of the sun, is an ancient city. It is divided into parts, i.e., the old city and the new city, and the tomb is situated in the old city. The people of Kashmir call it Rozabal, meaning the site of the tomb, and declare that it is a tomb of Yuzu-Asaph. This prophet came to Kashmir 1000 years ago, and preached the same parables of Christ.[189] Popular local tradition connects it with the tomb of Jesus Christ.[190] Some say it is the tomb of the Prophet of "the people of the Book."[191]

In the *Bagh-i-Sulaiman*, there is a poem about the tomb of Yuzu-Asaph, which is reproduced below:

> Here is the Tomb, so famous!
> Sepulcher of the Prophet,
> So illuminating!
> Whosoever bows before it,

Tomb of Yuzu-Asaph

Receives inner light, solace and contentment,
According to a tradition there was a prince,
Most accomplished, pious and great,
Who received the Kingdom of God.
He was faithful to the Lord.
Who commanded him to be the Prophet,
Through His grace he became the guide to the people,
Of this valley of Kashmir.
Here is the tomb of that prophet
Who is known as Yuzu Asaph.[192]

Decree 1194—A.H.

The Decree granted to the keeper of the Tomb, dated 1194 A.H. 1776 A.D., by the Grand Mufti of Kashmir declares that the tomb has two graves: one of Yuzu-Asaph sent as Prophet to the people of Kashmir during the reign of King Gopadatta; the other is of a descendant from the family of the Prophet of Islam.[193] The translation of the decree is given as follows:

THE SEAL OF THE JUSTICE OF ISLAM
MULLA FAZIL
1194-A.H.

In this High Court of Justice, in the Department of Learning and Piety of the Kingdom.

Present

Rehman Khan, son of Amir Khan, submits that: the kings, the nobles, the ministers and the multitude come from all directions of the kingdom to pay their homage and offerings in cash and kind at the lofty and the holy shrine of Yuz-Asaph, the Prophet, may God bless him.

Claims That

he is the only and absolute claimant, entitled to receive the offerings and utilize these, and none else has any right whatsoever on these offerings.

Prays That

a writ of injunction be granted to all those who interfere and the others be restrained from interfering with his rights.

Verdict

Now, this court after obtaining evidence, concludes as follows:

It has been established that during the reign of Rajah Gopadatta, who had built many temples and had repaired, especially, the Throne of Solomon on the hill of Solomon, Yuzu-Asaph came to the valley, Prince by descent, he was pious and saintly, and had given up earthly pursuits. He spent all his time in prayers and meditation. The people of Kashmir, having become idolators, after the great flood of Noah, the God Almighty sent Yuzu-Asaph as a Prophet to the people of Kashmir. He proclaimed oneness of God till he passed away. Yuzu-Asaph was buried at Khanyar on banks of the lake, and the shrine is known as Rozabal. In the year 871 A.H. Syed Nasir-ud-Din, a descendent of Imam Musa-Raza, was also buried beside the grave of Yuzu-Asaph.

Orders

Since the shrine is visited by the devotees, both high and common, and since the applicant Rahman Khan is the hereditary custodian of the Shrine, it is ordered that he be entitled to receive the offerings, made at the shrine as before, and no one else shall have any right to such offerings. Given under our hand, 11th Jamad-ud-Sani, 1184 A.H.

Signed and sealed:

| Mulla Fazil | Abdul Shakoor |
| Mohammad Aza | Mohammad Akbar |

Original Persian Decree 1766 A.D.

Hafiz Ahsan Ullah   Raza Akbar
Khizar Mohammad   Atta
Faqir Baba

The above Decree granted by the High Court in Kashmir, presided over by the Grand Mufti and other judges, clearly affirms that Yuz-Asaph was sent as a Prophet to the people of Kashmir.

Architecture of the Tomb

The present building built from bricks and mortar is raised on the ancient stone sepulchre. The building is rectangular with an attached entrance chamber. Towards the East of the structure lies the common graveyard.

The plinth of the present building is in reality a rectangular structure enclosed by walls made of chiselled stone blocks of big size. Very recently, the ancient stone walls have been plastered with cement, but the upper portion of the original door for access to the crypt is still visible. Its decorated stones have been plastered with

Wooden cross, sarcophagus of Yuz-Asaph, Rozabal, Srinagar (photo by author, 1975)

Metal disk hanging on the main door

Main door leading to the sarcophagus of Yuzu-Asaph

Wall of the tomb

These photographs were taken by Eva Maria Teja in 2004 at great risk. Now they do not allow any photography—inside or outside.

cement. The cella is an ancient structure decorated internally but access to it is blocked now by the road on the west side which was built some time ago. There is also a small niche to the north of this access door. This cella is the original sepulchre containing the remains of Yuz-Asaph. The structure above it contains the following:

1.Outer wooden sarcophagus.
2.Inner wooden sarcophagus.
3.Two artificial gravestones.
4.One stone slab with carved footprints.
5.One rectangular stone slab or gravestone.
6.One wooden cross.
7.One wooden incense stand.

The entrance to the tomb is from the south and the wooden door is elaborately carved. Strangely enough it depicts crosses. The ceiling consists of thin pieces of wood worked into geometrical patterns known as Khatumbandi style of Kashmiri architecture.

Sarcophagus

Stone of the sepulcher and the wooden cross

The surface is decorated with glazed tiles, in vogue before 1526 A.D. The windows are filled with elaborate wooden tapestry work, formed by joining together little pieces of wood in a geometrical pattern. The walls are constructed of bricks and mortar on the deco-rated wooden pieces projecting externally. The above would show that the original sepulchre, made of stone, is half-buried under the ground, above which the present brick, mortar and wooden struc-ture was raised in about the 16th century.[193]

This tomb was built in the Jewish style, with a room under-ground and having a side door. The shrine is quite distinct from Muslim shrines, which have the Buddhist style of conic domes.

Wooden
sarcophagus of
Yuzu-Asaph at
Rozabal

Historical inscription
at Rozabal

270 THE FIFTH GOSPEL

Near the grave is a stone slab engraved with footprints bearing traces of crucifixion marks; one foot impression has a small round hole and the other has a raised scar wound. These footprints were carved by some ancient unknown artist. As they represent crucifixion marks, it is possible that whoever carved them might have seen Jesus in person.[194]

Devotees and Pilgrims

Devotees and pilgrims to the Tomb of Yuz-Asaph visit it daily in the early morning and evening. They are accustomed to tear off a piece of their clothing or thread and bind these pieces around the wooden sepulchre as a token of homage.

Tombs and Relics

Archaeological excavations have revealed the existence of many Christian tombs and relics in the northwest of the Indian subcontinent. Such relics have been found in Ladakh, Afghanistan, and Central Asian regions, also. In Ladakh, at Tangste, there exist many stone boulders with Aramaic inscriptions with Georgian crosses. On some, the word Yuzu is also written.

In northern India, some crosses and tablets have been found during archaeological excavations at many places. Some remains of tombs have also been located, and it is asserted that these tombs were of the Nestorian Christians, who settled in these regions after their drift away from the Roman Catholic Church, some time around 428 A.D.[195]

Early Christian Tombs

It is interesting that early Christian tombs and graves have been located all along the Makran coast from Harmozia to Karachi. These tombs and graves are decorated with slabs bearing Christian symbols. Not only in Baluchistan, such Christian graves and relics have also been located in Kullu, Kangra, Mandi, and other Himalayan tracts. Similar tombs have been noticed in Kalat, also. The descrip-

Ancient Christian tombstones in northwest India

tion of such tombs given by the then Archaeological Survey of India is summarized as follows:

> Hinidan is situated on the right bank of the river Hab, near Las Bela in Sindh, Pakistan. At this site is an extensive cemetery, containing nearly one hundred sepulchres ornamented with yellowish sandstone slabs.
>
> Constructed with layers of carved slabs, these tombs give the general appearance of slender pyramids. A peculiar feature of the ornamentation is that the top slabs of some of these tombs carry the crude representation of the cross. In some cases, the design shows a human figure with widely outstretched arms, mounted on an ass, with representation of a crucifix. Some slabs show a knight-in-arms riding on a horse, but there is a Latin cross cut out above the head of the horse. Another slab shows a small cross on the face of the horseman. Another un-Islamic feature of these sepulchres is the peculiar form of their burial, which is Syrian, as well as Roman.[196]

The tombs may be divided into two categories: the sepulchres of early Christians, and the tombs of later Muslims. There may be a third category of Hindus, also. Representation of the cross on these slabs proves that some of the graves are from the Christian community. Horses, spears and swords symbolize travel and fighting with the enemies. The tombs with Arabic inscriptions proves that this community adopted Islam at a later stage. The symbol of a lotus on some slabs would indicate Buddhist leanings or a Hindu custom. However, the most important feature of these sepulchres is their Syrian and Roman form of burial, which is locally known as *Shami* and *Rumi*. This style of burial is quite unknown in India and has not been found anywhere except at the above-mentioned sites. This would show that the sepulchres belong to early Syrian or Roman Christians who migrated towards the East in search of Jesus Christ.

During archaeological excavations of some ancient sites in Afghanistan and Kashmir, potsherds of crockery of the Celadon type have been found. For this variety, the Jews were the inventors. This would show that Semites did settle in the region during ancient times and established small colonies. It is also astonishing that the base structures of many ancient monuments testify to their Semitic origin. Their main entrances are set in the eastern wall, which means that these monuments face the west. This is not the case with the Buddhist or Shaivist temples.[197]

Similarly, some graves have been located in Kashmir, laid in an east-west direction, which proves their Jewish origin. When Nadir Shah Durani marched toward India, the chief of the Yousafzai tribe presented him with a copy of the Bible written in Hebrew. He was also presented with several articles used for worship. Some of the soldiers of Nadir Shah Durani who professed Judaism at once recognized the articles of worship as belonging to their faith.[198]

In the open air gallery of the S.P.S. Museum, Srinagar, Kashmir, there is a stone slab for exhibition, 85 cm. square. This stone slab carries an engraving showing a six-cornered star in a circle, with a small circle in the center. Every wing of the star is 25 cm. in length. This figure is of two interlaced equilateral triangles, which is the Star of David, a Jewish symbol. Such symbols, engraved on stones, are found in different parts of the valley, and are used as a *pranali* stand for *lingam*.

In the architectural style, the dome became very popular during the rule of Muslim kings. In certain edifices, the style of dome over dome was adopted, which can be called doubled-dome architecture. We have only a few such double-domed edifices in the world. The earliest specimen is the Tomb of the Rock at Jerusalem; then we have the tomb of Timur at Samarkand. In Kashmir the tomb of the mother of Sultan Zain-ul-abidin and the *Dumut* near Sowara, Srinagar, have the same style of double domes.

Rider with a Cross

The coins of Demetrius of Syria, Alexander the Great, Eucratides the Great, Apollodotus, Hippostratus, Azilises, Lysian, Hyreodes, Spalyrises, Gondaphara and Abdagases are found in the valley of Kashmir and testify to the rule of the Greeks in Kashmir.[199] Kharoshti script, which is written from right to left like the Semitic scripts, was in vogue in the northwestern regions of India from the third century B.C. to the third century A.D. This script appears on the Greek, Scythian, Parthian and Kushana coins.[200] A Kushana seal shows a dignitary on his horse, holding a cross in his hand.[201] It is also a fact

King holding a cross,
first century

that the Scythian tribes who had adopted Christianity crossed the Indus and settled in the northwestern regions of India, including Kashmir.[202] It is interesting to note that the dignitary on this seal has been mentioned as Ra Dso, meaning Raja, in the Greek-Kushana legend. Hence, it is evident that the Raja or Raza of the Scythians, after having crossed the Indus, came to Kashmir along with his tribe with the aim of subjugating the people and forcing Christianity on the people.

The rider on the Central Asian horse wears a cap with two tassels, indicating a high rank. Holding the cross in his hand indicates that he is a Christian and is travelling with this emblem for the propagation of Christianity. His bridle is Central Asian and his belt is Greek.

Similar types of title decorations have also been located at Charsaddah, near Taxila, which depict crucifixion scenes, crosses and horses. These archaeological finds belong to early in the first century A.D.

Stone Footprints

The stone slab bearing impressions of the feet of Yuzu-Asaph which is in the corner of the inner tomb at Srinagar was examined by Kurt Berna, and his report is given as follows:

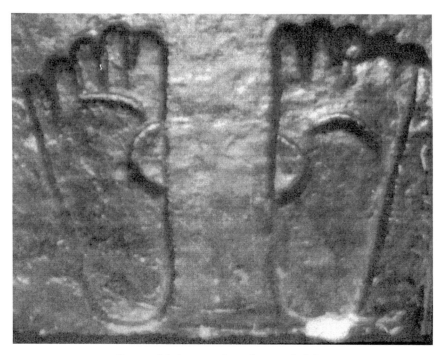

Stone slab impression of wounded feet

In this case, it is very interesting to find the nail-wound reproduction of the left foot near the toe. But the nail-wound reproduction of the right foot is full, at the place where it should be according to the classical view. It could be explained in this way: that the man was crucified with his left foot on top of his right foot, and that only one nail was struck through the both feet.

Secondly, the examination of the footprints reveals that these are not the real footprints of the man, but that the stone carver knew the facts of his crucifixion. As such, he wanted to indicate prominently the piercing of the feet by a nail through using distinguishing marks. He knew that the man had been put on the cross and that his feet, which bore nail marks, had been pierced. Accordingly, he carved the soles of the feet with these distinguishing signs.

Thirdly, it is a fact that when these impressions of the feet are compared with the Holy Shroud of Jesus Christ at Turin, we find that there also the crucifixion was done with the left foot put over the right foot and then the nail struck. After minute examination of the Shroud, it appears that the left knee was more stiff and bowed like the right leg.

In conclusion, indications suggest that the man in the Holy Shroud at Turin and the man buried in the tomb at Srinagar are the same.[203]

Chronology

It is very difficult to set dates for various events in the life span of Jesus Christ. However, an effort has been made below to fix a workable chronology.

Word made flesh	Paleolithic age.
Subsequent advent	6 B.C.
Fight to Egypt	4 B.C.
First journey	7 A.D.
Return to Jerusalem	28 A.D.
Baptism	33 A.D.
Ministry	35 A.D.
Crucifixion	36 A.D.
Reaches Taxila	49 A.D.
Reaches Kashmir	60 A.D.
Meets the King of Kashmir	78 A.D.
Demise	109 A.D.

The Christians of St. Thomas

As a result of the emergence of their empire, the valley of Kashmir came under the subjugation of the Kushanas. Whereas the new rulers patronized Buddhism, the Shaivites suffered innumerable difficulties and passed into oblivion. All religious edifices were taken over by the Buddhists, including the tomb of Yuz-Asaph. Thomas left the country for the south of India.

It is recorded that the Jews had reached the western coasts of India some time in 280 B.C. after the second desecration of the Temple of Jerusalem.[204] These tribes settled at Bombay, Goa, Daman, Dieu, Cochin, and Sri Lanka. Due to the political upheavals in the north Indian region, some more groups of Semites migrated towards the south of India, and this migration continued up to 175 B.C.[205]

These migrations continued for some time, and the king of the region, Airvi, gave them permission to settle in his kingdom. It is also recorded that Isappu Habban, the Chief Priest of the Jews, led them to the kingdom of Airvi.[206] It was during these migrations that Thomas left Kashmir and reached Maelapore. These immigrant Jews had come from Kashmir and they recounted the names of many other Jewish colonies in North India.[207]

We have mentioned earlier that it was Habban who accompanied Thomas during his sea voyage to India.[208] It is also recorded that these Israelite tribes moved down from the north and settled in the south of India. It is also probable that Thomas moved them from Kashmir. It is recorded that the Jewish tribes carried their scriptures with them. Information is available about the Book of Moses, written on leather, which they carried with them to south India from Kashmir.[209] After having settled at Maelapore, Thomas began his missionary activities. He established seven churches in the region, which was dominated by the Shaivite Brahmanas. The lower castes, such as the Shudras and the Vaishyas, were converted to Christianity. Thomas also succeeded in converting Tertia, the queen of Mazdal. The Brahmanas incited the masses against the king, with the result that Thomas suffered martyrdom in a communal riot.

The Church of Malabar founded by Thomas, though independent in certain respects, was connected with the Church of Edessa, and since 325 A.D. has been within the Patriarchal See of Antioch.[210] This Church has long been part of the Church of the east, to which Rome, in contempt, gave the name Nestorian, but which is really the Catholic Church of Assyria. It was once the Church of Persia, and even of China. In the fifth century A.D. this Church put itself under the jurisdiction of the Patriarch at Mosul. The Church has several branches, one being connected with Rome.[211]

The Christian community of South India call themselves Christians of St. Thomas who founded their church in the latter half of the first century A.D.[212] The tomb of Thomas is situated near Fort St. George in Madras, South India, where his relics are preserved. It may be mentioned that after the departure of Thomas from Kashmir, the valley witnessed many revolutions and political upheavals. The Kushanas, who patronized Buddhism, were replaced by the Huns, who patronized Shaivism. Subsequently, the Buddhists were exterminated from the soil, and they ran away towards the hilly regions of Ladakh. Hinduism held sway up to the fourteenth century, when the remnants of the Buddhists accepted Islam. The net result of all these persecutions under the rulers who preceded the Kushanas was that not a single Semite professing Judaism or Christianity remained in the valley of Kashmir. All of them were assimilated into Shaivism, Vaishnuism or Hinduism, and the orthodox ran away towards the south of India to join the Christians of St. Thomas.

No information is available about the early Christian community in Kashmir except that they changed their earlier beliefs and became adherents of the Nestorian thought. It has also been found that there existed Nestorian churches in Kashmir during ancient times, and there also existed Nestorian colonies.[213]

Barkat Ullah writes:

> Recently, several crosses have been found from graves lying in the valleys of North India. Their construction, art and engravings reveal that these are Nestorian crosses.
>
> It also stated that the graves are also of the Nestorians. This establishes that during ancient period, there existed Nestorian churches as well as settlements in Kashmir.[214]

It transpires that at the advent of the Prophet of Islam, there existed Jewish as well as Christian settlements in the valley of Kashmir. It is recorded:

> They had forty priests who were scholars, well read in the Talmud, the Torah, the Bible, and the Apocalypse of Abraham. They would sit in the royal court and give verdicts on cases referred to them by the Kashmiri king.
>
> At the time of the advent of the Prophet of Islam, they felt that mention about his advent existed in their scriptures. Hence, for enquiry, they deputed a mission under their representative "Ganam-Hindi" to Balkh, in Central Asia. After some time, he returned as a converted Muslim. After this event, the Kashmiri Christians joined the fold of Islam, in a collective manner.[215]

The above information, though scanty, collected from the Persian sources is both significant and important. It shows that prior to the fifth century A.D. there were Christian settlements in the valley of Kashmir.

Akbar, the Mughal emperor, began construction of his new capital at Fatehpur Sikri, twenty-two miles from Agra in 1569 and completed it within fifteen years. Of the religious buildings built by him, the most important are the Jamia Masjid, the mausoleum of

Saint Salim Chishti and the Buland Darwaza. Akbar had the following parable inscribed on the gateway:

> Jesus, the son of Mary, said:
> This world is a bridge;
> Pass over it;
> But build no house upon it:
> He who hopes for an hour,
> Hopes for eternity!
> This world does not last more than an hour;
> Spend it in prayers
> For what follows is unknown.

"This world is a bridge," saying of Jesus, inscribed stone slab,
Fathepur Sikri, Agra (The Archaeological Survey of India)

The Moslems of Jesus

We have definite evidence about the Christian communities in Persia, Afghanistan and northwest India in the third century. These Christians were called *Nasara* or the Followers of Jesus of Nazareth. Some of them were also named *Kristanis* or Christians.[216] We know about the followers of Yuzu-Asaph in Kashmir since the advent of the second century. But the most interesting information comes from the followers of Issa, Son of Miriam, who call themselves Moslems. O.M. Burke, who visited Afghanistan, has the following report about them:

> The followers of Issa, Son of Miriam, generally call themselves Muslims and inhabit a number of villages scattered throughout the

western area of Afghanistan whose center is Herat. I have heard of them several times, but considered that they were probably the people who had been converted by European missionaries from Eastern Persia, or else that they were a relic of the time when Herat had been a flourishing bishopric of the Nestorian rite, before the Arabs conquered Persia in the seventh and eighth centuries. But from their own accounts and what I could observe they seem to come from a much older source. There must be about a thousand of these Christians. Their chief is the Abba Yahiya who can recite the succession of teachers through nearly sixty generations to Issa, Son of Miriam, of Nazara, the Kashmiri.[217]

We already know that Jesus is known as Issa and Mary is known as Miriam in the East. Similarly, Nazareth is termed as Nazara or Nasara among the Oriental sources. But the reference to Issa, the Son of Miriam of Nazara, is very interesting and would mean Jesus, the Son of Mary of Nazareth and Kashmir. Here reference to Kashmir is very significant. Jesus, after his escape from the cross, reached Kashmir, where he was known as Yuz-Asaph. It is from that time that these Muslims of Issa seem to have gotten their message, and they still consider Jesus as belonging to Kashmir.

It was by chance that we located a printed publication in the Urdu language which also mentions Issa, the prophet of Allah, whose followers were Muslims. They call him Issa, the Son of Mary, who preached Islam as a religion for his followers.[218] In order to clear the issue, we reproduce some portions from this source.

The Word Made Flesh

1. His mother Miriam was a virgin from an Israelite family. She had not yet married when Allah decided to send his messenger without a father, so that the world would understand that Allah can do whatever He likes or wills. Allah is capable of creating a human being without the aid of a father.

2. When Miriam was fourteen, she went to take a bath in a spring. She had not finished her bath, when Allah ordered Gabriel to carry the first breath of Adam and blow it into the belly of Miriam.

3. When Miriam finished her bath and was about to leave, she saw a handsome young man. She felt afraid and thought that the young man might be from the tribe of goldsmiths and might have harbored bad intentions.

4. He came nearer and said: I have been sent by Allah. I have been sent to give you a handsome child.

5. Hearing this, she said: how can it happen when no man has even touched me until now.

6. The angel said that it is the will of God that a child is born to you without the aid of a father. It has been ordained like that. Then he blew the breath on her belly and disappeared.

7. Miriam came back to her home and engaged herself in prayers.

8. After a few months, signs of pregnancy appeared on Miriam. Then all from the tribe and her family began to cast aspersions on her; saying: you have sinned.

9. But Miriam refuted this, saying that she had never sinned; but none believed her. As such, she stopped going out of her home. When nine months were complete, the angel told her to go to a nearby forest. Issa was born in a natural way without any labor pains.[219]

The miraculous birth of Jesus is accepted by both the Christians as well as the Muslims. But here, the Moslems of Jesus claim that the breath of Adam was put into the womb, while the Gospel says that the Holy Ghost came upon Mary. However, in both the accounts, it is Gabriel who is sent by God to Mary.[220]

Jesus Begins His Ministry

1. When Jesus was young, he received the honor from Allah and revelations started reaching him through Gabriel. In accordance with the wishes of Allah, he asked people to shed evil and *kufur*. He invited them towards truth and Righteousness. The Bani-Israel stood, one and all, against him. They hurled abuses on him, saying that this young chap is shifting us from our religion.

2. Then they inflicted many hardships on Jesus. He felt sorry for them and left the city and sat on the bank of a river.

3. The place where Jesus sat was the place where washermen washed the clothes. Jesus said to them: "You wash filthy clothes, why not wash your hearts?" Then he said again: "You have drowned yourselves in the mud and filth of *kufur* and evil, why don't you come out of it?

Those washermen who heard Jesus came to him and asked: "Which is the soap for washing of hearts?" Jesus uttered this sentence: *"La-illaha-illul-lah, Issa Roh-Allah."* (There is no god but God; Jesus is the Spirit of God.)

4. Then all of them made this invocation: *"La-illa-ha-illullah, Issa Roh-Allah,"* and became Muslims.

5. When this news reached the other group of washermen, they came and asked for a miracle. Issa asked them: "What do you want to witness?" All cried with one voice: "Tell your God to send us a plate full of heavenly food and fruits, so that after eating it, we will recognize that you are a true messenger."

Jesus Performs Miracles

1. Issa prayed to the Lord God saying: "O Allah, these people are ignorant. Have mercy upon them! Let Thy will be done !" At that very moment a voice was heard from the sky: "We will send heavenly food for them who are blessed." At once, plates of heavenly food full of delicacies with roasted fish descended from the sky .

2. The people did not eat this dish but said: "We want another miracle from you. Let this roasted fish come to life." Issa lifted up his eyes towards the sky.

3. Suddenly, the roasted fish came to life and jumped with force into the river. Some felt puzzled, and died.

4, All believing persons sat to eat the heavenly food but the proud refused to partake of this dish. Those who were sick became healthy after eating this food, the poor became wealthy, the blind received eyesight; strangely enough, whatever one wished, one got.

5. For many days, this heavenly food descended from the sky and thousands ate it. Those who rejected this heavenly food with contempt, became victims of arthritis and their faces changed into ugly ones. Many accepted Issa as the prophet of God and became Muslims.

> The glory of truth shone,
> The flowers of belief blossomed,
> The infidels were defeated;
> The blind obtained eyes,
> The lame got legs to walk!

Jesus healing a blind man
(Mark 8: 22-6)

During a wedding feast at Cana
Jesus changes water into "wine"
(John 2: 1-10)

Jesus healing a so-called "leper"
(Mark 1: 40-42) In the ancient
world "leprosy" could denote
a variety of disfiguring skin
conditons.

Details from fifth-century
ivory from Palermo, Sicily,
now in the Victoria and Albert
Museum, London.

(Reproduced *from Jesus—the*
Evidence by Ian Wilson,
courtesy Harper San Francisco)

The sick were blessed with health!
The hungry got food,
Every one danced with joy!

In the above account, a definite statement is made in the fourth verse that, after making an invocation that Allah is the one God and Issa is His Spirit, they became Muslims. Here the author does not speak of the followers of Jesus as Christians but declares that "many accepted him as the prophet of God and became Muslims."[221]

O Woman, Great is Thy Faith

1. It so happened that in a city there lived a young woman with her husband and Allah had bestowed a baby son to them. One day when the father had gone out, the lady was offering the Nimaz, and her child slipped out of his cot and fell into a burning oven. This lady had great faith in her God.

2. She saw that this had happened but continued her prayers till she completed them. Then she proceeded towards the oven.

3. Strangely enough, the oven had turned into a bed of flowers. Her baby boy was safe and playing. She picked him up and kissed the boy. This song came to her lips:

O my Allah, Thou art the creator!
I offer my *Nimaz* to Thee five times:
Thou art my master,
Thou art my Protector
It is thee who saved my child.
O my Allah,
Thou art kind and full of mercy.
O my Allah, I am your dutiful maid;
Accept my gratitude, O Lord of Majesty

4. When Issa heard this episode, he hastened to the lady and asked, "How have you attained this position with God?"

5. The woman replied: "I know nothing except that I abide by the will of God. Under all conditions, I am a servant of Allah. He is my refuge!"

6. Hearing this Issa said: "O woman, great is thy faith. Had you been a man, Allah would have made you a prophet with a book!"

The Muslims offer *Nimaz*, which are obligatory prayers to be performed five times during day and night. Besides this, the Muslims have to join congregations on Fridays. The Christians have to go to church on Sundays only, and they are not required to offer *Nimaz* five times.

In the Gospels, Mary the Mother lives even after the crucifixion of Jesus Christ. But the Moslems of Issa believe that she passed away during the lifetime of Jesus. Here is the relevant account from the work under review.

The Death of Miriam

1. Once, Issa went with his mother Miriam on a long journey. She was very old and weak. It became impossible for her to move or walk.

2. Issa kept her at a place and himself went to the forest to search some herb.

3. In the meanwhile, Miriam became unconscious and died.

4. Allah, the Lord of Majesty deputed heavenly maids to wrap her in a heavenly shroud. She was buried by heavenly maids and angels.

5. When Issa came back, he did not find his mother. He cried: Mother, Mother, where are you?

6. From a nearby grave, a voice came:

> Dear son, I am before my God!
> Dear son, I am near the throne of God!
> Dear son, I am in paradise!
> Dear son, I am protected by the mercy of Allah!
> Dear son, You attend to the work of God!
> Dear son, You call people to the right path!
> Dear son, You come to me soon!

Jesus Preaches

1. Jesus departed from the tomb of Miriam and went to the city. He called the people towards Allah. Many joined his fold and became Muslims.

2. Everyone praised the Lord God but the rich became his enemies. Those who were evil-minded conspired against him. They were *kafir* and their hearts were black. They raised a cry: Issa is against Mossa! He has changed the religion of Mossa. Kill him, Kill him!

3. Issa said:

> O people! Mossa has fixed Saturday as the sacred day.
> It was incumbent on you to offer prayers to Allah on that day.
> It was forbidden to attend to worldly works on that day.
> It was written in the Torah.[222]
> But, now Allah has changed that day and fixed Sunday as his day.
> Consider Sunday as the sacred day.
> Now, the *Enjeel* [223] has come with the new order.
> As such, obey *Enjeel* and entertain no doubts in your heart!

While the Muslims obeyed his sacred orders, the kafirs did not. The Muslims declared that they would obey Issa with their heart and soul. But the evil-minded kafirs incited the masses against Issa. They alleged that Issa had desecrated Mossa and *Torah*. As such, they said, it was the duty of all followers of Mossa to kill Issa.

4. Now thousands of kafirs decided to kill Issa.

5. There were some good *yuhudis*,[224] who said: "Leave Issa alone. Do not kill him. Are you not the same persons who killed *Zakariya* [225] with a saw? Are you not afraid of Allah? Fear the wrath of God!"

6. But they did not listen to these wise words. They were bent upon killing Issa. They had become mad!

7. They went to the king and incited him against Issa. He declared: "Anyone who kills Issa will get a reward."

8. The evil-minded persons hatched conspiracies.[226]

The Departure of Jesus

1. The kafirs held a meeting and engaged a *yuhudi* to kill him. When Issa was in a house, they surrounded it so that they could kill him.

2. But Allah had willed otherwise! As ordained by God, Gabriel flew straight away to that house where Issa had absorbed himself in

prayers. The angel salaamed Issa and flew with him towards the sky. All the prophets welcomed him and Allah congratulated him for his work. Since then Issa is alive in the fourth heaven!

3. The *kafirs* who had surrounded the house, deputed one person named Shiyuh to search out Issa. He went in but could see none inside the house. When he came out, all cried: "Kill him." He felt bewildered because his face had transfigured and he looked like Issa.

4. They captured Shiyuh and put him on the gallows thinking that they had killed Issa.

5. Allah says that He has protected Issa and those who think he is dead are in the wrong.

These followers of Issa, Son of Miriam, call themselves Muslims. Once a week, they join a ritual meal in which bread and wine are taken as symbolic of the grosser and finer nutritions which are the experiences of attainment of nearness to Allah. They are convinced, too, that the day will come when the world will discover the truth about Jesus.[227]

Arabic inscription describing Jesus as "Al-Sayyid-Al-Masih"
(His Excellency—the Masiha) and as the crowned prince in the lap of
the Holy Mariam (Mary-ilee Mother), 1070 A.D.

Notes

CHAPTER ONE: SOURCES

1. Peak. *Commentary on the Bible*, pp. 681-744.
2. George Barker Stevens. *The Teaching of Jesus*, p. 21.
3. Eusebius. *Church History*, 111, p. 39, as quoted: Ibid.
4. Irenaeus. *Against Heresies*, III, I, p. 7, as quoted: Ibid.
5. Luke 1: 1–4.
6. John 21: 19.
7. Acts 4: 36.
8. Powell Davies. *The Meaning of the Dead Sea Scrolls*, p. 104.
9. *Ante-Nicane Christian Library*, Vol. 20, as quoted in *Jesus in Heaven on Earth*, p. 246. Addenda.
10. Warner Keller. *The Bible as History*, p. 407.
11. Muhammad Ahmad Mazhar. *Arabic*, p. 7.
12. *Bhavishya-maha-purana*, Vrs. 17–32.
13. *Studies in the History of Religions*, Vol. 18. 99, pp. 54–57.
14. The manuscript is in the collection of late Rev. S.S. Gergan, Gupkar Road, Srinagar, Kashmir.
15. Finding a name written in red ink—St. Issa—on pages 118 and 119, Professor Hassnain photographed them. After translation, it appeared that these two pages referred to the Buddhist scrolls found by Nicolas Notovitch in the Hemis Monastery, Ladakh.
16. Article in *The Nineteenth Century*, April, 1896.
17. Johan Forsstrom. *The King of the Jews*, p. 187.
18. Aurel Stain. *On Central Asian Tracks*, pp. 214–216.
19. Johan Forsstrom. *The King of the Jews*, pp. 230–231. See also *Jesus Died in Kashmir* by A. Faber Kaiser, p. 91.

CHAPTER TWO: GENESIS

1. The Septuagint Bible. Genesis 1: 1–27.
2. Genesis 6: l–3.
3. Genesis 6: 4.

4. Genesis 6: 4.

5. *The Concise Encyclopaedia of World History*, Ed. John Bowle, p. 13.

6. Sonia Cole. *Races of Man*, pp. 50–51.

7. Encyclopaedia Britannica, Micropaedia, Vol. VII.

8. John Bowle. Ibid. p. 42.

9. Giuseppe Tucci. *Transhimalaya*, p. 37.

10. Giuseppe Tucci. Ibid. p. 47.

11. Chakravarti. B. *A Cultural History of Bhutari*, p. 135.

12. Genesis 12: 14.

13. Genesis 21: 2.

14. Genesis 18: 9–14.

15. Genesis 21: 1–3.

16. Genesis 18: 5–8.

17. Genesis 18: 9–13.

18. Genesis 21: 1–2.

19. Duncan Greenlees. *The Gospel of Israel*, p. 19.

20. Chakravarti. B. *A Cultural History of Bhutan*, p. 127.

21. Exodus 3: 14–15.

22. Margolis & Alexander Marx. *A History of the Jewish People*, p. 16.

23. Exodus 20: 3–17.

24. Deuteronomy 5: 7–21.

25. Exodus. 34: 28.

26. Chakravarti. *Classical Studies in Ancient Races & Myths.* p. 89.

27. Genesis 18: 1.

28. Exodus 15: 20–21.

29. Numbers 12: 1–2.

30. The Septuagint Bible. Deuteronomy 32: 49–52.

31. Deuteronomy 34: 1–8.

32. Faber Kaisar. *Jesus Died in Kashmir*, p. 120. Peak's Commentary on the Bible quoted.

33. Margolis & Alexander Marx. Ibid. p. 180.

34. Josephus. *The Jewish War*, Chapt. 7.

35. Margolis & Alexander Marx. Ibid. p. 9.

36. Thomas Holditch. *The Gates of India*, p. 49.

37. Ezekiel 20: 32–38.

38. George More. *The Lost Ten Tribes*, pp. 145–48.

39. Tabaqat-i-Nasiri. p. 109.

40. Joseph Wolf. "Mission to Bokhara," as quoted in *Jesus in Heaven on Earth* by Nazir Ahmed, p. 287.

41. Margolis & Alexander Marx. Ibid. p. 48.

42. Khan Roshan Khan. *Tazkirah*, pp. 51–52.

43. *The Concise Encyclopaedia of World History*, Ed. John Bowles, p. 102.

44. Thomas Holdich. *The Gates of India*, p. 50.

45. Alexander Brunes. *Travels into Bokhara*, p. 139.

46. Khan Roshan Khan. Ibid. p. 74.
47. Khwaja Nazir Ahma. *Jesus in Heaven on Earth,* pp. 305–307.
48. Alexander Brunes. Ibid. p. 139.
49. Thomas Holditch. Ibid. p. 49.
50. Miguel Serrano. *The Serpent of Paradise,* pp. 140–142.
51. Interview dated 5th Jan. 1982 with the Head of Pashtoon Jirgah.
52. Roshan Khan: Tazkirah. *History of the Afghans,* p. 260.
53. Bernier. *Journey Toward Kashmir,* p. 430.
54. Katre. *The General History of the Mughal Kingdom,* p. 195.
55. Claudius Buknain. *Christian Researches in India,* p. 22.
56. Lawrence. *The Valley of Kashmir,* p. 318.
57. Hargopal Khasta. *Guidasta-i-Kashmir,* p. 19.
58. Zahoor-ul-Hassan. *Nigaristan-i-Kashmir,* p. 98.
59. George Moore. *The Lost Tribes,* p. 151.
60. Buknain. Ibid. p. 229.
61. Genesis 10: 1–6.
62. Baber. *Memoirs,* trans. Leyden & Erskine, p. 313.
63. William Jones. *Kashmir, India Researches,* I, p. 268.
64. Thomas Wardle. *Kashmir,* p. 290.
65. Kalhana. *Rajatarangini,* trans. Stein, I, pp. 286–287.
66. Khawaja Nazir Ahmad. *Jesus in Heaven on Earth,* pp. 302–307.
    Aziz Ahmad. Asrari-i-Kashir, pp. 337–343.
    Andreas Faber Kaiser. *Jesus Vivio y Murio en Cachemira,* pp. 113–128.
67. The Book of Esther T: 1–4.
68. Margolis & Alexander Marx. Ibid. p. 127.
69. *Cambridge History of India,* p. 421.
70. Hassnain, F. M. *Buddhist Kashmir,* p. 2.
71. Rhys Davids. *Buddhism,* p. 183.
72. Mirza Ghulam Ahmad. *Jesus in India,* p. 83.
73. Swete, H. B. *An Introduction to the Old Testament in Greek,* p. 16.
74. *The Crucifixion by an Eye-Witness,* p. 189.
75. Hassnain, F. M. *Hindu Kashmir,* p. 21.
76. Encyclopaedia Britannica . Micropaedia, Vol. VII.
77. Abdul Qadir. *Hashmat-i-Kashmir,* p. 7.
78. Mohammad Aazam. *Tarikh-i-Aazmi,* p. 84.
79. George Moore. *The Lost Tribes,* p. 137.
80. Epistle to the Hebrews. Ch. III, as quoted from *Jesus Died in Kashmir* by A. Faber Kaiser, p. 120.
81. Kalhana. Ibid. VIII, 2431.
82. Nil-toop means the peak of Mount Nabo. Nowall. *The Highlands of India.* V. 2. pp. 19–90.
83. Deuteronomy 34: 1–6.
84. Abdul Qadir. Ibid. p. 7.
85. Al-Beruni. *Kitab-ul-Hind,* V. l, p. 274.

86. Mohi-ud-din Hajini. *Maqalat*, p. 99.
87. Abdul Ahad Azad. *Kashmiri Zaban*, p. 10.
88. Bashir Ahmad. *Humayun*, Lahore, 1940.
89. Hassnain, F. M. *Hindu Kashmir*, p. 12.
90. Chakravarti, C. *Classical Studies in Ancient Races and Myths*, op. cit. p. 62.
91. Richard Temple. *Sayings of Lala Ded*, p. 65.
92. Genesis 31: 47–49.
93. Genesis 28 : 18–19.
94. Allan Menzies. *History of Religion,* p. 180.
95. Jawaharlal Nehru. *Glimpses of World History,* p. 86.
96. Kalhana. Ibid. Vol. II, p. 112.
97. Saadullah. *Tarikh-i-Sulaiman.* (Mss.).

CHAPTER THREE: THE SON OF GOD

1. John 1: 1–2.
2. John 1: 14.
3. John 3: 12–13.
4. Acts 1: 11.
5. Timothy 3: 16.
6. I Peter 1: 20.
7. Genesis 6: 14.
8. Timothy 3: 16.
9. Bhavishya-maha-pwana. Vrs. 17–32.
10. Mark 14: 36.
11. Matthew 1: 23.
12. Fuller, R. H. *New Testament Christology*, p. 23.
13. Luke 21: 8. *Kri or Chri* is a term used by Kashmiris for Christians.
14. Matthew 8: 8.
15. Luke 6: 46.
16. Nazir Ahmad. *Jesus in Heaven on Earth*, p. 81.
17. Matthew 2: 23.
18. Acts 24: 5.
19. Allegro, John. *The Sacred Mushroom and the Cross*, pp. 35–36.
20. Fuller, R. H. *New Testament Christology*, p. 29.
21. Joshua 1: 1.
22. Psalms 50: 73–83.
23. Mulla Nadri. *Tarikh-i-Kashmir*, folio 69.
24. Lepancer. *Mystical Life of Jesus Christ.*
25. von Daniken, E. *Miracle of the Gods*, p. 69.
26. Matthew 2: 1.
27. Luke 1: 36.
28. John 7: 52.

29. Matthew 26: 69–71.
30. Keller, Werner. *The Bible as History*, p. 346.
31. Matthew 1: 16.
32. Luke 3: 23.
33. Forbes Robinson. *The Apocryphal Gospel*, p. 1.
34. Luke 1: 5.
35. Yrjo Hiren. *The Sacred Shrine*, p. 206.
36. Luke 1: 28.
37. Luke 1: 32–33.
38. Luke 1: 35.
39. Luke 1: 30.
40. Luke 1: 5–38.
41. Luke 1: 40–42.
42. Gospel of James 8: 3, as quoted in Jesus *in Heaven on Earth* by Khawaja Nazir Ahmad, p. 134.
43. Matthew 1: 19.
44. Gospel of James 16: 1–2.
45. Nazir Ahmad. *Jesus in Heaven on Earth* , p. 136.
46. Romans 1: 3.
47. Galatians 4: 4.
48. Mark 10: 2–8.
49. William Phipps. *Was Jesus Married?*, p. 40.
50. *The Crucifixion by an Eye-witness,* pp. 40–41.
51. Genesis 6: 1–2.
52. Isaiah 7: 14.
53. Genesis 21: 1–2.
54. Schonfeld, Hugh J. *The Passover Plot,* p. 49.
55. Mark 10: 48.
56. Bhavishya-maha-purana. 17–32.
57. Peake. *Commentary on the Bible*, pp. 681, 700, 724, 744.
58. Galatians 1: 7–19.
59. Basileion. Samuel 11: VIII. 14.
60. Fuller. *The Foundations of New Testament Christology*, p. 202.
61. Allegro, John. *The Sacred Mushroom and the Cross*, p. 8.
62. Daniken. Eric von. *In Search of Ancient Gods*, p. 23.
63. John 1: 1–3.
64. John 1: 15.
65. Luke 2: 1–7.
66. Werner Keller. *The Bible as History*, p. 330.
67. A. Powell Davies. *The Meaning of the Dead Sea Scrolls*, p. 90.
68. Werner Keller. *The Bible as History,* p. 338.
69. Werner Keller. *The Bible as History*, pp. 332–336.
70. Matthew 2: 1–3.

71. Matthew 2: 1–2.
72. Matthew 2: 11.
73. Matthew 2: 12.
74. *The Septuagint Bible.* Ed. by C. Muses, p. XXI (Introduction).
75. Hassnain. *Ladakh the Moonland*, p. 74.
76. Matthew 2: 11.
77. Nicolas Notovitch. *The Unknown Life of Christ*, pp. 142–144.
78. *The Crucifixion by an Eye-witness*, p. 35.
79. Luke 2: 34-35.
80. *The Life of Saint Issa*, 111: 12.
81. Matthew 2: 1.
82. *The Crucifixion by an Eye-witness*, p. 35.
83. Hakim Ameen. *St. Mark and the Coptic Church*, p. 8.
84. Werner Keller. *The Bible as History*, p. 341.
85. Nazir Ahmad. *Jesus in Heaven on Earth*, p. 218.
86. *Encyclopaedia Britannica*, Art. Essenes.
87. *The Crucifixion by an Eye-witness*, pp. 41–43.
88. Nazir Ahmad. *Jesus in Heaven on Earth*, p. 114.
89. Eusebius. *Ecclesiastical History*, Vol. 11, XVII 2–23.
90. Allegro, John. *The Sacred Mushroom and the Cross*, p. 61.
91. Johan Forsstrom. p. 289.
92. Ulfat Aziz-us-Samad. *The Great Religions of the World*, p. 44.
93. Peter De Rosa. *Jesus Who Became Christ*, p. 109.
94. Levi. *The Aquarian Gospel of Jesus*, p. SO.
95. Luke 2: 42–46.
96. *The Crucifixion by an Eye-witness*, pp. 4W7.
97. Luke 2: 48–49.
98. *Encyclopaedia Britannica*. Micropaedia, Vol. 111, p. 965.
99. Mark 1: 7–8.
100. *The Crucifixion by an Eye-witness*, pp. 49–53.
101. Matthew 1: 1–16.
102. *Journale Asiatiqe*, 1869. Il, p. 439.
103. Matthew 1: 18.
104. Matthew 1: 20.
105. Mark 6: 3.
106. Ibid.
107. Ibid.
108. Nazir Ahmad. *Jesus in Heaven on Earth*, p. 138.
109. Matthew 2: 19–20.
110. Luke 2: 48.
111. Hastings. *Dictionary of the Bible*, p. 434, as quoted in Jesus *in Heaven On Earth*, p. 113.
112. Luke 2: 48–51.

113 . Luke 2: 40.
114. Nicolas Notovitch. *The Unknown Life of Christ*, p. 144.
115. Luke 2: 41–44.
116. *Himalaya: A Monograph*. Ed. Francis Grant Rerich, pp. 148–153.
117. Jami-ut-Tawarikh quoted by Johan Forsstrom in *The King of the Jews*, p. 176.
118. Johan Forsstrom. *The King of the Jews*, p. 176.
119. J. B. Segal. *Edessa, the Blessed City*, pp. 67–68.
120. Miguel Serrano. *The Serpent of Paradise*, pp. 142–43.
121. Janet Bock. *The Jesus Mystery*, p. 118.
122. Werner Keller. *The Bible as History*, p. 323.
123. Duncan Greenless. *The Gospel of Israel*, p. ixii.
124. Matthew 3: 1–3.
125. Luke 1: 13–20.
126. Luke 1: 36–42.
127. *The Crucifixion by an Eye-witness.* pp. 47–48.
128. Luke 1: 80.
129. Luke 1: 76.
130. Luke 3: 2–3.
131. Matthew 3: 2.
132. Luke 3: 10–14.
133. Luke 3: 16.
134. John 1: 29–33.
135. Luke 3: 22.
136. *The Aquarian Gospel of Jesus the Christ*, 64: 1, p. 106.
137. Matthew 4: 11.
138. Josephus. Wnr, 11, 136.
139. *The Aquarian Gospel*, pp. 83-85.
140. Werner Keller. *The Bible as History*, p. 347.
141. John 1: 35–36.
142. John 1: 49.
143. Luke 4: 1.
144. James W. Douglass. "The Yin-Yang of Resistance and Contemplation," *Gandhi Marg*, July, 1972.
145. Matthew 4: 3–4.
146. Luke 4: 5–7.
147. Matthew 4: 5–7.
148. Luke 4: 18–19.
149. Malcolm Muggeridge. *Jesus, the Man Who Lives*, p. 60.
150. *The Aquarian Gospel*, pp. 87–97.
151. John 1: 51.
152. Luke 6: 20–21.
153. John 3: 19–21.

154. Mark 12: 29–31.
155. John 8: 59.
156. Mark 2: 73.
157. Hugh Schonfeld. *The Passover Plot*, p. 70.
158. Lulce 4: 24.
159. Mark 6: 4.
160. Matthew 5: 19.
161. Luke 8: 2.
162. *The Crucifixion by an Eye-witness*, p. 531.
163. Johan Forsstrom. *The King of the Jews*, p. 128.
164. *The Crucifixion by an Eye-witness*, p. 54.
165. Werner Keller. *The Bible as History*, p. 347.
166. Matthew 11: 2.
167. Luke 7: 22.
168. Matthew 2: 9–10.
169. Luke 7: 28–33.
170. Werner Keller. *The Bible as History*, p. 348.
171. Mark 6: 22.
172. *The Aquarian Gospel*, p. 103.
173. Hugh Schonfeld. *The Passover Plot*, p. 256.
174. Mark 6: 27.
175. *The Aquarian Gospel*, p. 169.
176. John 10: 14.
177. Luke 6: 12.
178. Matthew 10: 1–4.
179. Luke 6: 16.
180. Mark 3: 16.
181. John 14: 22.
182. Schonfeld, Hugh J. *The Passover Plot*, p. 76.
183. Matthew 10: 6.
184. Luke 10: 2–10.
185. Mark 6: 8–9.
186. Matthew 10: 16–23.
187. Matthew 10: 9.
188. Matthew 10: 28.
189. Matthew 10: 34.
190. James W. Douglas. "The Yin-Yang of Resistance and Contemplation," article in *Gandhi Marg*, July, 1972.
191. Faber Kaiser. *Jesus Died in Kashmir*, pp. 22–24.
192. Luke 10: 1.
193. Matthew 10: 5–7.
194. Luke 10: 3–6.
195. George Barker Stevens. *The Teaching of Jesus*, p. 63.

CHAPTER FOUR: MINISTRY AND CRUCIFIXION

1. Werner Keller. *The Bible as History,* p. 350.
2. *The Aquarian Gospel,* pp. 112–113.
3. Matthew 4: 23–25.
4. John 7: 16–19.
5. Matthew 5: 3–10.
6. Luke 13: 1.
7. Matthew 5–47.
8. John 7:1.
9. Mark 7: 24.
10. Matthew 26: 6.
11. Luke 7: 36–39.
12. *The Crucifixion by an Eye-witness*, pp. 53–55.
13. *The Aquarian Gospel,* p. 161.
14. John 11: 5.
15. Johan Forsstrom. *The King of the Jews,* p. 126.
16. Johan Forsstrom. *The King of the Jews,* p. 128.
17. Johan Forsstrom. *The King of the Jews,* p. 128.
18. *Times*, London, March 8, 1963.
19. Luke 10: 41–42.
20. Matthew 26: 8–9.
21. *The Aquarian Gospel,* p. 151.
22. Luke 7: 44–47.
23. *The Aquarian Gospel*, p. 151.
24. John 11: 1–44.
25. *The Aquarian Gospel,* p. 152.
26. Mark 8: 30.
27. Matthew 16: 22–23.
28. Matthew 16: 24–25.
29. Mark 9: 2.
30. Luke 9: 30.
31. *The Aquarian Gospel,* p. 187.
32. Matthew 17: 4.
33. Mark 9: 7.
34. Matthew 17: 3–6.
35. Matthew 18: 24.
36. John 7: 3–4.
37. Luke 9: 52–56.
38. Luke 10: 1.
39. Luke 13: 33.
40. Matthew 23: 37–38.
41. John 11: 47–48.
42. *The Aquarian Gospel*, p. 194.

43. Matthew 26: 45.
44. John 11: 54.
45. Matthew 17: 25.
46. Mark 9: 35.
47. Luke 19: 9.
48. Mark 11: 7.
49. Luke 19: 38.
50. John 12: 13.
51. Luke 19: 40.
52. Mark 14: 17.
53. John 2: 13–14.
54. Luke 19: 46.
55. John 2: 18–19.
56. Matthew 24.
57. *Aquarian Gospel*, p. 220.
58. Matthew 28: 14–16.
59. Mark 14: 36.
60. Barnes, W. E. *The Testament of Abraham*, pp. 140–151.
61. John 18: 3.
62. Matthew 26: 53.
63. Mark 14: 48–49.
64. Matthew 26: 61.
65. Werner Keller. *Bible as History*, p. 355.
66. Matthew 27: 11.
67. Luke 23: 4.
68. Faber Kaisar. *Jesus Died in Kashmir*, p. 23.
69. Luke 23: 6–7.
70. Luke 23: 8–11.
71. Luke 23: 13–17.
72. John 19: 12.
73. Faber Kaiser. *Jesus Died in Kashmir,* p. 25.
74. Matthew 27: 24.
75. As quoted in *The Crucifixion by an Eye-witness*, pp. 29–30.
76. "Golgotha" in Hebrew means "the place of the skull."
77. Luke 23–27.
78. Mark 15: 21.
79. *The Crucifixion by an Eye-witness*, p. 58.
80. Luke 23: 28–29.
81. *The Crucifixion by an Eye-witness*, pp. 58-59.
82. Matthew 27: 34.
83. Mark 15: 23.
84. *The Crucifixion by an Eye-witness*, pp. 50-60.
85. John 18: 14–16.
86. Werner Keller. *Bible as History*, p. 359.

87. *The Crucifixion by an Eye-witness*, p. 64.
88. Dummelow. *Commentary on the Holy Bible*, p. 717.
89. Matthew 27: 45.
90. *The Crucifixion by an Eye-witness*, p. 64.
91. Mark 15: 34.
92. Matthew 27: 46.
93. Luke 23: 46.
94. John 19: 30.
95. Matthew 7: 1–8.
96. Mark 14: 36.
97. Luke 22: 43.
98. John 11: 41–42.
99. Puruckar, G. *Clothed with the Sun*, p. 40.
100. Psalms 22: 1–20.
101. Psalms 22: 1–5.
102. Psalms 22: 9.
103. Psalms 22: 16–18.
104. Psalms 22: 20–22.
105. Allegro, John. *The Sacred Mushroom and the Cross*, pp. 158, 199, 305.
106. William Hawird. *A Note Book on the Old and New Testaments of the Bible*, Vol. 1: p. 427.
107. Ram Dhan. *Krishen Bainti*, p. 72.
108. Hassan Shirazi. *Risala Tehqiqat-i-Garihabah*, pp. 21–24.
109. Imply, P. C. "Wonderful Stories of Islam," p. 249, *Star of Britannica*. London, Jan., 1954; *Mirror*, London, Feb. 1, 1954.
110. Bhatnagar, K. L. *Buddha Chamitkar, Ram Narayan*, Buddha Yougia, p. 54.
111. *The Crucifixion by an Eye-witness*, pp. 64–65.
112. John 23: 50.
113. Luke 23: 50.
114. Mark 15: 40.
115. Matthew 27: 56.
116. *The Crucifixion by an Eye-witness*, p. 62.
117. John 19: 39.
118. Mark 15: 45.
119. John 19: 39.
120. John 3: 1–3.
121. *Jewish Encyclopaedia*, Vol. 8, p. 250.
122. *The Crucifixion by an Eye-witness*, p. 74.
123. Luke 23: 44.
124. John 19: 32–33.
125. John 19: 34.
126. Ferrar. *Life of Christ*, p. 421.

127. *The Crucifixion by an Eye-witness,* pp. 65–75.
128. Exodus 20–8.
129. Ezekiel 46: 3.
130. John 19: 31.
131. Miguel Serrano. *The Serpent of Paradise,* p. 143.
132. Kalhana Panditta. *Rajatarangini,* Vrs. 11, 72–106.
133. John 19: 39.
134. Luke 23: 56.
135. *The Crucifixion by an Eye-witness,* p. 74.
136. Dummelov. *Commentary on the Holy Bible,* p. 808.
137. *Encyclopaedia Britannica.* Article on the Essenes.
138. *The Crucifixion by an Eye-Witness,* p. 153.
139. *The Crucifixion by an Eye-Witness,* pp. 78–93.
140. *Liber Almansoria* by Rhazes is also known as *De Pestilentia.*
141. *Canon of Avicenna,* Vol. 5, p. 93 (Urdu).
142. *Qarab-ud-Din-i-Kabir,* Vol. 2, p. 75.
143. *Minhaj-ul-Bayan.* Vol. 2, p. 576.
144. SyedAbddul Hye. *Marham-i-Issa Ansar Allah,* Rabwah, March, 1978.
145. *Life of Christ,* p. 79.
146. *Globo,* Brazil, dated March, 3, 1985.
147. Mark 15: 46.
148. John 19: 41.
149. Inayat-ullah Khan Al-Mashriqi. *Tazkirah* (Urdu), pp. 16–17.
150. J. B. Segal. *Edessa-the-Blessed City,* pp. 67–69.
151. From *Migne,* Vol. CXIII, Cols. 423–53 (Paris, 1857), copy in *The Shroud of Turin,* Ian Wilson, pp. 313–331.
152. Engraving on silk in the collection of Sherborne Castle, Dorset, England.
153. Ian Wilson. *The Shroud of Turin,* pp. 288–305.
154. Kurt Berma. *Jesus Nicht am Kreuz Gestorben,* pp. 102–142.
155. Ian Wilson. *The Shroud of Turin,* p. 276.
156. Luke 24: 1.
157. John 20: 1.
158. Matthew 28: 5.
159. Mark 16: 5.
160. Luke 24: 5–7.
161. Mark 16: 7.
162. Matthew 28: 8–10.
163. Mark 16: 8.
164. John 20: 2.
165. Luke 24: 12.
166. John 20: 7.
167. Luke 24: 12.

168. Peter 9: 35–40.
169. Mark 16: 5.
170. Matthew 11: 14.
171. *The Crucifixion by an Eye-witness*, p. 153.
172. Luke 24: 25–26.
173. Luke 24: 30.
174. Mark 16: 12.
175. John 20: 19.
176. Luke 24: 36–42.
177. John 20: 26–27.
178. John 21: 1–12.
179. John 21: 16.
180. Mark 16: 15.
181. Luke 24: 50.
182. Matthew 10: 23.
183. Luke 9: 27.
184. Matthew 16: 28.
185. Mark 9: 1.
186. Matthew 8: 23–27.
187. Mark 6: 48–49.
188. Luke 4: 33–36.
189. John 4: 46–51.
190. Luke 17: 11–14.
191. Mark 7: 31–37.
192. Luke 14: 1–6.
193. Mark 8: 1–8.
194. Matthew 16: 14.
195. Genesis 20: 17.
196. Numbers 11: 2.
197. Matthew 21: 22.
198. John 14: 16.
199. John 17: 9–20.
200. Matthew 26: 39.
201. A. Schweitzer. *The Quest of the Historical Jesus*, as quoted in A. Powell
    Davies, *The Meaning of the Dead Sea Scrolls*, p. 122.
202. Luke 22: 41–42.
203. Mark 14: 36.
204. John 10: 15–18.
205. *Barrassiha-ye-Tarikhi* (Historical Studies of Iran), V. 7, No. 3, 1942.
206. *Sitzungsberg der Berliner Akad*, Phil. Hist. Kl. 1925, p. 366.
207. Bull. *School Oriental Studies*, London, 9, 1938, p. 503.
208. S. S. Gergan. Letter dated April 4, 1976.
209. Guiseppe Tucci. *Transhimalaya*, p. 39.

CHAPTER FIVE: JESUS CHRIST IN THE EAST

1. A. Powell Davies. *Dead Sea Scrolls*, pp. 109–110.
2. *Encyclopaedia Britannica*, Art. "Essenes."
3. John 10: 39–40.
4. Edersheim. *The Life and Times of Jesus*, 1, 148.
5. *The Crucifixion by an Eye-witness*, p. 35.
6. Testaments of the Twelve Patriarchs. Joseph 1: 5–6 as quoted in A. Powell Davies, *The Meaning of the Dead Sea Scrolls*, p. 104
7. *The Crucifixion by an Eye-Witness*, p. 124.
8. Robertson Graves & Joshua Pedro. *Jesus in Rome*.
9. Acts 4–6.
10. Acts 9: 10–15.
11. Acts 9: 20–22.
12. Acts 12: 25.
13. *Encyclopaedia Britannica*. Micropaedia, Vol. VII.
14. Acts 13: 9.
15. *Encyclopaedia Britannica*. Micropaedia, Vol. VII.
16. Abu-Huraira. *Kanz-ul-Aimal*, II, p. 34.
17. Ibn-i-Jarir. *Tatsir Ibn-i-Jarir-at-Tabari*, Vol. 111, p. 191.
18. Luke 8: 2.
l9. Matthew 27: 26.
20. Luke 24: 10.
21. John 20: 12.
22. John 20: 16.
23. *Times*, London, March 8, 1963.
24. Hazrat Mirza Ghulam Ahmad. *Jesus in India*, p. 98. Jesus is surnamed as Ruh-Allah or "the Spirit of God" among the Muslims.
25. Mumtaz Ahmad Faruquii. *The Crumbling of the Cross*, p. 56, quotes from *The Heart of Asia* by Nicolas Roerich.
26. Mumtaz Ahmad Faruqui. *The Crumbling of the Cross*, pp. 55–56.
27. Josephus. *Antiquities*, XVIII, 9: 1–8.
28. Macmunn, Townsend. *The Holy Land*, Vol. II, p. 61.
29. Mir Khwand. *Rauza-tus-Safa*, Col. 1, p. 149.
30. J.B. Segal. *Edessa—the Blessed City*, p. 67.
31. Mumtaz Ahmad Faruqui. *The Crumbling of the Cross*, p. 67.
32. J.B. Segal. *Edessa—the Blessed City*, p. 69.
33. J.B. Segal. *Edessa—the Blessed City*, p. 68.
34. Farh~ng-i-Asafiyah. (Dictionary) Vol. I, p. 91.
35. Agha Mustafa. *Ahwal-i-Ahaliyan-i-Paras*, p. 219.
36. Meger G.R. *Witness of Antiquity*, p. 19.
37. Waddell. *Indo-Sumerian Seals Deciphered*, pp. 114–119.
38. Mir Khwand. *Rauzatus-Safa*, pp. 133–35.

39. Luigi Pareti. *History of Mankind,* Vol. II, p. 850.
40. Schonfield. *Saints against Caesar*, p. 142.
41. Matthew 23: 37–39.
42. Josephus. *Wars,* III, iv, 1. X, p. 9.
43. *The Life of Saint Issa,* VIII: 6–7.
44. Levi. *The Aquarian Gospel,* p. 79.
45. *The Life of Saint Issa,* VIII: 15–20.
46. *The Life of Saint Issa,* 12 13.
47. Faqir Muhamad. *Jame-ut-Towarikh,* Vol. II, p. 81.
48. *The Life of Saint Issa,* V. 9.
49. *The Aquarian Gospel of Jesus the Christ,* 25: 23–26.
50. *The Life of Saint Issa,* V. 16.
51. *The Life of Saint Issa,* V. 18.
52. *The Life of Saint Issa,* V. 20–23.
53. *The Aquarian Gospel of Jesus the Christ,* 31: 1–20.
54. *The Aquarian Gospel of Jesus the Christ,* 32: 42–43.
55. *The Life of Saint Issa,* VI: 4.
56. *The Aquarian Gospel of Jesus the Christ,* 33: 1–10.
57. *The Unknown Life of Jesus Christ,* VI: II.
58. *The Life of Saint Issa,* VI: 15.
59. *Studies in the History of Religions,* V. 18.
60. Ahamd Shah, the author of *Four Years in Tibet,* was deputed in 1894 by the then Christian Mission in India to refute the findings of Nicolas Notovitch.
61. *The Life of Saint Issa,* IX: 1–3.
62. *Nineteenth Century,* October, 1894. *Nineteenth Century,* April, 1896.
63. *The Museum, New Series,* published by the Newark Museum Association, 1972, p. 51.
64. Abhedananda. *Kashmir O Tibbate,* p. 269.
65. *The Life of Saint Issa,* VI: 4.
66. Meer Izzut-oolah. *Travels in Central Asia,* trans. Henderson, pp. 13–14.
67. Tokan Sumi. *Yakshas—the Guardian Tribes of the 4th Buddhist Council.*
68. Rhys Davids. *Buddhism,* p. 180.
69. Max Muller. *Sacred Books of the East,* Vol. XI, p. 318.
70. I-Tsing. *A Record of the Buddhist Religion,* trans. J. Takakwu.
71. Helmut Goeckel. *Die Messias Legitimation Jesu,* p. 514.
72. *The Illustrated Weekly of India,* Vol. CI 45, Dec. 21–27, 1980, p. 26.
73. Hasrat Mirsa Ghulam Ahamd. *Jesus in India,* p. 98.
74. Luke 12: 33.
75. John 10: 11.
76. *The Aquarian Gospel of Jesus the Christ,* 36: 11–36.
77. *The Life of Saint Issa,* VI: 6–12.
78. *The Life of Saint Issa,* VII: 5–9.
79. *The Aquarian Gospel of Jesus the Christ,* 37: 1–17.

80. John 20: 28.
81. Rapson, *Ancient India*, p. 174.
82. John 2: 16.
83. Vincent Arthur Smith. *The Early History of India*, p. 204.
84. *Acta Thomae*, Syriac Text, IV, p. 182.
85. Salmond. *The Writings of Hirpiclytus*, Vol. III, p. 131.
86. John Reland's *Library Bulletin*, Vol. XII.
87. Rapson. *Ancient India*, p. 174.
88. Stein. *Ancient Khotan*, Vol. I, p. 156.
89. Marshall. *A Guide to Taxila*, p. 14.
90. *The Imperial Gazetteer of India*, Vol. II, p. 288.
91. *Annual Report of the Archaeological Survey of India*, 1902–3, p. 167.
92. Qureshi, M. H. *Rahnuma-i-Taxila*, p. M44.
93. Nazir Ahmad. *Jesus in Heaven on Earth*, pp. 347–349.
94. Vincent Arthur Smith. *The Early History of India*, p. 20.
95. Klijin. *The Acts of Thomas*, p. 70.
96. *Acta Thomae*, Ante-Nicene Christian Library, Vol. XX, p. 46.
97. Nazir Ahmad. *Jesus in Heaven on Earth*, pp. 348–249.
98. Marshall, John. *Taxila*, Vol. I, p. 62.
99. John 20: 28.
100. Mark 3: 3–35.
101. John 2: 3.
102. John lg: 26–27.
103. Acts 9: 14.
104. Mumtaz Ahmad Farouqui. *The Crumbling of the Cross*, p. 62.
105. Mufti Mohamad Sidiq. *Qabr-Masih*, p. 26.
106. Khwaja Nazir Ahmad. *Jesus in Heaven on Earth*, p. 361.
107. Mumtaz Ahmad Faroqui. *The Crumbling of the Cross*, pp. 62–65.
108. I Chronicles 1: 8, 4: 40.
109. *Swarbica Journal*, Vol. I, 1978, p. 10.
110. Moonis Raza, Aijazuddin Ahmad, Ali Mohamad. *The Valley of Kashmir*, Vol. I, p. 11.
111. Thomas Holdich. *The Gates of India*, p. 31.
112. Lord, J. H. *The Jews in India and the Far East*, p. 23.
113. Sonia Cole. *Races of Man*, pp. 58–75.
114. Sonia Cole. *Races of Man*. pp. 58–75.
115. Alexander Brunes. *Travels into Bokhara*, Vol. II, p. 140.
116. Thomas Holdich. *The Gates of India*, pp. 49–50.
117. Bruknear, T. Nelson & Kurt Berna. *The Second Life of Jesus Christ*, p. 27.
118. Nilamata-purana, trans. *Ved Kumari*, Vol. I, p. 46.
119. Al-Beruni. *India*, trans., Edward & Sachau, Vol. I, p. 206.
120. Kal, R. C. *Ancient Monuments of Kashmir*, p. 75.
121. Abdul Qadir. *Hashmat-i-Kashmir*, p. 68.
122. Bernier. *Travels in the Mughal Empire*, p. 430.

123. Johnston, Keith. *Dictionary of Geography*, Art., Kashmir.
124. Wilson, Henry. *Travels in Himalayan Provinces*, p. 129.
125. Regarding the etymology of the name Kashir, see Tuzak-i-Babari. *Memories of Babar*, trans. Leyden & Erskine, p. 313.
126. Hassnain. *Hindu Kashmir*, pp. 18–19.
127. Vincent Smith. *The Early History of India*, p. 235.
128. Rapson, E. J. *The Cambridge History of India*, Vol. I, p. 582.
129. Wheeler, J. H. *History of India*, p. 239.
130. *Bhavishya-maha-purana*, verses 17–32.
131. Mulla Nadri. *Tarikh-i-Kashmir*, folio 69, Haider Malik Chaudura. *Tarikh-i-Kasmir*, II, 12–56, Hassan Shah, Tarikh- i-Kashmir, Vol. III, p. 25.
132. *Bhavishya-maha-purana*, V. 1–32.
133. Mulla Nadri. *Tarikh-i-Kashmir*, folio 69.
134. Haider Malik Chandura. *Traikh-i-Kashmir*, folio 11–12.
135. Cole. *Illustrations of Ancient Building in Kashmir*, p. 8.
136. Al-Shaikh Al Said-us-Sadiq. *Ilkmal-ud-Din*, p. 359.
137. Matthew 5: 10.
138. Luke 2: 28.
139. Al-Shaikh Al-Said-us-Sadiq. *Ikmal-ud-Din*, p. 359.
140. Luke 12: 31.
141. Al-Shaikh Al-Said-us-Sadiq. *Ikmal-ud-Din*, p. 359.
142. Chronicles.
143. Ecclesiastes 8: 8.
144. Al-Saikh Al-Said-us-Sadiq. *Ikmal-ud-Din*, p. 359.
145. *Sufi Studies: East and West,* edit. Rushbrook Williams, p. 202.
146. Ibid. p. 358.
147. George Barker Stevens. *The Teaching of Jesus*, p. 39.
148. Mark 4: 3–8.
149. Al-Saikh Al-Said-us-Sadiq. *Ikmal-ud-Din*, p. 327.
150. Kalhana. *Rajatarangini*, II: 90.
151. Ibid. p. 72.
152. Ibid. p. 85–86.
153. Ibid. p. 90.
154. Ibid. p. 106.
155. Ibid. p. 110.
156. Sufi, M. D. *Kashmir*, Vol. I, p.
157. Haider Malik Chaudura. *Tarikh-i-Kashmir*, II, 12–56. Hassan Shah. *Tarikh-i-Kashmir*, III, p. 2. *Rajataran-gini*, Vol. 1, p. 63.
158. Psalms 22: 1–28.
159. Matthew, Mark, Luke, John. *The New Testament*.
160. Rajatarangini, trans. Stein. 11: 72–106.
161. Werner Keller. *The Bible as History*, p. 360.
162. John 13: 36.
163. Mark 14: 37–72.

164. Matthew 16: 18–19.
165. Acts 1: 6–15.
166. Acts 2: 41.
167. Acts 4: 4.
168. Acts 5: 2.
169. Acts 5: 17–40.
170. Acts 9: 32–34.
171. Acts 12: 1–4.
172. Galatians 2: 11.
173. Peter 1: 1.
174. Peter 2: 9–10.
175. Peter 5: 12–14.
176. John 13: 36.
177. Shaikh Abdul Qadir. Art. in weekly *Badar,* Qadian, India, dated 17th May, 1979.
178. Report of the Archaeological Survey of India, Frontier Circle, 1912
179. Benjaman Roland. *St. Peter in Ghandhara,* see also, *The East & West,* Rome, Vol. 4, no. 4, 1953.
180. Shaikh-al Said-us Sadiq. *Kamal-ud-Din,* p. 358.
181. Kanzul-Ammai. Vol. II, p. 34.
182. Sheikh-al-Said-us-Sadiq. *Kamal-ud-Din,* p. 357.
183. Matthew 13: 55. Mark 6: 3.
184. Nazir Ahmad. *Jesus in Heaven on Earth,* pp. 3–6.
185. Shaikh-al Said-us-Sadiq. *Kamal-ud-Din.* p. 357.
186. *The Week End,* London, July, 17–24, 1973.
187. *Decree of Rozabal,* Srinagar, Kashmir.
188. Francis Buchanan. *A Journey from Madras,* Vol. 2, p. 391.
189. Younghusband. *Kashmir,* p. 112.
190. Enrique. *The Realms of the Gods,* p. 25.
191. Abdul Qadir. *Hashmat-i-Kashmir,* p. 68.
192. Saad-ullah. *Tarikh-i-Bagh-i-Sulaiman,* as quoted in Qabr-I-Massin, p. 48.
193. Ghulam Nabi. *Wajeez-ul-Tawarikh,* Vol. II, p. 279.
194. Faber Kaiser. *Jesus Died in Kashmir,* p. 100.
195. Barkat Ullah. *History of the Indian Churches,* p. 157.
196. Report of the Archaeological Survey of India, 1912–14, pp. 213–216.
197. Aziz Ahmad. *Asrar-i-Kashir,* p. 266.
198. Ferrier, J. P. *History of the Afghans,* p. 4.
199. Bleazby, G. B. *List of Coins & Medals in the S.P.S. Museum,* Srinagar, Kashmir, pp. 1–3.
200. John S. Deyell. *A Guide to the Reading of Ancient Indian Coin Legends,* Wisconsin, NI: 1,'19.
201. Kushan Gem. British Museum, London.
202. Sutta. *Bhaivishya-maha-purana,* p. 287.

203. Kurt Berna. D-7140 Ludwigsburg, West Germany. Letter dated 6th July, 1978.
204. Claudius Buchanan. *Christian Researches in India*, p. 141.
205. Milman. *History of the Jews,* Vol. 1, p. 442.
206. Joseph Benjamen. *Eight years in Asia and Africa*, p. 134.
207. Claudius Buchanan. *Christian Researches in India*, p. 224.
208. Vincent Arthur Smith. *The Early History of India*, p. 204.
209. Claudius Buchanan. *Christian Researches in India*, p. 229.
210. Decision of the Supreme Court of Travancore, South India, in the case of Dionysus Joseph Vers Mar. Athanansius Thomag, 1871.
211. George Macmuon. *The Religions and the Hidden Cults of India,* pp. 106–108.
212. *The Encyclopaedia Britannica.* Under the heading, "Thomas."
213. Barkat Ullah. *History of Churches in India*, p. 120.
214. Barkat Ullah. *History of Churches in India*, p. 151, trans. from the Urdu by the author.
215. Safi Sharah-Asool-i-Kafi. Vol. 3, p. 304, *Ikmal-ud-Din*, p. 243.
216. Richard Fre. *Heritage of Persia*, p. 268, note 31.
217. Burke, O.M. *Among the Dervishes*, p. 12.
218. The gospel is entitled *Mujuzat-i-Masih,* edit. Farocq Argalli (Urdu).
219. *Mujuzat-i-Masih*, edit. Farocq Arg, p. 3.
220. Luke 1: 26.
221. *Mujuzat-i-Masih*, edit. Farocq Argalli, pp. 7–9.
222. Torah.
223. Bible.
224. Follower of Judaism.
225. Zechariah.
226. Mujuzat-i-Masih, edit. Farocq Arga., p. 23.
227. Burke, O.M. *Among the Dervishes*, p. 109.

Bibliography

Biblical Sources

The Holy Bible: Old and New Testament. King James Version., 1611.

The Holy Bible with Commentary. John Murray. London, 1899.

Pelboubet. Select Notes on the International S.S. Lessons. Boston, 1918.

The Epistles of the Apostles.

The Acts of the Apostles.

Commentary on the Holy Bible. Dummelow. London, 1928.

The New Testament in the Original Greek. Ed. Westcott. London, 1891.

Penticost Bible Studies. London, 1891.

The Four Gospels in Research and Debate. Ed. Bacon. New Haven, 1918.

Pagan Sources

Josephus, Flavius. *Antiquities of the Jews: A History of the Jewish Wars and Life of Flavius Josephus, Written by Himself.* Tr. W. Whiston. London, 1872

Josephus, Flavius. *Antiquities of the Jews (Historia Antiqua Judaico).* Ed. Loeb. London & Cambridge, MA, 1924ff.

Josephus, Flavius. *The Jewish Wars.* Tr. W. Whiston. London, 1872.

Josephus, Flavius. *The Jewish Wars.* Tr. G. A. Williamson. Penguin, Harmondsworth, 1978.

Josephus, Flavius. *The Wars of the Jews.* T. Nelson & Sons, London,1873.

Philo, Judaeus. *Every Good Man Is Free.* Tr. F. H. Colson. London & Cambridge, MA, 1962, 1967.

Philo, Judaeus. *Works.* Ed. Loeb, Loeb. Classical Lib., Heinemann, London, and Harvard Univ. Press, Cambridge, MA, 1960.

Pliny the Elder. *Natural History.* Tr. J. Rackham & W. H. S. Jones, 10 vols., London, 1938–42.

Pliny the Elder. *Natural History.* Loeb. Classical Library, Heinemann, London, and Harvard Univ. Press, Cambridge, MA, 1969.

Pliny the Younger. *Letter to the Emperor Trajan.* Ed. Loeb, Loeb. Classical Library, Harvard Univ. Press, Cambridge, MA, 1964.

Jewish Sources

Albright, W. F. *Archaeology and the Religion of Israel.* Hopkins, Baltimore, 1953.

Authorised Jewish Prayer Book. Eyre & Spottiswoode. London, 1916.

Black, A. *The Prophets of Israel.* Edinburgh, 1882.

Charles, R. H., tr. *The Book of Enoch,* 2 vols. Clarendon Press, Oxford, 1893, 1912.

Charles, R. H., tr. *Testament of the Twelve Patriarchs.* A. & C Black, London, 1908.

Driver, S. R. *Introduction to the Literature of the Old Testament.* 1892.

Encyclopaedia Judaica. Jerusalem, 1971.

Greenlees, Duncan. *The Gospel of Israel.* Adhyar, Madras, 1955.

Haupt, P., ed. *Sacred Books of the Old Testament in Hebrew.* New York, 1898.

Moore, G. F. *Judaism in the First Century of the Christian Era.* Cambridge, 1930, Vol. 1, p. 20.

Ryle & James, eds. *The Psalms of Solomon.* Cambridge, UK, 1891.

The Talmud. Standard Edition, Macmillan, London, 1938.

Bani Israel

Barakat, Ahmad. *Muhammad and the Jews.* Vikas, New Delhi, 1979.

Barber, Izekiel. *The Beni Israel of India.* Washington, DC, 1981.

Bell, A. W. *Tribes of Afghanistan.* London, 1897.

Bellew, H. W. *Are the Afghans Israelites?* Simla, India, 1880.

Bruhi, J. H. *The Lost Ten Tribes.* London, 1893.

Khan, Roshan. *Tazkirah* (History of the Afghans). (Urdu) Karachi, 1982.

Kehimkar, Haeem Samuel. *Bani Israel in India.* Tel Aviv, 1937.

Lord, Rev. J. H. *The Jews in India and the Far East*. SPCK, Bombay, 1907.

Margolis, Max & Marx, Alexander. *A History of the Jewish People*. Temple Books, MA, 1969, 1978.

Mir Izzut-oolah. *Travels in Central Asia*. Tr. Henderson. Foreign Dept. Press, Calcutta, 1872.

Mohammad, Yasin. *Mysteries of Kashmir*. Srinagar, 1972.

Moore, George. *The Lost Ten Tribes*. Longman Green, London, 1861.

Moore, George. *Judaism in the First Century of the Christian Era*. Cambridge, UK, 1930.

Qureshi, Aziz Ahmad. *Asrar-i-Kashir* (Urdu). Srinagar, 1964.

Rose, George. *The Afghans and the Ten Tribes*. London, 1852.

Wolf, Joseph. *Mission to Bokhara*, 2 vols. London, 1845.

Wolf, Joseph. *Researches and Missionary Labours among the Jews and Mohammedans and Other Sects*. London, 1835.

Apocrypha

The Ante-Nicene Christian Library, 25 vols. T & T Clark, Edinburgh, 1869.

Andrews, A. ed. *Apocryphal Books of the Old and New Testament*. Theological Translation Library, London, 1906.

Anjeel-i-Barnabas (Arabic). Al-Minar Press, Cairo, 1908.

Barnabas Ki Anjeel (Urdu). Markazi Maktaba Islami, Delhi, 1982.

Bonnet, Max, tr. *Acta Thomae*. Leipzig, 1883.

Charles, R. H., tr. *The Old Testament Apocrypha and Pseudepigrapha*, 2 vols. Clarendon Press, Oxford, 1913.

Charles, R. H. *Religious Development Between the Old and the New Testament*. Henry Holt, 1913.

Cureton. *Ancient Syriac Documents*, 24 vols. London, 1864,

Gartner, Bertil. *The Theology of the Gospel of Thomas*.

Gospel of the Hebrews. Edenite Soc. Inc., Imlaystown, NJ, 1972.

Hennecke, E. & Schneemelcher, W. *New Testament Apocrypha*. Philadelphia, 1963–66.

James, Montague. *The Apocryphal New Testament*. Oxford, 1924, 1953.

Klijn, A. F. J., tr. *The Acts of Thomas*. E. J. Brill, Leiden, 1962.

Lost Books of the Bible. World Publishing Co., New York, 1944.

Pagels, Elaine. *The Gnostic Gospels.* New York, 1979.

Pratten, tr. *Syrian Documents Attributed to the First Three Centuries.* Ante-Nicene Christian Library, Vol. XX, Edinburgh, 1871.

Ragg, Lonsdale & Laura, tr. *The Gospel of Barnabas.* Oxford Univ. Press, 1907.

Robinson, Forbes. *The Coptic Apocryphal Gospels.* Methuen & Co., London, 1902.

Robinson, James M., ed. *The Nag Hammadi Library.* New York, E. J. Brill, Leiden, 1977.

Schonfield, Hugh. *The Authentic New Testament.* London, 1956.

Swete, H. B., ed. *The Gospel of Peter.* Macmillan, London, 1893.

Walker, Alexander, tr. *Acts of Barnabas.* Ante-Nicene Christian Library, Vol. XVI, T& T Clark, Edinburgh, 1970.

Wilson, R. M., ed. *The Gospel of Philip.* London, 1962.

Wright, W. *Apocrphal Acts of the Apostles.* Soc. for Publ. of Oriental Texts, London, 1871, Vol. II.

Christology and Theology

Ahmad, Mirza Ghulam. *Jesus in India.* Ahmadiyya Muslim Mission, Qadian, India, 1944.

Ahmad, Mirza Ghulam. *Massih Hindustan Mein* (Urdu). Qadian, 1908.

Bock, Janet. *The Jesus Mystery.* Aura Books, Los Angeles, 1980.

Bornkamm, G., tr. *Jesus of Nazareth.* Hodder & Stoughton, London, 1956.

Bultmann, Rudolf. *Primitive Christianity and Its Contemporary Setting.* Tr. R. H. Fuller. Collins, Glasgow, 1960.

Cadoux, C. J. *The Life of Christ.* Pelican, London, 1948.

The Crucifixion by an Eye-Witness. Indo-American Book Co., Chicago, 1907.

Dummelow, Rev. J. R. *Commentary on the Holy Bible.* Macmillan, London. 1917.

Faber-Kaiser, Andreas. *Jesus Died in Kashmir.* Gordon & Cremonesi, London, 1977.

Faruqi, Mumtaz Ahmad, *The Crumbling of the Cross.* Lahore, 1973.

Ferrar, Dean F. W. *The Life of Christ.* Cassell, Peter & Galpin, London, 1874.

Forsström, Johan. *The King of the Jews.* Nugedoga, Sri Lanka, and East West Books, Hango, Finland, 1987.

Fuller, R. J. *The Foundations of New Testament Christology.* Collins, London, 1965.

Goeckel, Helmut. *Die Messias-Legitimation Jesu.* Liber Verlag, Mainz, 1982.

Graves, Robert. *The Nazarene Gospel Retold.* Cassell, London, 1953.

Gregory, A. *The Canon and Text of the New Testament.* New York, 1907.

Hastings, J. *Dictionary of the Bible.* T & T Clark, Edinburgh, 1904.

Hastings, J. *Dictionary of Christ and the Gospels.* T & T Clark, Edinburgh, 1908.

Holy Bible, King James Version, reference ed. with Concordance. New York, London.

Kamal-ud-Din, Khwaja. *The Sources of Christianity.* MMI Trust, Woking UK, 1924.

Kashmiri, Aziz. *Christ in Kashmir.* Roshni Pubs., Srinagar, 1984.

Keller, Werner. *The Bible as History.* Hodder & Stoughton, London, 1956.

Kersten, Holger. *Jesus Lived in India.* Element, Shaftesbury, UK, 1986.

Levi (H. Dowling). *The Aquarian Gospel of Jesus the Christ.* De Vorss, Marina del Ray, CA, 1972.

Lewis, Spencer H. *Mystical Life of Jesus.* AMORC, San Jose, CA, 1929.

The Life of Christ, Rev. Ed., Mazdaznan Elector Corp, Los Angeles, 1960. Reprinted by Stockton Doty Press, Whittier, CA, 1969.

Muggeridge, Malcolm. *Jesus, the Man Who Lives.* Collins, London, 1975.

Muses, G.A., ed. *The Septuagint Bible.* Falcon's Wing Press, CO, 1954.

Nazir Ahmad, Khwaja. *Jesus in Heaven on Earth.* Azeez Manzil, Lahore, 1973. First published by Muslim Mission and Literary Trust, Woking, UK, 1952.

Notovitch, Nicolas. *The Unknown Life of Christ.* Rand McNally, Chicago, 1894 and Hutchinson, London, 1895.

Peake, A. S. J. *Commentary on the Bible.* London, 1920.

Peloubet's Select Notes on the International Lessons. Boston, 1918.

Prophet, Elizabeth Clare. *The Lost Years of Jesus.* Summit Univ. Press, Malibu, CA, 1984.

Robinson, J. M. *New Quest for the Historical Jesus.* London, 1959.

Sadiq, Mufti Muhammad. *Qabr-i-Masih* (Urdu). Talif-o-Ishait, Qadian, 1936.

Serrano, Miguel. *The Serpent of Paradise.* Harper, New York, 1972.

Shams, J. D. *Where Did Jesus Die?* Baker & Witt, London, 1945.

Schweitzer, A. *Quest for the Historical Jesus.* London, 1945.

Stroud, William. *On the Physical Cause of Death of Christ.* London, 1965.

Talmud Immanuel. Freie Interessengemeinschaft, Switzerland, 1974.

Wehrli-Frey. *Jesat Nassar,* 2 vols. Drei Eichen Verlag, Munich, 1965.

Wilson, Ian. *The Turin Shroud.* Penguin, Harmondsworth, 1978.

Yosuf, Chalpi. *Mashihat* (Urdu). Majlis Tehqiqat, Lucknow, 1976.

The Shroud

Berna, Kurt. *Jesus ist Nicht am Kreuz Gestorben.* Hans Naber, Stuttgart, 1957.

Berna, Kurt. *Christ Did Not Perish on the Cross.* Expositions Press, New York, 1975.

Berna, Kurt. *Das Linnen.* Stuttgart, 1957.

Forsyth, William H. *The Entombment of Christ.* Cambridge, UK, 1970.

National Geographic, Vol. 157, no. 6. Washington, DC, June 1980.

Reban, John (Kurt Berna). *Inquest of Jesus Christ.* London, 1967.

Rinaldi, Peter M. *Is It the Lord?* New York, 1972.

Segal, J. B. *Edessa, the Blessed City.* Oxford. 1970.

Vignon, Paul. *The Shroud of Christ.* London, 1902.

Wilcox, R. K. *Shroud.* Macmillan, New York, 1977.

Wilson, Ian. *The Turin Shroud.* Penguin, Harmondsworth, 1978.

Anthropology & Archaeology

Al Beruni. *Kitab-al-Hind, India.* From Arabic, tr. Edward Sachau, 2 vols. Trubner, London, 1888. Reprint, S. Chand & Co., Delhi, 1964.

Aziz-us-Samad, Ulfat. *Great Religions of the World.* Lahore, 1976.

Bowle, John, ed. *Concise Encyclopaedia of World History.* Hutchinson, London, 1958.

Chakraberti, C. *Classical Studies in Ancient Races and Myths.* Puja Publications, New Delhi, 1979.

Cole, Major H. H. *Illustrations of Ancient Building in Kashmir.* W. H. Allen, London, 1869.

Cole, Sonia. *Races of Man.* British Museum, London, 1965.

Kak, Ram Chandra. *Ancient Monuments of Kashmir.* London, 1933.

Kellet, E. E. *Short History of Religions.* Pelican, Harmondsworth, 1972.

Khwand, Mir Muhammad. *Rauzat-us-Safa* (Persian). 7 vols., translated in *The Garden of Purity,* tr. E. Rehatsek, 5 vols. Royal Asiatic Soc, London, 1892.

Marshall, John et al. *Taxila,* 3 vols. Cambridge, 1951.

Rapson, Prof. E. J. *Ancient India.* CUP, Cambridge, UK, 1911.

Roerich, Nicholai. *Altai Himalaya.* New York, 1929.

Roerich, Nicholai. *The Heart of Asia.* New York, 1929.

Smith, Arthur Vincent. *The Early History of India.* Clarendon Press, Oxford, 1904.

Smith, Sir George Adam. *Historical Geography of the Holy Land.* Hodder, London, 1894.

Dead Sea Scrolls

Allegro, John. *The Dead Sea Scrolls: A Reappraisal.* Penguin, Middlesex, 1964.

Allegro, John. *Dead Sea Scrolls: Thy Mystery Revealed.* New York, 1981.

Allegro, John. *The People of the Dead Sea Scrolls.* Routlege, London, 1959.

Allegro, John. *The Dead Sea Scrolls and Christian Myth.* Abacus, London, 1981.

Barthelemy, D. & Milik, J.T. *Discoveries in the Judaean Desert.* Oxford Univ. Press. 1955.

Brownlee, W. H. *The Dead Sea Manual of Discipline.* BASOR, New York, 1951.

Brownlee, W.H. *The Meaning of the Qumran Scrolls for the Bible.* New York, 1964.

Burrows, M. *The Dead Sea Scrolls.* Viking Press, London, 1956.

Burrows, M. *More Light on the Dead Sea Scrolls.* London, 1958.

Davies, Powell. *The Meaning of the Dead Sea Scrolls*. Mentor Books, New York, 1956.

Dupont-Sommer, A. *The Dead Sea Scrolls*. New York, 1956.

Schonfield, Hugh. *The Scret of the Dead Sea Scrolls*. New York, 1960.

Vermes, G. *The Dead Sea Scrolls in English*. Pelican, Middlesex, 1962.

Wilson, Edmund. *Scrolls from the Dead Sea*. Oxford, 1955.

Yadin, Y. *The Ben Sira Scroll from Masada*. Jerusalem, 1965.

Christians of St. Thomas in India

Brown, L. W. *The Indian Christians of St. Thomas*. Cambridge, 1956.

Buchanan, Claudius. *Chrstian Researches in Asia*. Cambridge, 1811; Ogle, Edinburgh, 1912.

Geddes, M. *History of the Christian Church of Malabar*. Walford, London, 1894.

Farquhar, J. N. *The Apostle Thomas in North India*. Manchester, 1926.

Keay, F. E. *History of the Syrian Church in India*. Madras, 1938.

Matthew, P. V. *Acta Indica*. Cochin, 1986.

Medlycott, A. E. *India and the Apostle Thomas*. London, 1905.

Menacherry, George, ed. *The St. Thomas Christian Encyclopaedia of India*. Madras, 1973.

Milne, Rae. *Syrian Church in India*. Edinburgh, 1892.

Mingana, A. *Early Spread of Christianity in India*. Manchester, 1926.

Plattner, F. A. *Christian India*. Vanguard Press, New York, 1957.

Raulin. *Historia Ecclesiae Malabartica*. Rome, 1745.

Essenes

Dupont-Sommer. *The Jewish Sect of Qumran and the Essenes*. Macmillan, 1956.

Kosmala, H. *Hebraer, Essener, Christen*. Leiden, 1959.

Larson, Martin A. *The Essene Heritage*. New York, 1967.

Szekely, Edmond Bordeaux. *The Essene Code of Life*. San Diego, 1977.

Szekely, Edmond Bordeaux. *The Essene Humane Gospel of Jesus*. Santa Monica, 1978

Szekely, E. B. *The Essene Jesus*. San Diego, CA, 1977.

Szekely, E. B. *The Essene Teachings of Zarathrustra*. 1973.

Szekely, E. B., tr. *The Gospel of the Essenes*. C.W. Daniel, Saffron Walden, UK, 1978.

Szekely, E. B. *The Gospel of Peace of Jesus Christ by the Disciple John*. C. W. Daniel, London, 1937 & 1973.

Szekely, E. B. *The Teachings of the Essenes from Enoch to the Dead Sea Scrolls*. C. W. Daniel, London, 1978.

Islamic

al-Bukhari, Imam. *Al-Jami-al-Sahih*, 3 vols. Cairo.

al-Jajjaj, Muslim bin. *Al-Sahih*, 18 vols. Cairo.

Al-Sahih of Muslim, 2 vols. Ghulam Ali & Sons, Lahore, 1962.

Bashir-ud-Din, Mahmood Ahmad. *Introduction to the Study of the Holy Quran*. London, 1949.

Ibn-i-Jarir-at-Tibri. *Tafsir*, 30 vols. Kubr-ul-Mara Press, Cairo, 1921.

Mohammed Ali, Maulana, tr. *The Holy Quran*. Ahmaddiyya Anjuman, Lahore, 1951.

Mohammad Ali, Maulana. *A Manual of Hadis*. Lahore, 1949.

Sale, George. *The Koran*. London, 1939.

Yusuf Ali, Abdullah, tr. *Holy Quran*. Lahore, 1961.

ORIENTAL MANUSCRIPTS AND WORKS
Arabic

Ibn-i-Hazam. *Almallal-o-Alnahal*. Cairo.

Ibn-i-Tamima, Shaikh-ul-Islam. *Al-Jawab-al-Sahi-Liman-Badil-Din-al-Masih*, 4 vols.

Mohammad Abdul, Shaikh, *Al-Islam-al-Nasrania*. Cairo.

Shahrastani, Mohammad ibn Abdul Karim. *Kitab al-Milal wa al-Nihal*. Soc. for Publ. Oriental Texts, London, 1842.

Persian

Abdul Qadir. *Hashmat-i-Kashmir*. Persian MS, no. 42, f7, Royal Asiatic Soc. of Bengal, Calcutta.

Dehlvi, Syed Ahmad. *Farhang-i-Asafiyah*. Persian dictionary, Hyderabad, 1908.

Khwaja Muhammad Azam Deedamari. *Tarikh-i-Azami* (in Persian). Muhammadi Press, Lahore, 1747.

Khwand, Mir Muhammad. *Rauzat-us-Safa* (Persian), 7 vols. Translated in *The Garden of Purity*, tr. E. Rehatsek, 5 vols. Royal Asiatic Soc., London, 1892.

Mustafa, Agha. *Ahwal-i-Ahalian-i-Paras* (Persian). Teheran, 1909.

Said-us-Saddiq, Al Shaikh. *Kamal-ud-Din.* Sayyid-us-Sanad Press, Iran, 1881. Translated into German by H. Muller, Heidelberg Univ., Germany, 1901.

Urdu

Ahmad, Mirza Ghulam. *Jesus in India.* Ahmadiyya Muslim Mission, Qadian, 1944.

Ahmad, Mirza Ghulam, *Massih Hindustan Mein.* Qadian, 1908.

Argali, Farooq, ed. *Mujazat-i-Masih (Miracles of Jesus).* Delhi.

Qadir, Abdul Shaikh. *Ashab-i-Kahf-kay-Sahijay (The Scriptures of the Cave-Dwellers).* Lahore, 1960.

Sadiq, Mufti Muhammad. *Qabr-i-Masih (The Grave of Jesus).* Talif-o-Ishait, Qadian, 1936.

Shams Tabriz Khan, tr. *Masihat (Christianity).* Lucknow, 1976.

Sanskrit

Bhavishya Mahapurana. MS, Oriental Research Library, Univ. of Kashmir, Srinagar.

Bhavishya Maha Purana. tr. & comm. in Hindi. Oriental Research Inst., Poona, 1910.

Kumari, Ved, tr. *Nila-Mata-Purana.* Cultural Academy, Jammu, 1968.

Natha Namavali Sutra. Natha Yogis. Vindhya Chal.

Shastri, Vidyavaridi Shiv Nath, tr. *Bhavishya Maha Purana* (Hindi). Venkareshvaria Press, Bombay, 1917.

Stein, M.A., tr. *Kalhana's Rajatarangini,* 2 vols. Constable, London, 1900. Reprints New Delhi, 1961 & 1979.

Tibetan

Le-zan Chhes-kyi Nima. *Grub-tha Thams-chand kyi Khuna dan Dod-Thsul Ston-pe Legs Shad Shel-gyi Melong* (Tibetan, translated from Chinese) or *The History of Religions and Doctirnes—The Glass Mirror,* in the collection of S.S. Gergan, Srinagar, Kashmir.

Bengali

Abhedananda, Swami. *Kashmir O Tibbate.* Ramakrishna Vedanta Math, Calcutta, 1927.

Ghose, Ashutosh. *Swami Abhedananda—the Patriot Saint.* Ramakrishna Vedanta Math, Calcutta, 1967.

About the Authors

Haji Prof. Fida M. Hassnain
**M.A. (Hist.), Ll.B., D. Arch.,
Doctor Indology**

PROFESSOR HASSNAIN was born in 1924 in Srinagar, Kashmir. His parents were school teachers. Professor Hassnain was placed under the charge of the Immam at Tral, Kashmir, at the age of three and learned the Holy Quran. He was put in a modern school at the age of six and completed his matriculation at the age of sixteen. At the age of twenty he graduated from the Punjab University. He obtained his Master's Degree from Muslim University, Aligarh.

Professor Hassnain took up studies in law and received his Ll.D. in 1946. Returning to his home town, he joined the bar and worked as a lawyer for a few years. He soon felt disgusted with this profession because his conscience would not allow him to defend an offender.

Professor Hassnain then took up social work among the poor, started painting and wrote poetry. Soon the hard realities of life forced him to seek a job, and he became a Lecturer at S.P. College in Srinagar. Later, he rose to the position of Professor of History and Research.

Professor Hassnain became the Director of the State Archives, Archaeology Research and Museums in 1954 and continued as such until his retirement in 1983. His study tours resulted in the salvaging of several hundred manuscripts in Arabic, Sanskrit and Persian, which were housed in the Archives and Oriental Research Libraries. As an expert archaeologist, he has conducted several excavations.

In 1969 he was invited by some educational institutions of Japan to speak on Buddhism. Since then he has visited Japan six times for lecture tours. His scholastic achievements have won for him the title of Doctor of Indology.

Professor Hassnain visited Ladakh (Western Tibet) for the first time in 1960, and since then has been to this land of Tantric Lamaism a number of times. Here, he came into contact with Shamanic Tantric practices being made use of by a Tibetan hermitess. His anthropological interest induced him to study the past of the Brukpa tribes, in whom he found traces of the Greek remnants of Alexander the Great.

During his official tours in Kashmir, Jammu and Ladakh, he came into contact with several Sadhus, Faqirs, Lamas, Majzoobs and Sufis. He felt much impressed by Swami Lakshman Joo, Sayyid Mirak Shah, Kausar Sahib, Sharif Sahib, Yogni Chomoji, Sultan Sahib, Swami Nanda Mutto, Sayyid Babaji and Lassa Mutto.

Avoiding his official work, he began to spend his days and nights with the last named three mendicants. This gave his two official colleagues an opportunity to involve him in official bungling, which resulted in his suspension from service. This calamity produced a profound shock to him and he felt forsaken by God. Suspicions about the existence of God crept up in his mind. But this phase lasted only for a few months! A Sadhu from South India, on pilgrimage to Shri Amareshwar Lingam in Kashmir, visited the house of Professor Hassnain to tell him that God was great.

When Professor Hassnain started throwing challenges, the Sadhu said, "God has removed both your enemies from the scene." In a strange coincidence, both the officers who had implicated Professor Hassnain disappeared, along with their families. To his amazement, he learned later on that the chief enemy had migrated to Pakistan with his family, leaving his hearth and home in Kashmir. The other enemy was found, after twelve years, roaming in the hills like a pauper. This event was a turning point in his life. Soon after, he was reinstated in his post and continued until his retirement.

Professor Hassnain has widely traveled in Europe and Asia. He is a member of many national and international organizations pertaining to philosophy, religion, mysticism, history, anthropology and culture. After retirement, he was initiated into the Sufi Way and, with the permission of his Master, he conducts Sufi Meditation sessions as a therapy in psychiatric clinics.

Professor Hassnain has written numerous articles on varied subjects. His published books are *Buddhist Kashmir* (1973), *British Policy* (1974), *Ladakh Moonland* (1975), *Hindu Kashmir* (1977), *History of Ladakh* (1977), *Gilgit* (1978), *Heritage of Kashmir* (1980), *Kashmir Misgovernment* (1980), *The Abode of Shiva* (1987), *Freedom Struggle in Kashmir* (1988), and others. He has lectured extensively and has been a visiting professor to several universities. He was granted the title of Rastra Sanskriti Samrat, or the Emperor of National Culture, in 1987. He lives with his family at 32. Dastgir Villa, Umar Enclave, Parray Pora, P.O. Sanat Nagar Srinagar-19005, Kasmir, India. fidahassnain@myasa.net

Rabbi Dahan Levi
President, Alliance d' Abraham, Order National du Merite

RABBI DAHAN LEVI was born on December 8, 1920 in Morocco. He was the last of six sons. His education started with the study of the Bible. He was so diligent that at the age of eight he questioned the views given in various commentaries. He began his studies of the Talmud at the age of eleven and obtained admission to the Yeshiva when he was barely fifteen years old.

At the Talmudic University, Rabbi Levi's inquisitive mind led him to ask questions of his teachers, which sometimes perplexed them. His teachers believed in traditional methods of teaching and endeavored to persuade him to follow them in theory and dogma. While the teachers laid stress on commentaries, Dahan Levi wished to go to the essence of the scriptures.

A time came when Dahan Levi's academic discussions earned for him the dislike of his teachers. Instead of answering his questions, they would simply ask him to leave the classroom. However, he continued his theological studies with critical analysis, with the result that he obtained in 1940 the degree of Talmudic Teacher and Rabbin. After long study, he had come to the conclusion that it was easy to understand the scriptures without the help of controversial commentaries.

Rev. Levi now made plans for further study and research into the myths of the Old Testament world but he was called upon to perform compulsory military service. He joined the army and completed his term in Tunis and Libya as a member of the French Legion. During all these years, his heart longed to visit the Holy Land. He was nominated as "almoner to the battalion" in the British Legion, and so he got an opportunity to proceed to Egypt.

Rev. Levi wandered all over the land of the Pharaohs and then traveled in Palestine, Syria and Iraq for three months. He left army service in 1942 and became a Titular of Talmud and ritual sacrificer in the city of Oran in Algeria.

Rev. Levi married in 1948 when he was twenty-eight years old. Another important event in his life was to move to Paris—and his stay there. He took up various jobs and later got an administrative job of the third subdivision in state service. In 1950, he became the Founder President of the "Alliance d' Abraham," an organization which aims at the survival of historical links between the three monotheist faiths, Judaism, Buddhism and Islam. It also aims at educating Muslims in the technique of the rite of circumcision.

Rev. Dahan Levi is the Vice-President of the Israeli community from the third administrative subdivision of Paris. In 1972, he was honored with the Decoration of the City of Paris. For his excellent work, he was honored in 1977 with the "Order National du Merite."

He is a searcher for the truth in history and culture. With the Bible in hand, he visited Occidental Arabia and toured India in 1986. During this period, he visited Delhi, Bombay, Calcutta, Agra, Jaipur and Srinagar in Kashmir. It was destiny that he met Professor Fida Hassnain, and they became good friends.

Both Rev. Levi and Professor Hassnain are searchers for truth. Both have sensitive hearts and both are open-minded. Despite the barriers of mother-tongue, both of them have had many fruitful discussions. Rev. Dahan Levi is the type of man who works without any fear and has hope in the future. Both he and Professor Hassnain have joined hands to investigate and find truth, which for them, means the "search of God." Their work is not the final word—for two reasons: shortage of human life span; and the nature of their work, which has never received attention from their contemporaries. Since childhood, Rev. Dahan Levi has been inquisitive and he continues to be so during his lifetime.

IT IS MY GREAT PLEASURE to be a contributor towards the publication of this great work, *The Fifth Gospel,* by Prof. Hassnain and Rev. Levi, and published by Blue Dolphin. I have revised and edited this book.

Prof. Hassnain is my father, a friend, and my teacher. I always consult him during any difficulty, and he is always there to help me with his prayers and his spiritual powers. He is a great scholar known all over the world, and I am proud to be his son. My contribution towards the publication of this book is my humble gesture to respect my father and my guru. Sincere thanks are due also to my friend, Ms. Claire Miller, for her help in bringing out this book.

Ahtisham Fida,
President, Fida Corporation Co., Ltd.
Japan

Made in the USA